Integration Through Foreign Direct Investment

Integration Through Foreign Direct Investment

Making Central European Industries Competitive

Edited by

Gábor Hunya

Senior Research Economist, The Vienna Institute for International Economic Studies (WIIW), Austria

In Association with The Vienna Institute for International Economic Studies (WIIW)

Edward Elgar
Cheltenham, UK • Northampton, MA, USA

Published by
Edward Elgar Publishing Limited
Glensanda House
Montpellier Parade
Cheltenham
Glos GL50 1UA
UK

Edward Elgar Publishing, Inc.
136 West Street
Suite 202
Northampton
Massachusetts 01060
USA

HG
5430.7
.H3
I53
2000

A catalogue record for this book
is available from the British Library

Library of Congress Cataloguing in Publication Data

Integration through foreign direct investment : Making Central European
    industries competitive / edited by Gábor Hunya.
    (In association with The Vienna Institute for International Economic Studies)
        Includes index.
        1. Investments, Foreign—Europe, Eastern.   2. Europe, Eastern—
    Foreign economic relations—European Union countries.   3. European
    Union countries—Foreign economic relations—Europe, Eastern.
    I. Hunya, Gábor.   II. Title: Making Central European industries
    competitive.   III. Series: Vienna Institute for International Economic
    Studies series.
    HG5430.7.A3I53   1999
    332.67'3'0943—dc21   99–21910
                                                                        CIP

ISBN 1 84064 156 8

Printed and bound in Great Britain by Creative Print and Design Wales

Contents

Figures

Tables

Contributors

Christian Bellak is Lecturer in Economics at the University of Economics, Vienna

Andrea Éltető is Scientific Researcher at the Institute for World Economics of the Hungarian Academy of Sciences, Budapest

Gábor Hunya is Senior Research Economist at The Vienna Institute for International Economic Studies (WIIW), Austria

Mark Knell is Research Fellow in the Business School at DeMontfort University, Leicester and Research Associate at The Vienna Institute for International Economic Studies (WIIW), Austria

Josef Pöschl is Senior Research Economist at The Vienna Institute for International Economic Studies (WIIW), Austria

Slavo Radoševic is Research Fellow at Science and Technology Policy Research Unit (SPRU), University of Sussex, Brighton, UK

Matija Rojec is Senior Research Fellow at the Centre of International Relations of the Faculty of Social Sciences, University of Ljubljana

Miklós Szanyi is Scientific Researcher at the Institute for Economics of the Hungarian Academy of Sciences, Budapest

Waltraut Urban is Senior Research Economist at The Vienna Institute for International Economic Studies (WIIW), Austria

Foreword

The process of economic development is nowadays increasingly moulded *externally*, that is, by the forces of global capitalism. It is all trite to say that foreign direct investment (FDI) and technology transfer are the critical features of economic development in emerging economies. There is no such thing as an autonomous (closed economy) process of industrialization and modernization in this age of globalization. The collapse of the Soviet empire was a persuasive testimony to the futility of such an attempt. Global capitalism demands the openness of an economy in trade, FDI and short-term capital flows by way of deregulation, liberalization and marketization. Cross-border homogenization of the institutions and rules of the game of international business will be the ultimate outcome of the spread of capitalism.

Multinational corporations (MNCs) are the vanguard of globalization. They serve as *creators and suppliers (appropriators)* of new knowledge they are capable of developing through technological and organizational activities. They innovate increasingly in the context of their far-flung networks of multinational operations. Their knowledge production is thus no longer confined to, and derivable from, the home market alone. Indeed, this gives them greater advantage as compared to uni-national (home-confined) firms. 'Learning-by-investing abroad' is a new way of accumulating knowledge; it is in addition to and supplementary with 'learning-by-operating at home'.

To produce directly in foreign markets, MNCs bring a package of superior corporate assets of their own. However, they do not – and *cannot* – bring and transport all the necessary assets that make their local production competitive and profitable. They ineluctably require locally available assets as complements. This is the very nature of *multinational* (cross-border) production that necessarily combines individual corporation-specific assets with locally available assets in the host country-specific business milieu. Hence, the qualities of both local assets and the business environment offered to MNCs are crucial, since they ultimately circumscribe the rationale and profitablitity of MNCs' overseas investment. They thus determine the attractiveness of a host country as a location of production and learning.

On the other hand, emerging economies are badly in need of knowledge for their efforts to close the gap in economic development. They thus *demand and absorb* knowledge. The unique 'public good' nature of knowledge and the emerging host economies' low organizational and technological capacity to absorb knowledge make arm's-length transactions (such as licensing) unpractical in many instances. In general, FDI is a more suitable alternative, since it can reduce the transaction costs of contracting, implementing and monitoring. In order to attract FDI, however, a host country must be able to offer complementary local assets as well as an attractive business environment (inclusive of the legal system of private property protection). Host governments have a decisive role to play in providing these 'host-goods'.

The above style of open-economy structural transformation can be conceptualized as a paradigm of 'collaborative growth' (or 'MNCs-cum-host-government-assisted growth'). In this host-focused approach, MNCs need to be conceived as 'development catalysts' at policy level, even though they are individually profit-seeking corporations.

Collaborative growth is not frictionless. After all, MNCs are known as 'creatures of market imperfection' with a dual character of organizational efficiency and market restraint. The host governments, therefore, must adopt judicious policy measures to maximize the social gains of inward FDI as an instrument of structural upgrading and minimize any accompanying social costs.

This book edited by Dr Gábor Hunya contains 11 chapters written by eight distinguished scholars specialized in the issues of inward FDI and economic development in central and eastern Europe. They explore the various aspects of collaborative growth in the Czech Republic, Hungary, Slovakia and Slovenia as well as in Austria. The underlying theme is a comparative analysis of the differential performance of business activities between foreign investment enterprises (FIEs) and domestic enterprises (DEs). Here, the host countries are faced with a 'dual' gap; one is an inter-regional gap between the central European transition countries and the EU, and the other an intra-country, inter-firm gap between FIEs and DEs. Both gaps, however, generate *integrative forces* by way of macroeconomic and microeconomic restructuring and upgrading. MNCs are thus agents of development arbitrage at both firm and regional levels.

The book persuasively points out that what really attracts FDI is not so much special investment promotional measures but the overall economic and legal environment (that is, a FDI-friendly and inducing host milieu), a business environment compatible with the workings of global capitalism. The book goes a long way towards understanding a host of key issues related to the emerging pattern of MNC-cum-host collaborative growth in central and eastern Europe.

Terutomo Ozawa
Colorado State University
March 1999

1. Introduction: integration through FDI making central European industries competitive

Gábor Hunya

The central European countries (CECs) in transition are involved in a process of economic and political integration with the European Union (EU). One of the major impediments to a rapid accession is the large gap between the EU and the central European accession countries in terms of the level of economic development, the legal system, the efficiency of market institutions and the competitiveness of companies. Narrowing the gap by a higher rate of economic growth depends on the international competitiveness of companies and industries in small open economies, poor in natural resources. This book explores whether foreign direct investment (FDI) can contribute to competitiveness and to narrowing the development gap between the CECs and the present EU members.

CECs, the Czech Republic, Hungary, Slovakia and Slovenia have attracted a substantial amount of FDI since the beginning of the transition to a market economy and even more can be expected as they prepare to join the EU. FDI would accelerate economic growth and thus support the accession process. FDI can benefit a host country in several important ways: direct transfer of investment means, transfer of technology, know-how and management skills; thus it enhances macro- and micro-economic restructuring and creates positive externalities. All these improve the competitiveness of individual firms and stimulate growth in the economy as a whole. Recent theories stress that the access to technology and to knowledge in a wide sense is even more important than the amount of invested capital.

As technological development takes place to a large extent within multinational enterprises, economic growth depends on the successful integration of a country's enterprises into international corporate networks. Countries relying heavily on FDI in the take-off period of economic growth can benefit from imported technology while focusing domestic research on adaptation. The case of Austria, an advanced but net capital importing country, can be taken as a relevant example. EU firms in CECs also enhance the adaptation of EU-conforming market behaviour. Intensive foreign capital penetration is a sign of progress in transformation especially in the field of economic liberalization and the strengthening of ownership rights.

This book is the result of a project which linked researchers from five countries to set up a joint framework to examine the impacts of FDI penetration in the central European transition countries, the Czech Republic, Hungary, Slovakia and Slovenia, as well as Austria.[1] We investigated the trends of FDI inflows into the manufacturing sector, the economic policy environment of FDI and the lessons of other research projects in the field. We have set up a unique database comparing the performance and characteristics of foreign affiliates, or 'FIEs', with domestically owned enterprises in the manufacturing industries.[2] The research results presented refer to the foreign penetration patterns, industrial and foreign trade specialization, capital and technology transfer and the prospects of EU integration. While the majority of publications on FDI rely either on the theory of multinational enterprise, or the survey of a limited number of companies, the approach of this book is different. It relies mainly on the theories of economic growth and structural change and it uses aggregate data for the manufacturing industries in the foreign and the domestic sectors. Another feature is that our approach is strictly comparative avoiding single country issues. The only exception is Austria which provides lessons useful for central European transition countries.

Chapter 2 summarizes background knowledge on the central European region as a target of FDI and reflects on its role in catching-up and EU accession. The trend of FDI into the region shows that only less than half of it goes into the manufacturing sector, thus our conclusions do not necessarily apply to the whole foreign investment sector. This chapter also summarizes some policy conclusions of the project. In Chapter 2 the catching-up by FDI is discussed mainly based on its effect on increasing investment means, macro- and microeconomic restructuring. This approach is further developed in Chapters 7 and 10. The place of our research in theory and in comparison to the results of other research projects are summarized in Chapters 2, 3 and 4.

Chapter 3 (complemented by Chapter 9) stresses the importance of technology and knowledge transfer based on the new growth theories.

> An exogenous increase in investment, whether from home or abroad, would increase the amount of capital (and output) per person, but this would only be temporary as diminishing returns would impose a limit to this growth. Foreign investment can only offset this limit if it includes the transfer of new technological knowledge in form of new goods, new markets or new processes.

Chapter 4 discusses scores of case studies and company surveys which were prepared in the last few years and reveals important features of FDI in central European transition countries. It identifies three major types of foreign direct investments:

- the domestic market-oriented (based on local suppliers);
- the assembly-type export-oriented (greenfield investment with intra-firm trade dominance);
- the export-oriented local supply-based company (usually privatized firms or joint ventures that also sell on the local market).

The impact of FDI on host countries is different for the three categories and a positive international competitiveness impact is mainly expected from export-oriented subsidiaries. Chapter 5 gives an overview of a developed country's, Austria's, experience with inward FDI and draws lessons for CECs.

Further chapters rely on the database comparing performance indicators of foreign affiliates with domestic companies and reflect on various aspects of the impact of FDI in a CEC:

- Foreign penetration by industries and basic features of the foreign sector are discussed in Chapter 6. This chapter also deals with some methodological problems of the database on FIEs.
- As a follow-up, Chapter 7 provides a systematic comparison of the performance indicators of domestic companies and foreign affiliates.
- Structural change in manufacturing production is analysed in relation to exports and FDI in Chapter 8.
- The role of FDI in the transfer of knowledge and technology is discussed in Chapter 9.
- Foreign trade and balance-of-payments impacts of FDI are the subjects of Chapters 10 and 11.

Although each chapter is a research paper on its own, these papers build on each other, utilize the same set of data, and use the same distinction between FIEs and domestic enterprises (DEs). Findings are presented in a coherent way despite the national and theoretical diversity of the authors. Some of the most important results are summarized below.

The analysis of the data of FIEs in comparison to DEs shows that FDI upgrades a host economy's comparative advantages through its allocative efficiency impact, by changing the distribution of industrial investment (macroeconornic restructuring), and through its industry (technical) efficiency impact, by increasing productivity through microeconomic restructuring and through spillover effects. Four major conclusions on the allocative and industry efficiency impact of FDI can be made (Chapter 7):

1. FIEs feature much better performance indicators than DEs in terms of labour productivity, capital productivity and profit margins. The comparison of operating profit per equity and value added or sales per employee indicates that a considerable portion of FIEs' superior performance is due to their higher allocative efficiency.
2. The distribution of FIEs among the manufacturing industries is radically different from that of DEs, indicating that macroeconomic restructuring takes place through FDI. By allocating investment differently than the existing distribution of assets in host countries' manufacturing sectors, FDI fosters macroeconomic restructuring.
3. FIEs' above-average profitability, value added per employee, export orientation and also assets per employee indicate that FDI fosters microeconomic restructuring.
4. As indicated by the analysis of revealed comparative advantages, FDI fosters restructuring of the manufacturing sector in accordance with the analysed host countries' comparative advantages.

The better operating indicators of FIEs compared to DEs can be explained by the facts that FIEs are much larger in size, more capital-intensive, show a much more intensive investment activity and are more export-oriented. Of these four areas, only the difference in export orientation can by definition be attributed to the presence of 'foreign ownership', that is the fact that FIEs are part of international production systems. This enables them to get better access to foreign markets including exports to other subsidiaries of the parent company. The other three distinctive features, larger company size, higher capital intensity and more intensive investment activity, are not necessarily correlated to 'foreign ownership', but are characteristic of foreign subsidiaries world-wide. In developed market economies the differences in behaviour of domestically owned and foreign-owned firms can be mostly explained by differences in the firms' structure and organization and not by ownership categories. In CECs foreign investors are, on average, of a different quality in terms of technology and organization. Restructuring without FDI, that is without the import of specific know-how and technology, is generally slow.

While at the beginning of transition to a market economy the process of structural adjustment in the CECs was a passive one, enforced by the collapse of the Council for Mutual Economic Aid (CMEA) and the massive drop in domestic demand, it became more active after 1992, when overall growth, in particular growth of investment, gained momentum (Chapter 8). Major winners of restructuring after 1992 were the relatively sophisticated engineering branches while the losers were the food industry, and the labour-intensive branches. Findings indicate that – not only at the aggregate level, but at the level of individual industries as well – foreign trade with the EU has become an engine of growth in most CECs after 1992. There is a certain positive impact of FDI on structural change but not for every industry.

Capital-importing countries aim at getting access to recent technology through the activity of multinational corporations (MNCs). The productivity gap between FIEs and DEs shows the superiority of technical knowledge in MNCs (Chapter 9). Previous chapters stress the importance of this superiority in raising the general productivity and income level of the capital-importing country. Mark Knell has a more forward-looking approach suggesting that spillovers are even more important. Spillovers occur when the productivity gap between FIEs and DEs decreases. This is the case only in the Czech Republic between 1993 and 1996 and the increase of the gap is especially large for Hungary and Slovakia.

In export-oriented branches where important foreign investments were realized, production and exports increased rapidly, while other branches mostly stagnated or declined (Chapter 10). This causes increasing concentration of the commodity and geographical structure of exports in a few foreign-dominated industries. While foreign penetration helps CEC industries to integrate with Western production systems, the concentration of exports caused by FDI makes these economies vulnerable to external shocks.

The analysis of the balance-of-payments impact of FDI led to the conclusion (Chapter 11) that even large current account deficits should be of little concern if they reflect strong private investment. Equity financing, especially FDI, is more secure than debt financing. Massive capital inflow has a positive impact on currency reserves and in this sense lowers the vulnerability to currency crises. On the other hand, if it continues over a longer period of time, it tends to increase the monetary base with an upward pressure on inflation. It also tends to push the exchange rate towards appreciation, which may threaten the competitiveness of domestic producers of tradables on domestic and international markets.

Based on the analysis of FDI in Austria (Chapter 5) and taking into account the FDI-related problems in other chapters, some policy lessons for CECs can be drawn:

- Greenfield FDI is to be preferred to merger and acquisition. FDI policy should give priority to initial investments, since these carry a potential for future expansion and domestic firms may develop in co-operation with foreign affiliates. However, in the process of privatization the positive effects of foreign take-over (fast restructuring) must be acknowledged.

- Those technologies which are relevant for growth are principally developed by multinationals and accessed through subsidiaries, but they can only be accessed if the host country location has something to offer to multinationals willing to invest. A constant upgrading of local knowledge and skill, as well as investments in infrastructure, are necessary for attracting more sophisticated production processes. A lock-in position can be avoided through diversification which can be increased by improving information flows, creating competition and fostering small business development.
- Direct incentives to attract FDI should be avoided as they do not only distort competition but cannot, in fact, substitute a proper institutional framework. A simplification of government regulations and a stable fiscal regime can be effective as they lower the compliance costs for foreign investors.
- Governments should stay firm in public debates and not give in to populism. Public debate on the alleged unfavourable impact of FDI ('selling out the country', 'one-sided dependence on foreigners') may continue long after the benefits of FDI have been proved.

At the end of 1996 the share of FIEs in manufacturing sales was over 60 per cent in Hungary, over 50 per cent in Austria and about 20 per cent in the Czech Republic, Slovakia and Slovenia. Reduced sovereignty of companies and national economic policies is the result of foreign penetration. An economy of foreign subsidiaries is limited in its choice of development targets, in the use of profits and the domestic availability of some high-quality jobs. For maintaining its position as a frequented investment target a country must constantly upgrade its international attractiveness as a location for production and for spending incomes. How much control can a state give up, how much should it keep? To what extent does the nationality of a private owner matter if both foreign and domestic owners are allowed to transfer earnings abroad? Our investigations cannot answer these questions. The answers often lie beyond the scope of economics. However, the analyses in this book suggests that economies in transition can become more competitive and overcome their backwardness more rapidly and more profoundly with the help of FDI than without it.

NOTES

1. The research was carried out in the framework of the Phare-ACE research project P-96-6183-R. The selection of countries was influenced by the availability of funding and research contacts. I would like to thank all participants of the project and especially those whose papers have not been included in this volume, Alena Zemplínerová, Czech Republic and Daneš Brzica, Slovakia for their valuable contribution and friendly co-operation.
2. The database was published in: Gábor Hunya (ed.), *Database on Foreign Investment Enterprises in Central European Manufacturing: Austria, the Czech Republic, Hungary, Slovakia, Slovenia 1993–96*, The Vienna Institute for International Economic Studies, September 1998.

REFERENCES

Knell, M. (1997), 'Knowledge transfer through foreign direct investment and technology licensing in Central Europe', paper written in the framework of the Phare-ACE project P-96-6183-R, mimeo.

Zemplínerová, A. (1997), 'Policies and climate for FDI', paper written in the framework of the Phare-ACE project P-96-6183-R, mimeo.

2. Central Europe catching-up through FDI?

Gábor Hunya

---

1 THE REGION

As mentioned in Chapter 1 this book covers five CECs, the Czech Republic, Hungary, Slovakia, Slovenia (CECs) and Austria. They share a long common historical past in the framework of the Austrian empire, but were separated and to a large extent alienated after World War I. Later they found themselves on the two opposing sides of the post World War II Iron Curtain. Austria became an advanced market economy deeply integrated into the European corporate networks and joined the EU in 1995. The others, CMEA members or Yugoslav countries, became 'centrally planned economies' developing non-competitive and autarchic economic structures. They started with the economic transformation towards a functioning market economy in 1989–90.

The CECs are the most advanced among the transition countries in terms of per capita gross domestic product (GDP) and, together with Estonia and Poland, also in progressing economic transformation. They have association agreements with the EU which means basically free trade for non-food manufactured goods and the possibility to join the EU in the future. They started accession negotiations in April 1998, with the exception of Slovakia, which was left out mainly for political reasons. The CECs are connected to each other by the trade liberalization pact CEFTA (Central European Free Trade Association).

All the five central European countries are small, open economies. Small domestic markets drive them to international specialization. They are open both in terms of foreign trade, and in terms of the affiliation of their companies to international alliances. All of them, including Austria, have been net direct capital importers. They use the inflow of FDI, technology and skills as a vehicle of economic modernization. CECs are among the leading targets of FDI among the transition countries. They are also the oldest target countries which allows us to investigate their experience with FDI over several years.

The links among the five countries are less intensive than to their common primary trading partner, Germany. Companies from Germany, together with US-based companies, MNCs, are among the most important direct investors in all the five countries (Table 2.1). However Austria is also a prominent trading partner and foreign investor for the CECs. For the two smaller countries – Slovenia and Slovakia – Austria is the first and second largest investor, respectively, with about one quarter of the foreign capital invested there. For Hungary and the Czech Republic, larger countries with more diversified international links, Austrian FDI is at place four and seven, with below 10 per cent of the invested capital. (The capacity of Austria as an investing country is not subject to our analysis which deals only with inward FDI in the five countries.) There has been a recovery of trade and investment among the CECs in recent years without reaching the artificially high trade shares of the CMEA years.

2   CECS CATCHING-UP?

A major task for the CECs, eager to join the EU, is to diminish the development gap between their economies and the EU. The gap is apparent in several fields: income, institutions, technology, human capital and so forth.

Table 2.1   FDI in CECs by major investing countries' FDI stock as of December 1996, shares in per cent

	Czech Republic	Hungary[a]	Slovakia[b]	Slovenia
Germany	27.9	23.8	22.6	14.1
Austria	7.3	14.5	20.9	34.3
USA	13.2	17.1	6.3	1.3
Netherlands	13.8	9.5	9.9	2.0
Switzerland	10.6	2.3	1.3	3.5
France	7.8	7.8	6.8	7.5
Italy	2.1	3.8	1.3	7.4
United Kingdom	n.a.	5.8	11.2	4.7
Other countries	17.3	15.4	19.8	25.2
EU	76.2	71.2	74.9	76.7
Total	100.0	100.0	100.0	100.0
Total (US$ mn)	6763	8778	1517	1934

Notes:
[a]   1996, data based on sample survey.
[b]   Data of national bank including banking sector.

Source: National publications and WIIW Database.

Table 2.2   GDP (real change in per cent against preceding year and per capita compared to Austria)

	1994	1995	1996	1997	1998	Index 1998 1999 = 100	Per capita in per cent of Austria 1997 at exchange rate	at PPP
Czech Republic	3.2	6.4	3.9	1.0	−2.7	95.3	20	53
Hungary	2.9	1.5	1.3	4.6	5.1	95.1	17	34
Slovakia	4.9	6.9	6.6	6.5	4.4	99.7	14	39
Slovenia	5.3	4.1	3.1	3.8	3.9	104.1	36	54
CECs	3.6	4.7	3.4	3.1	2.8	95.0		

Note: PPP: purchasing power parity.

Source: WIIW Database relying on national sources and WIFO.

CECs' income levels are considerably lagging behind the EU average. Even the two most advanced applicant countries, the Czech Republic and Slovenia, have real per capita GDPs somewhat below 60 per cent of the EU average at purchasing power parity (PPP), and half of that at the exchange rate (Table 2.2 compares CECs' and Austrian per capita GDP levels). The CEC income level is less than currently in both Greece and Portugal (67 per cent of the EU average), but not much different from the level before these countries' accession to the EU. Slovakia (43 per cent of the average EU per capita GDP) and Hungary (37 per cent) are even less developed. As the income gap is larger than the human capital gap, competitive advantage appears in the field of high-quality labour-intensive production. The analysis of FIEs confirms the tendency for intensive foreign penetration in such branches.

Economic growth in transition countries has been neither very rapid nor a constant process in the last 10 years. The early transformation literature concentrated on the speed and sequence of reforms under the headings of shock therapy and gradualism. It was assumed that by either method the transition to market economy would be a straightforward process leading to sustained economic growth in a shorter or longer period of time. The experience of the last few years shows, however, that the fragile market economies emerging in the wake of the transformation are subject to various setbacks and crises. Initial transformational recessions were frequently followed by recovery periods which resulted in mounting external and internal deficits (Hungary 1994, the Czech Republic 1996, Slovakia 1998).

Restructuring of enterprises and institutional reform being usually slower than monetary stabilization, the microeconomic foundations for sustained economic growth have not been established.

Hungary had to correct excessive current account and budget deficits in 1995 which was accompanied by a slow-down of economic growth and and acceleration of inflation. In 1997 and 1998 the Czech Republic suffered from a slow-down of output as a result of insufficient structural reforms. High current account deficits triggered currency depreciation which resulted in temporary import controlling measures in both countries. Slovakia has had rapid economic growth fuelled mainly by public investments which led to external imbalance and increasing indebtedness. Corrective measures triggering a slow-down of growth appeared in the second half of 1998. Slovenia had a cautious policy, avoiding too rapid restructuring as well as internal and external imbalances.

Table 2.3 Labour productivity in industry, change in per cent against preceding year

	1994	1995	1996	1997	1998	Index 1998 1989 = 100
Czech Republic	5.1	10.6	8.6	9.2	5.1	119.4
Hungary	15.7	10.2	9.4	13.6	12.0	170.9
Slovakia	7.2	4.0	2.5	4.8	9.5	110.2
Slovenia	13.2	6.3	9.2	4.4	5.4	135.6

Source: WIIW Database relying on national sources.

Table 2.4 Unit labour costs (ULCs) in industry (wages and productivity), exchange rate (ECU) adjusted change in per cent against preceding year

	1992	1993	1994	1995	1996	1997	1997 1989 = 100
Czech Republic	23.7	33.3	11.4	6.2	8.0	−2.4	131.0
Hungary	20.1	4.6	−9.6	−15.8	−5.3	−2.9	108.8
Slovakia	21.3	21.2	4.1	9.7	11.2	8.0	130.8
Slovenia	−1.3	8.9	−2.5	9.7	−5.7	0.9	87.8

Source: National statistics; WIIW estimate.

Progress of restructuring in industry must be expressed in rising labour productivity (Table 2.3). This has been especially rapid in Hungary over the whole transformation period. Slovenia showed much progress in initial years, the Czech Republic later. In Slovakia labour productivity progressed the most slowly among the countries compared. As we discuss later, this sequence of countries corresponds to the inflow of foreign capital which can be seen as a major driving force of productivity development. To compare competitive positions, labour productivity must be viewed in relation to wages.

A significant comparative advantage of the CECs is the relatively low wage cost level. The average gross monthly wage in 1997 amounted to US$ 900 in Slovenia, and to only US$ 300 in the Czech Republic and Hungary, as compared with almost US$ 2500 in Austria. Although labour productivity in the CECs is also much lower than in the EU, average ULCs in the CECs are still very low. Compared to the Austrian level, ULCs in the Czech Republic, Hungary and Slovakia amount to less than 30 per cent and in Slovenia to 50 per cent in 1997. ULCs grew after the first stabilization and the labour cost competitiveness gradually deteriorated contributing to a loss of international competitiveness and triggering external imbalances. After renewed stabilization measures in Hungary, an improvement of ULCs set in after 1995, reflecting the progress in industrial restructuring due mostly to the activity of foreign investors. Hungarian labour cost competitiveness has surpassed other CEC competitors in most manufacturing industries.

Catching-up with the EU's average income level by the year 2015 (assuming 2 per cent annual growth in the EU) would require 5 per cent annual growth in the two more advanced countries, Slovenia and the Czech Republic, and about 7–8 per cent growth per year in Slovakia and Hungary. Attaining 75 per cent of the EU's average GDP by 2015 would demand lower and, therefore, more realistic annual growth rates: Czech Republic 3.4 per cent, Hungary 6.1 per cent Slovakia 5.2 per cent, and Slovenia 3.4 per cent (Richter *et al.*, 1998). High growth rates and shorter catching-up scenarios may become feasible in case of massive capital imports and stepped up restructuring.

3   THE ROLE OF FDI IN CATCHING-UP

Theory gives no general guideline concerning the catching-up effects of FDI. Neoclassical theory maintains that international factor movements lead to overall welfare gains provided the production factors are fully mobile. International factor movements are induced by factor-price differentials. As a consequence low-income regions will catch up, provided they attract those factors which, because scarce, have a high-marginal productivity.

Under liberalized conditions the rate of return on capital together with a risk-related premium determines the size and direction of international capital flows. Besides factor costs, transaction costs appear on the cost side. Legal, political, economic provisions and conditions influence the magnitude of risk. On the basis of changing cost and risk perception, foreign capital is in constant search for favourable locations. Once the initial factor-price advantage shrinks (for example, wages go up) production may move to new locations. Other activities may result instead which use a different combination factors for example, instead of simple labour, more knowledge).

Modern approaches on catch-up and convergence (Nunnenkamp, 1997) argue that even under conditions of full factor mobility, agglomeration tendencies and a polarization between high- and low-income regions are possible. The tendency to agglomeration emerges because of technological externalities and limited diffusion of knowledge, which create spillover in those regions where human capital and technology are abundant factors. Consequently, mobility of production factors will not lead to convergence, but may instead aggravate the lagging behind of low-income regions. In addition, the mobility of production factors is usually limited. Foreign direct investors acquire a controlling position in subsidiaries and usually integrate the affiliates into their international production networks. For these reasons costs and risks are considered in a longer-term perspective and from the specific viewpoint of the international strategy of MNCs. Cost and risk factors influence the location of new investment projects more than established ones which are not very flexible to move, although relocations are on the increase world-wide.

International competition has two specific impacts on the role of foreign capital and the position of business in a country. First, the deepening economic integration of markets and states, by reducing transaction costs, opens new possibilities for internalizing transactions into companies internationally and thus favours large MNCs. Second, it gives impetus for an increased mobility of firms optimizing their international portfolio via relocation. Both features imply that firms have several immobile elements in the value-added chain, which cannot be separated easily from the business location (for example, localized learning, institutional environment, human capital). Only financial capital is footloose – real capital has a high degree of location specificity. The opportunity for business locations, including the CECs, lies in the fact that the location-specific elements often are the high value-adding elements.

FDI can contribute to closing income and other gaps through a bundle of impacts on CEC host economies. We mention here five, not in the order of importance. The first of the impacts is the direct capital transfer adding to available investment means. The second is the transfer of knowledge in the form of management, know-how and technology contributing significantly to the restructuring of firms. As a result of these inflows microeconomic restructuring takes place which results in increasing profits and improved growth potential. Third, FDI rearranges the industry structure and foreign trade structure, and thus the specialization patterns of a country and the enhanced allocation of resources contributes to growth. Fourth, the interest of foreign capital for a country is a good proof for its advance in transformation, tolerable investment risk and good economic growth potential. FDI can be a self-generating process through demonstration effect and agglomeration effects. Fifth, the inflow of FDI capital may ease the foreign financing constraints of an economy.

Measuring these impacts are far from easy. Subsequent chapters in this book deal with various impacts on restructuring, foreign financing and technology. With regard to the direct transfer of capital, this is only in part effecting the sum of available investment resources. As half or more of the FDI in CECs was spent on privatization acquisition, the efficient investment of public revenues from privatization in part determined the impact of FDI. Correcting FDI inflow figures for the sum spent on acquisition of existing assets the direct contribution of FDI to gross fixed capital formation can be calculated. Own calculations and estimations show that the contribution of direct capital inflows to gross fixed capital formation 1993–96 was 10–16 per cent in Hungary, 2–3 per cent in the Czech Republic and Slovenia and 1 per cent in Slovakia. These shares are small with the exception of Hungary and in relationship with the achieved rate of economic growth. Positive effects can be expected from follow-up investments of MNCs in the enterprises acquired through privatization. If most of the productive lines and the organization are changed by the new owner, privatization-related acquisition has some features of a greenfield investment ('brown field investment').

Technological development takes place to a large extent within multinational enterprises (MNEs), thus economic growth depends on the successful integration of a country's enterprises into international corporate networks. Countries relying heavily on FDI in the take-off period of economic growth, like Austria, can benefit from imported technology while focusing domestic research on adaptation. While multinationals may not bring the most advanced technology to their investments in medium developed countries, such as the CECs, they mostly transfer more advanced technologies than those locally available.

However, technology import inside MNCs can be limited as they try to prevent leakages and positive externalities (Meyer, 1998). Thus, while the firm may gain from relocation to CECs, the target country may not. Borensztein *et al.* (1995) emphasize the crucial role of human capital and suggest that while FDI is, in fact, an important vehicle for the transfer of technology, contributing to growth in larger measure than domestic investment, FDI is more productive than domestic investment only when the host country has a minimum threshold stock of human capital. Thus catching-up is most likely from low-medium to high-medium techno-logical levels. The successful country must have a sufficient local knowl-edge base and learning and adaptation capacity to cope with technology import. The CECs generally have these conditions which makes them (including Poland and Estonia) different from south-east European and Commonwealth of Independent States (CIS) countries. The CECs having the appropriate knowledge base are more successful than others in terms of economic transformation, catching up and attracting FDI. There seem to be positive feedbacks between these three processes although their progress may differ.

Priewe (1997) raises doubt that positive effects of FDI suggested by theory will materialize in transition countries because of (a) the conflict between motives of investors and expectations of host countries; (b) replacement rather than expansionary FDI; (c) transfer of low-end value-added stages; (d) limited spillover from FIEs to domestic firms. His arguments are mainly based on the experience of less-developed east European countries and are less valid to more advanced transformation economies, but all these characteristics do exist in the case of the CECs (Chapter 4). The evaluation can be more positive if the counter-scenario of non-investment is considered. Even a limited impact of FDI can be positive compared to a situation where the position of a country is deter-mined by ailing domestic companies. There is also some evidence pointing to an improving situation over time, FIEs investing into higher value-added production and generating spillover.

A further major problem associated with FDI is its possible negative impact on competition. As pointed out by Dunning (1993), MNCs tend to use their superior market power in order to reduce competition. They can be subject to greater competitive pressure globally than in individual country markets, but monopolistic behaviour can cause welfare loss even if it appears only on a regional segment of the market. CECs will have to fully adopt EU-conforming legislation and practices to control the abuse of market power.

In CECs the liberalization of markets and the entry of foreign firms is ahead of the application of strict controlling norms. Environmental standards, consumer protection and labour norms do not usually conform with EU laws, or if these norms are enacted, they are not properly applied. Public opinion is more critical towards foreign investors than domestic companies when good practices are not applied. In fact, looser production and employment standards are part of the cost advantages CEC locations provide. The gradual implementation of EU norms for the environment and working conditions will increase production cost and thus diminish the competitiveness of some CEC companies if they cannot compensate for it with efficiency increase. Implementation of stricter norms usually need more investment which may actually hit financially weaker domestic investors more than foreigners.

Economic liberalization and integration enlarge the possibilities for a country to gain international capital flows, but does not ensure that the effects will be positive in the long run. The long-term impact of FDI on development is critically dependent on three variables:

1. the type of FDI undertaken;
2. the structure of the indigenous resources and capabilities of countries concerned;
3. the macroeconomic and organizational policies pursued by governments.

The type of FDI has to do with the spillover effects and the possibility of a subsidiary to upgrade its competitive position. Local resources and skills must be maintained and continuously improved. The host country must conduct policies which lead to an upgrading of the country as a business location in order to benefit from FDI in the long run. These policies, if applied to all companies, can benefit domestic firms as well. They are, in fact, policies which a country needs anyway if it aims at sustainable economic growth.

4.   BASIC FEATURES OF FDI IN CECS

The CECs received 1 per cent of global FDI and the central and east European countries combined received about 3 per cent in 1994–96 (UNCTAD, 1998). The seven countries listed in Table 2.5 attracted some US$ 10.7 billion in 1995, US$ 9.2 billion in 1996 and almost US$ 11.7 billion in 1997. The recent upswing is due to more privatization sales in Poland, Romania and Bulgaria. In line with theory-based expectations, more advanced, stable and open countries have been the most attractive FDI targets also among the CEECs (Central and Eastern European countries) in the 1990s. The Czech Republic, Hungary and Slovenia, as

Table 2.5   FDI in CEECs: inflow 1994–97 and stock end-1997

	Inflow US$ mn				Inflow 1997 as % of fixed capital formation[a]	Stock 1997 US$ mn	as % of GDP[a]
	1994	1995	1996	1997			
Czech Republic	869	2562	1428	1300	8.1	6763	13.0
Hungary	1319	4571	2040	2107	21.5	17529	39.3
Poland[b]	1493	2511	4000	5678	19.7	17705	12.5
Slovakia	185	181	667	301	4.0	1537	9.0
Slovenia	377	414	190	532	14.3	2120	12.7
Bulgaria	214	163	234	510	51.0	1252	12.5
Romania	568	313	609	1224	18.0	3433	9.0
CEEC	5025	10714	9168	11652	–	50340	–

Notes: Different national methodologies. Flows do not add up to stocks. For a detailed description of methodology see Hunya and Stankovsky (1998).
[a]   Preliminary.
[b]   Projects with more than US$ 1 million invested capital.

Source: National publications and WIIW Database.

well as Poland and Estonia, have attracted considerable amounts of FDI either in volume or in comparison to their size. That the seven countries have been more attractive than others is the result of their better macro-economic performance and stability together with a faster pace of institutional transformation. The relative amount of FDI within the group has mainly to do with the progress and method of privatization.

International comparisons of FDI are seriously limited by the incompatibility and frequent changes of national statistical methodologies. Although most CECs make efforts to implement international standards, deviations from standardized reporting are still substantial. For measuring FDI flows the major problem is to include all inflows in cash and kind as well as reinvested earnings. Methodological changes, as in Slovakia in 1996, Slovenia in 1994 or Romania in 1997, limit comparability over time. For measuring stocks, the way flows are aggregated is important. According to international standards, aggregation should be done in local currency and converted into US$ using the end-of-period exchange rate. A strengthening dollar can thus 'devalue' past stocks. Some of the CEECs, notably Poland, Bulgaria and Romania, report only accumulated dollar inflows which increases their stocks in comparison to other countries. An attempt to recalculate Polish 1997 FDI stocks using cumulation in local currency yields US$ 15.7 billion, substantially less than the locally calculated 20.5 billion (including small ventures).

The size of FDI inflow can be compared to gross fixed capital formation, and FDI stocks to GDP. The world average of FDI inflow compared to gross fixed capital formation was 5 per cent in 1995 and 1996 and there were only 20 countries where it exceeded 20 per cent (UNCTAD, 1998). Hungary stands out with a rate of over 20 per cent FDI per gross fixed capital formation in each year between 1992 and 1997. The Czech Republic in 1995 and Poland in 1997 came close to this mark but also the others, except Slovakia, are above the world average. Extremely high rates can appear due to a depression of nationwide investments, such as in Bulgaria in 1997. The world average for FDI stocks to GDP is about 10 per cent, which is exceeded by five countries out of the seven CEECs in Table 2.5. Hungary is in the group of countries with the highest FDI stock per GDP in the world. The Czech Republic and Slovenia are average countries and, out of the CECs, only Slovakia is lagging behind.

The distribution of FDI by economic activities (Table 2.6) reflects the opening up of individual sectors to foreign investment. Initially, most FDI went into trade and manufacturing; also later the financial sector caught up. In countries where new sectors have been opened to foreign investment through the advance of privatization, the share of manufacturing declined below 40 per cent. The most notable cases were telecommunications in the Czech Republic and also the gas and energy sectors in Hungary. In Slovenia, where several activities are still closed to foreign investors and the manufacturing sector was privatized mainly to domestic owners, the energy sector has a remarkably high share due to the atomic power station jointly owned with Croatia.

The method of entry is a characteristic feature of FDI in CEECs. About half of the FDI in CEECs was invested through privatization-related acquisitions. Some 10–20 per cent were greenfield investments, the rest being investment into existing FIEs. Mass privatization by vouchers, sale to insiders, or to the management have hindered foreign take-overs, whereas in direct sale tenders foreigners usually outbid domestic investors (Hunya, 1997). The main applied method of privatization supported FDI in Hungary and hindered it in the Czech Republic, Slovenia or Slovakia. Foreign sales were allowed in the latter countries, too, but were restricted to a few individual cases. With time passing, the motivation of entry becomes less important, subsidiaries may take other functions, enlarge or shrink their original task in the MNC's network.

*Table 2.6   FDI in CECs by industries (NACE) FDI stock as of December
1996, shares in per cent*

NACE Code		Czech Republic	Hungary	Slovakia	Slovenia
A, B	Agriculture, forestry, fishing	–	1.2	–	–
C	Mining and quarrying	–	1.2	–	–
D	Manufacturing	37.4	39.6	47.5	35.2
E	Electricity, gas, water supply	*	14.2	–	*
F	Construction	8.3	3.7	3.1	–
G	Trade, repair of motor vehicles	8.1	11.9	18.0	9.2
H	Hotels and restaurants	*	2.5	1.4	*
I	Transport, communications	22.1	8.8	2.1	6.6
J	Finance, insurance	*	8.9	25.5	11.3
K	Real estate, renting	*	7.3	1.9	8.3
L	Public administration, defence	–	–	–	–
N	Health and social work	–	0.1	–	–
O	Other community, social services	–	0.6	0.5	–
	Not classified activities (*)	24.1	–	–	29.4
	Total	100.0	100.0	100.0	100.0
	Total, US$ mn	7060.9	9787.2	1326.2	1642.8

Source: National publications and WIIW Database.

5   FDI AND EU EASTERN ENLARGEMENT

This book covers three of the five candidates which have been selected to
join the EU ahead of others. Slovakia was left out mainly for political
reasons from the first round of enlargement and hopes to catch up under
the new coalition government inaugurated in autumn 1998.

Joining the EU can be considered as the culmination of an integration
process which started with the systemic changes in central and eastern

Europe. Since the liberalization of East–West trade and capital flows, an intensive microeconomic integration is on the way between the present and future EU members. EU investors in CECs benefit from the access to new markets and from low-cost production facilities. As shown by data for three of the first tier accession countries and Slovakia, foreign investors make use of the lower labour cost, but their primary targets are capital-intensive industries with a generally high degree of internationalization (for example, the motor industry and the production of electric machinery).

FDI has generated trade between CECs and EU countries with a deficit on the eastern side. Through the trade with CECs, EU countries generated income on their current account and their economies benefited from a demand pull. The current account surplus was partly balanced by increasing capital export to CECs. Part of the FDI projects helped to supply the markets of CECs especially in the food industry as well as in financial services and retailing. These investments generated additional business and also jobs in the home countries of the investors. Another part of FDI aimed at sourcing out part of the production to lower-cost locations. While this generated further exports of components, it also strengthened the international competitive position of EU firms. This is especially the case for small- and medium-size companies in Germany and Austria for which the proximity of new markets and production locations matter more than for global-oriented multinational corporations.

Successful foreign investment projects in CECs increase the profits of investing firms and if repatriated, also the tax base in EU countries. On the other hand, host countries of intensified FDI activity undergo accelerated restructuring of capacities, jobs and regional specialization. In the process of restructuring, local and temporary loser companies, areas and branches appear both in the EU and in CECs. The treatment of the emerging problems can, therefore, be local and temporary without hindering the overall deepening of integration.

When discussing the impact of regional integration on FDI, Dunning (1994) distinguishes between primary and secondary effects. As a primary effect intra-regional trade becomes more attractive, and companies outside the integration move part of their production within the borders of the integration thus FDI increases. Companies inside the integration would adjust locations to benefit from free trade and as a consequence FDI would decrease in some countries and increase in others. As a secondary effect appearing later in time, reduced risk and lower transaction costs would increase the overall mobility of capital in the integrated area. Cantwell (1992) pointed out that as a reaction to the single European market, MNCs developed regional corporate networks and alliances. Blomström (1997) points out that an integration between developed and less-developed areas can generate a boom of FDI both from within and outside the integrated area, while this is not the case if only developed or less-developed countries, set up an integration. The more change an integration agreement generates in terms of trade and investment liberalization between the member countries, the more change in investment patterns can emerge. As Rojec (1997b) points out, the impact of the EU accession on FDI in CECs can be judged if compared to the association agreements which already stipulate free trade of manufacturing products. They also guarantee that no new restrictions on international capital movements, including FDI, would be imposed.

What changes of the direct investment activities in CECs can be expected due to EU accession? Becoming part of the internal market may boast trade and FDI activities between CECs and the EU. Based on the experience of Portugal and Spain, a general upswing of FDI can be expected already during the accession negotiations and also when the accession takes place. However, a real surge of FDI such as in the case of the Iberian countries, cannot be expected due to already advanced trade and investment liberalization in most CEEC candidates.

Factors attracting FDI will generally change for the better, such as the level of investment risk, the size of a freely accessible market and the size of the host country local market. The investment risk of accession countries will certainly be lower than that of left-out CECs due to higher political and economic stability. Lower risk is a benefit for investors and host countries alike in the form of lower risk premium and higher potential FDI. The size of a freely attainable market will grow for certain products. Although most of the trade with manufacturing products was already liberalized by the Europe agreements, the lifting of border control can further reduce costs. Domestic demand is expected to increase in the accession countries more rapidly than in the present EU member States. Although FDI supports the catching-up of CECs in terms of economic development and wage levels, the gap will remain there for a considerable time and attract labour-intensive production to CECs.

It can be expected that a reorganization of multinational corporate networks will take place when CECs become part of the internal market. There will be more intensive production integration of the new members and also some rationalization of locations. Domestic market-oriented affiliates in CECs may become more internationalized, others may be closed down. Some of the activities of multinational enterprises may become more concentrated in one of the new EU member States and move out from less favourable locations.

It can be concluded that further FDI, EU accession and catching-up reinforce each other. The benefit of the three processes to the present EU members is both an enhanced political and economic stability in Europe and higher dynamism and competitiveness. These aims can best be achieved if CECs can catch-up fast with the EU in terms of economic growth as well as legal and institutional harmonization. EU membership is, therefore, to be considered as a vehicle and not the final result of the catching-up process.

6   THE ROLE OF POLICY AND THE PROSPECTS OF FDI IN CECS

Economic and political stability are the most important basic conditions for attracting FDI. The maintenance of an environment conducive to sustained economic growth is the best FDI policy. The second condition is the creation of a business environment, including an efficient institutional structure, which would allow for an efficient operation of economic agents. Special investment promotion measures come only last in importance.

During the first years of the transition process, all governments provided tax holidays and other incentives to foreign investors. Despite that, relatively modest amounts of FDI could be attracted. Insufficiencies in the overall economic and legal environment could not be corrected by special FDI incentives. Later, most special incentives were abolished and domestic treatment became valid for foreign investors. In the Czech Republic all incentives were abolished as of 1993 and FDI increased nevertheless. This was due to the economic upswing and to some major privatization deals. Hungary was the last to unify incentives for domestic and foreign investors in 1995. CEC governments keep in mind that both protective and stimulating policies discriminating FIEs against DEs violate the principles of the EU single-market rules and competition rules in particular and thus might be an obstacle to closer relationships with the EU. All the four countries have made progress in implementing EU regulations in the field of FDI liberalization but there are still some protected industries in some countries. Independently, whether a CEC becomes a member of EU or not, the freedom both to protect domestic industries and to subsidize inward FDI is limited under international competition rules.

EU competition policy is also shaping the behaviour of non-members as far as their trade with the EU is concerned. Further effects can be expected from the envisaged Multilateral Agreement on Investment of OECD which most likely will further reduce national policy discretion in this field. Practice has allowed for three major diversions from the general principles of non-incentives: in the case of privatization deals, general investment incentives which can be mainly utilized by foreign investors, and special case-by-case incentives for large investments. As most of the initial FDI in manufacturing came to the CECs as a privatization acquisition, the terms laid down in the privatization agreements can be considered as a major part of industrial and FDI policy.

Future opportunities for acquisition in the privatization process differ from country to country. In Hungary, a country with almost completed privatization and dominating foreign ownership will provide few new opportunities: only some problematic companies in industry expect privatization as well as residual shares in already privatized companies. However, the high degree of foreign presence makes this country attractive for FDIs due to agglomeration effects. A steady high rate of FDI inflow will take the form of greenfield projects and capital increase in existing ventures.

The rest of the CECs, countries with shallow privatization, face a second drive of ownership changes. As the owners who received property rights in various distribution schemes will not have the means to restructure the companies, they may invite foreign investors to do the job. In addition, there are important activities, especially utilities and banks, where major privatization deals are still ahead.

At the same time, there is competition between CECs for further greenfield projects. A new system of direct investment incentives was approved by the Czech government in April 1998 (Zemplínerová, 1998, 1999). Incentives are available for domestic as well as foreign investors. However, there exists a minimum amount to be invested: US$ 25 billion which, in fact, excludes potential domestic investors. The major argument in favour of the incentive programme was to 'equalize the conditions for FDI in the Czech Republic with other countries': to counterbalance the disadvantages of the country *vis-à-vis* other potential host countries of FDI and increase the inflow of foreign capital. In the case of large multinational investors, incentives are often negotiated on an individual basis between multinationals and the government. Incentives can be 'sold' for higher privatization revenues or for future investment promises. The most outstanding example for this approach was the Škoda–Volkswagen joint venture (JV) which also demonstrates that promises of foreign investors are not necessarily kept.

The CECs may further benefit from their geographic proximity to EU markets. Some relocations from low-cost Asia to low-cost Europe can be observed (Philips car-audio from Singapore to Hungary). Cost-sensitive production can move from the EU core to the CECs. This relocation can be direct (for example Electrolux white-ware from Italy to Hungary) or indirect effecting only the expansion of production (carmaker Audi to

Hungary, Volkswagen to Slovakia). Also non-European investors (Japanese, South Korean) consider CECs as a European location and expand production for local and EU markets.

Specific features of industrial structures connected with the small size of the CECs, in the case of Slovenia and Slovakia even more than in the other two, may strengthen in the future. With increasing liberalization and joining the EU internal market, local market-oriented investments will be less and less attracted to the manufacturing sector. Subsidiaries may also become more and more specialized, which may raise the problem of overspecialization and a too high dependence of certain markets.

A large part of domestic companies in the CECs are still in a transitional phase and have relatively weak international competitiveness based on low wages and low capital cost due to non-investment. They need both massive capital investments and the integrating force of foreign capital to improve their position by access to knowledge and international networking. This may or may not happen in the form of direct investment, but the acceptance of foreign control is indispensable in certain industries.

The role of policy in the future can be seen in stabilizing the positive effects of foreign penetration and stimulating spillovers to the rest of the economy. The impact on the development of indigenous capabilities and on restructuring and upgrading of dynamic comparative advantages of domestic companies can be improved by increasing domestic private and public investment in these fields. Attracting the right kind of investment with targeted incentives and advantageous privatization deals can be a help. An increase of competition and efficiency in all sectors of the economy can be a benefit. The existence of a large state sector absorbs financial means, human capital and administrative capacity. FDI helps to change industrial structures in conformity with European trends, but for the future, the development path of subsidiaries in international productive networks is more important.

CEC manufacturing industries are for the time being increasingly competitive due to their integration into multinational production networks via FDI. They will be able to utilize their labour cost advantage for attracting FDI for quite some time, as did Austria in the 1960s and 1970s. However, they must be aware of the increasing competition when their labour costs start rising. As to the future impact of FDI, the development path of subsidiaries in international productive networks is more important. They must move to higher value-added products within the framework of the multinational corporate network.

In Austria a cluster-oriented location policy has been frequently proposed, partly implemented, in order to support complementary investment, which may then accumulate know-how and networks between suppliers and customers and competition between cluster firms (Bellak, 1998). Among the various general location policies, the optimization of the national innovation system has priority. This should ensure not only technology transfer and technology creation in foreign subsidiaries but also attract additional investment. A steady process of upgrading human capital is also seen as a necessary condition to ensure inward FDI. Other methods include business parks and regional initiatives. Future subsidies by the EU may complement local policies. Hungary has a recent programme supporting domestic subcontracting to FIEs and to attract greenfield FDI with industrial parks. The duty-free zone status of exporting FIEs remains one of the major factors of attraction (Hunya, 1996; Éltető, 1998a).

Assembling plants with a mass production of specific products via comparatively low production cost and high productivity tend to be subject to a substantial pressure to relocate if costs increase. CECs benefit from this type of relocation for the time being and EU countries are the losers. The future of a country as a business location should, therefore, be based on the immobile, at the same time high value added, elements of the value added chain of large MNCs. Austria is moving in this direction and can generally stand the pressure of international competition for inward investment, paralleled with further reductions of the share of production cost in total cost.

BIBLIOGRAPHY

Amsden, A.H., J. Kochanowicz and L. Taylor (1994), *The Market Meets its Match: Restructuring the Economies of Eastern Europe*, Cambridge: Harvard University Press.
Baldwin, R. *et al.* (1997), 'The costs and benefits of eastern enlargement: the impact on the EU and central Europe', *Economic Policy*, **24**.
Bellak, Ch. (1998), 'Lessons from Austria's post-war pattern of inward FDI for CEECs', *WIIW Research Reports*, no. 251, The Vienna Institute for International Economic Studies, November.
Blomström, M. (1997), 'Regional integration and foreign direct investment', *NBER Working Paper*, no. 6019, New York, April.
Borensztein, E., J. DeGregorio and J.W. Leed (1995), 'How does foreign direct investment affect economic growth?', *NBER Working Paper*, no. 5057.
Brzica, D. (1998), 'Foreign direct investment in the Slovak Republic: theory, policy, facts and future', final report, Institute of Slovak and World Economy, mimeo, June.
Cantwell, J.A. (1992), 'Innovation and Technological Competitiveness', in P.J. Buckley and M. Casson (eds), *Multinational Enterprises in the World Economy*, Aldershot: Edward Elgar, pp. 20–40.
Dunning, J.H. (1993), *Multinational Enterprises and the Global Economy*, Wokingham: Addison Wesley.

Dunning, J.H. (1994), 'Reevaluating the benefits of foreign direct investment', *Discussion Papers in International Investment and Business Studies*, no. 188, University of Reading.

Dunning, J.H. (1996), 'Governments and the macro-organization of economic activity: an historical and spatial perspective', *Discussion Papers in Economics and Management*, no. 352, University of Reading.

Dunning, J.H. and R. Narula (1996), 'The investment development path revisited', in J.H. Dunning and R. Narula (eds), *Foreign Direct Investment and Governments*, London: Routledge.

Éltető, A. (1998a), 'Economic policy background of foreign investments in Hungary', *WIIW Research Reports*, no. 244, The Vienna Institute for International Economic Studies, April.

Éltető, A. (1998b), 'The economic performance of firms with foreign investment in Hungary', *Working Papers*, no. 94, Institute for World Economics, Budapest, July.

Havlik, P. (1996), 'Exchange rates, competitiveness and labour costs in central and eastern Europe', *WIIW Research Reports*, no. 231, The Vienna Institute for International Economic Studies, October.

Hunya, G. (1996), 'Foreign direct investment in Hungary: a key element of economic modernization', *WIIW Research Reports*, no. 226, The Vienna Institute for International Economic Studies, February.

Hunya, G. (1997), 'Large privatization, restructuring and foreign direct investment', in S. Zecchini (ed.), *Lessons from the Economic Transition*, Boston: Kluwer Academic Publishers.

Hunya, G. (1998), 'Integration of CEEC manufacturing into European corporate structures via direct investment', *WIIW Research Reports*, no. 224, The Vienna Institute for International Economic Studies, May.

Hunya, G. and J. Stankovsky (1998), 'WIIW-WIFO Database. Foreign Direct Investment in Central and East European Countries and the Former Soviet Union', The Vienna Institute for International Economic Studies (WIIW) and Austrian Institute of Economic Research (WIFO), July.

Inotai, A. and P. Marer (1995), 'Foreign direct investment in Hungary: trends, policies, impacts and recommendation', Blue Ribbon Commission, Budapest, December.

Landesmann, M. (1996), 'Emerging patterns of European industrial specialization: implications for trade structures, foreign direct investment and migration flows', OECD Seminar on Migration, Free Trade and Regional Integration in Central and Eastern Europe, Vienna, February.

Marin, D. (1995), 'Learning and dynamic comparative advantage: lessons from Austria's post-war pattern of growth for eastern Europe', *CEPR Working Papers*, no. 1116, London.

Markusen, J. and A. Venables (1997), 'Foreign direct investment as a catalyst for industrial development', *NBER Working Paper*, no. 6019, New York, October.

Meyer, K.E. (1995), 'Direct foreign investment, structural change and development: can the east Asian experience be replicated in east central Europe?', *Discussion Paper Series*, no. 16, London Business School, CIS-Middle Europe Centre, January.

Meyer, K. (1998), 'Direct Investment in Economics in Transition', Aldershot: Edward Elgar.

Nunnenkamp, P. (1997), 'Aufhol- und Abkoppelungsprozesse im europäischen Binnenmarkt', *Die Weltwirtschaft*, **2**.

OECD (1996), *Globalisation of Industry: Overview and Sector Reports*, Paris: OECD.

Ozawa, T. (1992), 'Foreign direct investment and economic development', *Transnational Corporations*, **1**.

Pfaffermayr, M. (1995), 'Direktinvestitionen im Ausland und ihre Wirkung auf die Exporttätitgkeit', mimeo, Johannes Kepler University, Linz.

Pöschl, J. (1998), 'Central and east European countries: prone to currency crises?', *Discussion Paper*, FS II 98-601, Wissenschaftszentrum Berlin für Sozialfragen, October.

Priewe, J. (1997), 'Direktinvestitionen im Transformationsprozeß – Hoffnungsträger oder Mythos? Zum Stellenwert von Direktinvestitionen in GUS-Ländern', *Wirtschaft und Gesellschaft*, **23**, (2).

Pye, R. (1997), 'Foreign direct investment in central Europe: results from a survey of major western investors', *Finance Working Paper*, A.97/1, City University Business School, London, April.

Radošević, S. (1995), 'Technology transfer and restructuring of technology capability in global competition: the case of economies in transition', paper presented at the workshop 'Transfer of Technology, Trade, and Development: the Newly Industrialised Economies in the Global Competition', Venice, April.

Richter, S. *et al.* (1998), 'EU eastern enlargement: challenge and opportunity', *WIIW Research Reports*, no. 249, The Vienna Institute for International Economic Studies, July.

Rojec, M. (1997a), 'The development potential of foreign direct investment in the Slovenian economy', *WIIW Research Reports*, no. 235, The Vienna Institute for International Economic Studies, April.

Rojec, M. (1997b), 'Foreign direct investment – how much does NATO and EU membership enhance investments by non-EU investors', mimeo.

Rojec, M. (1998), 'Restructuring with foreign direct investment: the case of Slovenia', Institute of Macroeconomic Analysis and Development, Ljubljana.

Szanyi, M. (1997) (co-ordinator), Documents of the Phare-ACE project P95-2225-R, 'Industrial investments: cornerstones in the next stage of central European transition', mimeo.

Szanyi, M. (1998), 'The role of foreign direct investment in restructuring and modernizing transition economies: an Overview of Literature on Hungary', *WIIW Research Reports*, no. 244, The Vienna Institute for International Economic Studies, April.

UNCTAD (1998) *World Investment Report 1998*, New York and Geneva: United Nations.

Zemplínerová, A. (1998), 'Die Rolle der ausländischen Direktinvestitionen im Restrukturierungsprozeß der tschechischen Wirtschaft', *Leipziger Beiträge zu Wirtschaft und Gesellschaft*, **8**, Leipzig.

Zemplínerová, A. (1999), 'Impact of foreign direct investment on the restructuring and growth in manufacturing', *Prague Economic Papers*, **1**.

Zemplínerová, A. and V. Benáček (1995), 'Foreign direct investment east and west: the experience of the Czech Republic', mimeo, ACE Project Workshop, Prague, 6–8 April.

3. FDI, technology transfer and growth in economic theory

Mark Knell and Slavo Radošević

1 INTRODUCTION

FDI can play an important role in closing the technology gap between central Europe and the EU. While endogenous growth theory has provided several arguments for why technological learning and technical change will stimulate growth in the long run, the role of FDI in this process is not well understood. FIEs provide a potentially important channel for the diffusion of knowledge-based, firm-specific assets. Yet these firms can still undermine the development of local markets and dynamic competitive advantage in central Europe. This requires a more systematic investigation into the relationship between inward FDI and the transfer of technology.

There are at least three motivations for investing in central Europe: (1) cutting production costs; (2) market presence; and (3) technological capabilities. Traditional theories of foreign investment stress the first motivation over the latter two, mainly because in the mass production economy cost cutting was more important than the creation of technological capabilities. However, given the changing nature of technology and production and the inability of single firms to innovate across a broader range of technologies, multinationals became increasingly interested in technological collaboration with a partner with complementary capabilities. This trend explains why most global investment is contained within the Organization for Economic Cooperation and Development (OECD) countries. In the 1990s, more than 50 per cent of production in the major OECD countries is knowledge-intensive. This suggests that strategic investment will depend on the complementarity of knowledge-based assets of the firm, especially in industrial sectors that require a highly skilled labour force.

This chapter discusses the relationship between foreign investment, technology transfer and growth in economic theory. In the narrow sense FDI is one of many channels to transfer technology. Other sources of technology transfer include JVs, technology licensing, capital good imports, strategic alliances and subcontracting (Mowery and Oxley, 1995; Radošević, 1997b). FDI is complementary to these sources of technology transfer and together they form a network of intra- and extra-multinational company links. The main difference between equity and non-equity relationships is that technology tends to transfer more easily within the firm when equity is at stake. In addition non-equity forms of technology transfer will be more prevalent whenever patent rights are easy to establish and defend, while ownership is more prevalent when knowledge is tacit and not easy to copy. FDI is also less prevalent in the high-tech industries since it requires a close interaction among companies and involves more risk and uncertainty. This suggests that it is difficult to isolate equity relationships out of the specific industry context. In reality equity relationships are complemented with a variety of non-equity relationships that jointly engender the patterns of production and global integration. Central Europe is not isolated from these trends and the aim of this chapter is to shed new light on the patterns of integration through FDI.

2   FDI AND MODERN GROWTH THEORY

The relationship between FDI and traditional growth theory is rather simple. In the traditional 'production function' approach pioneered by Solow (1956), long-run growth can only result from advances in technological knowledge. Without technological progress, diminishing marginal returns to both domestic and foreign investment would eventually limit economic growth. An exogenous increase in investment, whether from home or abroad, would increase the amount of capital (and output) per person, but this would only be temporary as diminishing returns would impose a limit to this growth. The implication for the global economy is that foreign investment can only offset this limit if it includes the transfer of new technological knowledge in the form of new goods, new markets or new processes. Policies to attract foreign investment would only have a transitory effect on growth, unless they include incentives to encourage innovation.

In endogenous growth theory, FDI can affect growth in different ways. Most endogenous growth models focus on the production and use of new knowledge in the presence of increasing returns, non-convexities and monopoly power including a technology parameter that recognizes new ideas in the form of research and development (R&D) and human capital. As a technology parameter, foreign investment can generate growth and increasing returns through global knowledge transfers and domestic knowledge spillovers. Through these knowledge transfers, the theory predicts that foreign investment will increase the stock of knowledge by creating new products and processes, introducing new management practices and organizational arrangements, and improving the skills of the labour force. Even without majority ownership, foreign investment can lead to knowledge spillovers through minority JVs and licensing.

While Rebelo (1991) demonstrates that it is not necessary to assume diminishing returns to physical capital to generate economic growth, most endogenous growth models offset the negative feedback by including various externalities associated with increasing returns into the production function. The models of Romer (1986) and Lucas (1988) suggest that growth rates differ because the positive feedback generated by technological learning external to the firm (diffusion) may exceed the negative feedback engendered by diminishing marginal returns internal to the firm. Romer (1986) introduces a technology parameter in the production function that exhibits increasing returns to knowledge and constant returns in knowledge accumulation. This allows the model to generate growth through learning-by-doing and knowledge spillovers.

Technical knowledge is generally public (or non-rival) and at least partly excludable, tacit knowledge is private or firm-specific (rival) and is excludable in that it requires certain rights to access it. The main interest of the firm, therefore, is to enforce these rights to gain monopoly profits, yet for society it is the inability of the firm to protect these rights that may lead to certain 'positive externalities' or 'knowledge spillovers' that can offset the marginal diminishing returns to physical capital. FDI can play an important role in facilitating these knowledge spillovers across national boundaries, but this will depend not only on obtaining the right to use the technical knowledge and the ability to transfer tacit knowledge from the parent firm to the subsidiary. If individuals possess this knowledge as Lucas (1988) suggests, then human capital is a rival good that can spill over as a result of a contractual arrangement between individual and firm or organization. In this context foreign firms may be attracted to a country or region because of the high skill levels and potentially high growth rates. As a lead variable, inward FDI can close the technology gap and generate economic convergence in these models, but as a lag variable it is just as likely to widen the technology gap as to close it (Krugman and Venables, 1995).

The role of multinational activity in facilitating economic growth is perhaps better understood in Romer (1990). In this model Romer generates growth through the creation of human capital, differing from Lucas in that it represents the endowment of human capital as the intensity of R&D. This model also suggests that research contains positive feedback that increases the variety of intermediate inputs by creating general knowledge and inducing the amount of human capital needed for subsequent innovations. Since the growth rate is an increasing function of the amount of human capital dedicated to R&D, the choice between production and research determines the pace of growth. Thus, an increase in the intensity of research generates growth through a cumulative rise in product innovation. This product differentiation reflects the increased specialization of labour across an increasing variety of activities, whether domestic or international. As the economy grows, producers introduce new intermediate goods that increase the productivity of labour and capital.

Aghion and Howitt (1992) and Grossman and Helpman (1991) generate growth in a similar way as Romer (1990) but consider technological progress as an improvement in the quality of existing producer products. Old technology becomes obsolete through the introduction of new technology. Grossman and Helpman (1991) represent this process as a quality ladder that firms climb depending on the stochastic nature of the R&D process. Firms obtain monopoly profits from the introduction of new producer goods that force lower quality goods to exit the market. Intertemporal improvements in the quality of production goods imply that the market outcome may not be optimal, but they may lead to either a higher or lower growth rate than is socially optimal since the knowledge spillovers can appear as a positive or negative externality. The inclusion of foreign investment and technology licensing into the model increases the range of factor endowments where price equilization is possible. International knowledge spillovers occur as firms with high technological capabilities and high factor prices find it profitable to locate or license high technology production to a country with lower capabilities and lower factor prices. Over time the country with high technological capabilities may become a net importer of high-tech products, as the affiliates export their finished products home, but also receive additional income from increased licence fees and the repatriation of profits.

Endogenous growth models have attempted to incorporate various channels of technology transfer. Dollar and Wolff (1993) show that international R&D spillovers play a significant role in explaining productivity growth across industries. Coe and Helpman (1995) describe how trade flows can facilitate the transfer of technology through R&D spillovers. Building on the model of Romer (1990) and Grossman and Helpman (1991), this model shows that a country's total factor productivity depends not only on its own R&D activity, but also on the R&D activity of its trading partners. Keller (1998) shows, however, that randomly generated trade flows can lead to similar or even higher international spillover effects on productivity compared with using

actual trade shares. The implication of this analysis is that other channels of technology transfer may describe R&D spillovers better than
trade flows. Borensztein *et al.* (1998) develop and test an endogenous
growth model in which FDI affects growth through the transfer of technology. Though not statistically significant, the results of the test show
that FDI has a positive impact on economic growth and is dependent on
the level of human capital in the host country.

3 TECHNOLOGY GAPS AND FDI

Gerschenkron (1962) developed the idea that technological differences
explain differences in growth rates and hence the possibility of catching-
up and convergence. The size of the gap creates an opportunity for
catching-up with the technology leader, but this opportunity will depend
on whether the relatively backward country can successfully imitate the
technological leader. Abramovitz (1989) developed this argument further
by arguing that the realization of this opportunity for closing the technology gap depends not only on the relative backwardness of the region, but
also on the 'social capability' of each individual country to absorb new
technology from abroad. Abramovitz and David (1996, p. 50) define social
capability as the 'attributes, qualities, and characteristics of people and
economic organization that originate in social and political institutions'
that influence economic behaviour. These institutional arrangements may
include the education system and the organization of firms of that country, but could be defined more specifically as technological capabilities or
competencies. Backward countries, therefore:

> have the potentiality for generating growth more rapid than that of more
> advanced countries, provided their social capabilities are sufficiently developed
> to permit successful exploitation of technologies already employed by the tech-
> nological leaders (Abramovitz, 1989).

The realization of this potential for central Europe to catch-up with
the EU will depend both on the presence of social capabilities and the
size of the technology gap.

Social capability also includes the absorptive capacity of firms to
assimilate technical knowledge from abroad. This social capability
appears as an externality in neoclassical endogenous growth theory and
as a joint product in the classical growth theory (Parrinello, 1993). Romer
(1990) and Grossman and Helpman (1991) include international knowledge spillovers by distinguishing between a purely 'local' or national
good and a 'global' or international good, but leave out the cost of build-

ing an absorptive capacity. According to Cohen and Levinthal (1989, p. 569) an absorptive capacity is the 'firm's ability to identify, assimilate and exploit knowledge from the environment'. When a firm wants to apply knowledge transferred from technological spillovers, it must enter into a time-consuming and costly process of investing in its absorptive capacity if it wants to imitate or improve. In this context, the idea of absorptive capacity becomes a connecting device between the potential for catching-up (technological opportunities) and its realization (appropriability conditions). This later factor is a necessary condition for firms to have incentives to invest in learning.

It is possible to restate the approach of Abramovitz (1989) so that catching-up in its complex form is the outcome of the existing technology gap, social capability and a variety of independent causes. From this perspective, factors of technology transfer should be considered as partly independent of those governing potentiality itself, and partly as a reflection of national social capability, in this case the capability to absorb and effectively use and innovate imported technology. This is in sharp contrast to the growth literature where the issue of how technology transfer contributes to growth is of no concern. The very mechanics of growth, or how technological, social and other independent factors interact and contribute to divergence/convergence processes, are not of prime concern. However, from a technology transfer perspective it is the mechanics (or process) that are the main concern. The approach which tries to take into account the interaction of these factors is the so-called national systems of innovation approach (see Lundvall, 1992; Nelson, 1993; Edquist, 1997). However, this approach lacks a strong underlying theoretical basis (Radošević, 1998).

Verspagen (1991) presents a simple (non-linear) bifurcation model that captures the essence of Abramovitz and describes how social capability and the size of the technology gap can influence the potential for catching-up. This model shows that the technology gap tends to close when a country has a high learning capability or low initial gap and tends to widen when a country has a low learning capability and high initial gap. International technology spillovers will increase in the catching-up economies and then decrease slowly until there is some convergence of technology levels. Complete convergence occurs as the economy moves from an imitator to innovator and increases the domestic R&D levels up to a level comparable with the technological leader. FDI can potentially play an important role in facilitating the knowledge spillovers and increase the likelihood that the economy will bifurcate into the 'convergence club'.

Developing the capability to absorb new technologies was essential in every case of catching-up this century. Empirical studies show that few countries have these technological capabilities. While the developed OECD countries have been converging over time (see also the case of Austria in Chapter 5), Baumol (1986) shows that this group of countries have also tended to grow faster than the world economy. Barro and Sala-i-Martin (1995) argue that the only convergence that occurs is so-called conditional convergence, by which they mean convergence after controlling for differences in steady states or situations in which a limited set of growth-related variables grow at a constant rate. The further an economy is below its steady state, the faster it should grow and vice versa; the further an economy is above its steady state, the slower the economy should grow (Jones, 1998). This suggests that the economic growth is a much more complex country-specific process, not easily amenable to generalizations.

The technology gap literature does not deal explicitly with technology transfer issues mainly for methodological reasons. This would require modelling a process with institutional variables in a dynamic context. While evolutionary modelling has made considerable progress in the last few years, it still has not reached a sufficient level to encompass the co-evolution of institutions and technologies. Moreover, it is difficult to separate the technology transfer from endogenous capability-building. Dunning (1994) has started to conceptualize the dual role they may play in the virtuous and vicious cycles of increasing and decreasing technological capability. Solvel and Zander (1995) point out that a common perspective in the new models is that the FIEs build increasingly complex organizational structures and management processes which allow technological learning and development across national borders. In that respect they function as a 'global learning vehicle'. However, taking into account the diversity of transfer channels and the different forms in which technology appears, it is probable that conceptualizations which link the catching-up process with technology transfer will remain very limited and vague.

Finally, the technology gap approach of Abramovitz (1989) and Verspagen (1991) shows how complex such an attempt would be. An alternative approach to analysing links between transfer and growth is to reduce it to measuring the costs and benefits in the host economy. We analyse this approach in the next two sections, which focus mainly on FDI. Other forms of technology transfer, like subcontracting and alliances, are far more difficult to analyse as the technology content is implicit in these arrangements.

4   ECONOMIC DEVELOPMENT THROUGH FDI AND TECHNOLOGY TRANSFER

The development literature of the 1960s and 1970s did not consider FDI as the best channel for growth and catching-up. Generally the share of equity capital that a foreign firm could own was often restricted because of the belief that equity relationships contained greater social costs than benefits. An assumed inverse relationship between the costs of transfer and the degree of foreign ownership led to a hierarchical ranking of channels according to their assumed benefit for a recipient. JVs were preferred over majority FDI, licensing over JVs and direct purchase over licensing. Hoffman and Girvan (1990) argue that an implicit assumption in the literature was that suppliers willing to agree to non-equity relationships would be smaller in size and have less bargaining power than FIEs, and, therefore, would agree to less costly contractual terms.

This hierarchy goes from less packaged towards more packaged forms of technology transfer, neglecting informal channels and alliances. Also, channels are seen as excluding each other. The absolute level of licensing is negatively related to the level of FDI so that these two strategies are seen as substitutes rather than complements. On the other hand, the rise of alliances shows the complementary rather than substitutive relationship among channels (Mowery and Oxley, 1995). The mainstream view in the literature on technology transfer is that unbundling the technology package is preferable to obtaining it bundled at a premium price. Ernst and O'Connor (1990) conclude that this may mean choosing a licence rather than joint ventures. Pack and Kamal (1997) also argue that licensing should generally be preferred to FDI even if it is hedged with some restrictions. However, they all place certain reservations on this view. Contractor (1985) shows that technology licensing can be disadvantageous for a seller and advantageous for a buyer, if measured in terms of the net technology margin. Ernst and O'Connor (1990) point out that unbundling and licensing a particular technology may reduce the costs of acquisition, but it may raise absorption (learning) costs if the licensee does not have sufficient internal expertise. Finally, empirical evidence suggests that the technologies transferred to foreign affiliates are newer than those for outside licensing and joint ventures (Mansfield and Romeo, 1980).

There are two explanations for why differences in technology transfer channels may be of secondary importance in the literature. The first argument focuses on the ability of firms to successfully absorb the new technology. Technological benefits gained from foreign technology depend less on the method selected for the transfer than on how the method is implemented – especially with regard to building a firm's technological capabilities. There is evidence that there are small differences in transfer conditions between FIEs and domestic-owned firms. Based on research into 47 technology transfers from the UK to India, Alam and Langrish (1981) suggest that there is no significant difference in the conditions of transfer (sophistication, royalty, import) between FIEs and domestic-owned firms. However, while this evidence suggests that technology transfer channels are of secondary importance, these studies tend to neglect the role of policy and the firm in facilitating technology diffusion. Dahlman *et al.* (1987, p. 768) concludes, therefore, that 'the technological benefits to be gained from foreign technology depend less on the method selected for the transfer, more on how the method is implemented'.

The second explanation focuses on the impossibility to differentiate between the relative success and failure of different technology transfer channels. Examining the effectiveness of different channels on countries' aggregate performance, Mowery and Oxley (1995) conclude that the mix of channels through which an economy obtains technology from foreign sources appears to be less important than the overall effort to exploit foreign sources of technology. Mowery and Oxley (1995) also suggest that channels alone are far from sufficient to explain the dynamic effects of technology transfer on the host economy. The secondary importance of technology transfer channels might be particularly pronounced at a macro-level, especially in high-growth economies, as the increasing absorptive capacity of these economies plays down all the factors which are seemingly important in a static framework (primarily costs), and the main concern of firms and policy makers is with the dynamic potential of specific technologies, irrespective of short-term costs.

Stewart (1981), Antonelli and Perosino (1992) and Vernon (1986) suggest that it is difficult to reach definite conclusions regarding technology transfer mechanisms. As Stewart (1981) states, 'there are many factors that contribute to the overall breakdown, including recipient country policy, industrial composition, country source of supplies, etc'. The choice of channels contains specific firm, industry and country elements that are difficult to ignore. This mixture of firm, industry and country-specific factors playing a role in the selection of technology transfer channels is confirmed also by several empirical researches. Reddy and Zhao (1990) identify several factors in choosing the method of transferring technology: the competition faced by the supplier firm; the age of the transferred technology; the nature of the transferred technology; and the importance of the technology to the supplier firm. Cortes and Bocock (1984) found that the type of product, and the country characteristics of both the recipient and supplier were important determinants of technology transfer in the Latin American petrochemicals industry. Davidson and McFetridge (1993) found close relationships between the mode of transfer and the characteristics of the technology, the parent firm and certain demographic and geographic characteristics of receiving countries. There was a looser relationship between the mode of transfer and selected public policies of the receiving countries and no relationship at all between transfer mode and the economic characteristics of receiving countries.

The notion of different transfer mechanisms relate to corporate governance mechanisms. The proposition that we introduce is that intra-industry modes of governance determine typical technology transfer channels. For example, it is difficult to expect that in the textile industry, where the dominant governance mode is an arm's-length relationship, FDI might be the dominant technology transfer channel. Similarly, in the aviation industry it is difficult to expect that licences could be the dominant technology transfer mode. As Hollingsworth (1993) points out, modes of governance are contingent on markets, technology and customer characteristics, with markets being a cyclical component and technology and demand a longer-term, structural component. On that basis he develops a taxonomy of governance modes consisting of hierarchies, obligational networks (subcontracting and co-operative alliances) and markets.

Pavitt (1984) shows how technology transfer can be industry- and technology-specific. In supplier-dominated sectors technology mainly comes already embodied in production machines. In production-intensive sectors key technologies relate to constructing and operating large-scale plants and are transferred internationally mainly through know-how agreements. In sectors supplying production equipment, technology is transferred internationally mainly through 'reverse engineering' and through local linkages with the production engineering departments in production-intensive user firms. In science-based firms the key technology emerges mainly from industrial R&D and in some cases from academic research. In information-intensive sectors (finance, retailing, publishing, travel) the technology transfer channel is purchase of equipment and software and 'reverse engineering'.

5 STATIC EFFECTS OF MULTINATIONAL ACTIVITY

If the private costs and benefits to technology exporters were the same as the social costs and benefits to host countries, any form of technology import would automatically provide the right kind of technology for the host country. Benefits would outweigh costs if the social rate of return from inward investment (equal to the value-added less profit accruing to the foreign owners) is greater than the opportunity cost of the resources used. Dunning (1994) outlined the different costs and benefits that FDI has on the competitiveness and growth of the firm. He identified at least eight potential benefits from inward foreign direct investment:

1. additional resources and technological capabilities;
2. new entrepreneurship, management styles and work cultures;
3. spillover effects in the domestic economy;
4. effective demand;
5. tax revenue;
6. improving balance of payments through export growth and import substitution;
7. access to global network;
8. corporate governance.

He also identified at least seven cost factors that can offset these benefits:

1. wrong kind of resources and assets;
2. inability to adapt to local customs and culture;
3. lock-in to low innovative dynamism;
4. transfer pricing;
5. worsening the balance of payments;
6. abuse of power;
7. the global interests of the multinational may be inconsistent with the dynamic competitive advantage.

Costs and benefits are never confined only to enterprises involved in technology transfer; they spill over into other enterprises and other sectors. The costs and benefits of FDI or licences are augmented by those of suppliers of capital equipment and intermediary products to the foreign affiliates or domestic producers. This undoubtedly makes the calculation of costs and benefits rather complex. Even if it is possible to resolve the problems of measurement, time horizon and choice of discount rate, the problem of the dynamic potential of transfer, which is not reflected in current costs and benefits, remains. The dynamic potential of transfer is unknown because it is highly dependent on the domestic generation of knowledge. That is the primary reason why similar policies of technology transfer usually produce rather different results in different countries. A country may acquire, at high cost, a wide range of technological capabilities in different sectors, yet these will not necessarily result in augmented innovative capability.

In view of these problems, it is perhaps not surprising that none of the studies on technology transfer to developing countries have come up with satisfactory estimates of direct costs. Hoffman and Girvan (1990) identify four direct costs associated with technology transfer:

1. direct costs;
2. costs resulting from restrictions on the recipient's production and marketing;
3. indirect costs associated with repatriated profits;
4. costs associated with the purchase of inputs from suppliers.

Direct costs are charges for the right to patents, licences, know-how and trademarks (recurrent payments and lump-sum payments). It is assumed that direct costs on average amount to 2–5 per cent for contracts using gross sales as a royalty base. Costs resulting from the restrictions on export and production are multiple and include contract obligations, restrictions on production, export restrictions, price fixing and the inefficient use of imported technology.

UNCTAD (1975) carried out the most systematic estimates of direct costs in the 1970s. They estimated that in 1968 the direct costs of technology transfer to developing countries were around US$ 1500 million in royalties and fee payments, equivalent to around 0.5 per cent of GDP. Stewart (1981) estimated that technology payments were more than US$ 5 billion in 1977. IMF estimates for royalties were, as expected, far lower than those of UNCTAD (generally of the order of 0.5 per cent to 1 per cent of exports). Stewart also assumed that tied purchase of capital goods added 30 per cent to the costs of capital equipment, as may be suggested by the evidence on tied aid. So, for countries with around 75 per cent of their inputs tied by technology contracts, the additional cost would be over 20 per cent of the cost of capital equipment. Stewart (1981) states that the share of agreements containing such provisions in most countries is between 62 and 83 per cent (1961), except in India where it was 15 per cent (1961) and 5 per cent (1964). On these grounds Stewart justifies the significant foreign exchange savings that could be made by developing countries if they regulated technology imports.

There were no estimates of this kind carried out during the 1980s, except via the normal process of technology balance-of-payments statistics. An alternative approach to the issue of costs and benefits of technology transfer are cross-sectional studies which measure performance of domestic and foreign-owned affiliates. The assumption is that the higher labour productivity or more capital-intensive techniques or higher employment creation of foreign affiliates positively affects the host economy, including technology transfer. For example, Karake (1990) found, in the case of the Egyptian industrial sector, a positive and substantially larger impact from foreign than domestic technology, measured by marginal productivity of foreign capital. The analysis also revealed that the contribution of total factor productivity to output growth is small relative to the contribution of physical inputs.

Helleiner (1989) cites only two case studies that show reductions in the host country's national product in the presence of FDI. FDI lowered national income and welfare in the host country though it earned profits for the private foreign investor. He concludes that the incidence of bad FDI projects and lower social rates of return were systematically associated with higher levels of domestic protection against imports. Administratively determined input prices like subsidized energy also played a significant role in these results. His conclusion is that FDI has mostly generated positive economic effects for host countries.

Studies reviewed in UNCTAD (1997) suggest that foreign affiliates are often more efficient in production than their domestic counterparts. Labour productivity in foreign affiliates tended to be higher than that in domestic firms in the same industry. This review also recognized that in some cases these differences diminished when the data were controlled for size of firm, suggesting that the productivity differences observed relate to differences in capital intensity and scale as well as in technology, and organizational capabilities.

Jenkins (1990) suggests that evidence does not support any strong statement about the relative performance of FIEs and local firms. He ascribes this to the inherent limitations of cross-section studies which often failed to reveal any clear-cut general pattern. The implicit assumptions of cross-section analysis is that the behaviour of local firms and foreign subsidiaries are independent of each other, and that there are differences between foreign and local firms which are universally valid. Jenkins goes on to suggest that a more fruitful approach is to be found in longitudinal studies. This approach would show that the behaviour between local and foreign firms is mutually dependent and that differences between them are often sector-, country- or technology-specific. This interaction creates dynamics which are difficult to reveal through cross-section analysis. Dunning (1993) points out that 'the dynamic view on technology transfer costs and benefits would bring out more clearly the trade-off between the wish to minimize real costs and to maximize technology contribution'.

6 DYNAMIC EFFECTS OF MULTINATIONAL ACTIVITY

The main reason why countries attempt to attract foreign investment is the desire to obtain new technology. Even if multinational firms carry out foreign activity in wholly owned affiliates, technology is to some extent a public good. Benefits to the host economy can take the form of various externalities, or what is often called 'productivity' or 'technological' spillovers. In neoclassical economic theory, these spillovers are usually associated with market imperfections and the inability of firms to appropriate the full benefit of their own R&D activity in neoclassical theory. The inability to protect this proprietary knowledge could either reduce business R&D activity is suggested by Nelson (1959) and Arrow (1962) or increase it as Cohen and Levinthal (1989) maintain. By definition spillovers create a dichotomy between private and social returns. Bernstein and Nadiri (1988) define social returns as private rate plus the inter-industry marginal cost reductions due to spillovers. Technology spillovers are important if local firms are able to appropriate this public knowledge that foreign affiliates have generated. Subcontracting, competition and the labour market can play an important role in facilitating these spillovers, (Blomström and Kokko, 1998).

Mohnen (1990) identifies two general approaches to defining technology spillovers in the literature: (1) the spillover is an unweighted sum of the R&D stock of all other sectors in the economy or in the industry; and (2) the spillover is a weighted sum of all the other R&D stock, with different proximity measures used to construct weights. Depending on the proximity measure used, Mohnen further distinguishes the weights proportional to the flows of intermediate purchase, to the flows of patents, or the flows of innovations between the sectors, or the correlation of the position vectors of these sectors in a technology space. In this last group the stock of each potential source of R&D spillover is entered separately into the production function.

Empirical analysis that follows the first approach initially estimated the social returns to a well-defined innovation, but later focused more on the effects spillovers have on productivity. In his pioneering work, Griliches (1958) calculated current and future consumer surplus flows, discounted them back to the present, and compared them to the cumulated research cost. Technology impact studies also used a similar methodological approach. If the imported technology is embodied in a domestic product or range of products, then it is possible to measure the social returns to the particular stream of imports by the sum of the product and consumer surplus generated by it. Private rates of return to R&D capital are the returns to the R&D performers, and social rates of return are the returns to the R&D users. To demonstrate the extent of spillovers, Griliches shows that the social rate of return is several times greater than the private rate in almost all cases. Imported knowledge influences downstream industries through declining real factor prices, a pecuniary externality. It is more difficult, however, to measure the impact that knowledge flows have on productivity. This is a non-pecuniary externality that is not embodied in a particular service or product, though it may be covered by a licence. To measure these directly, it is necessary to assume either that their benefits are localized in a particular industry or range of products or that one can detect the path of spillovers. It is also necessary to consider the time lags in the realization of effects in other sectors, which always take more time than the direct effects of transfer.

The second approach to spillovers developed regress-based estimates of overall returns to a particular stream of outside R&D expenditures. These estimates relate R&D capital or R&D intensity (R&D to sales ratio or value added) to the growth rate of output or total factor productivity across firms or industries (Griliches, 1991). Spillovers appear in these models as the sum of current expenditures of firms or industries on R&D, the sum of R&D capital stock, R&D stock weighted by patents, or R&D desegregated according to each distinct potential spillover source (Bernstein, 1991).

Studies of developing countries suggest that spillovers can either complement or substitute domestic R&D activity. While there is little evidence as to the nature of spillovers, they can appear substantial both within and between industries, but they may also be insignificant or even non-existent (Mohnen, 1990; Blomström and Kokko, 1998). The evidence on spillovers in multinational activity suggests that they are country-specific and often only in one direction. In a review of 12 studies from developed and developing countries, Dunning (1985) concluded that multinational affiliates had a beneficial effect on resource allocation at least in a static sense, although about half of the studies stressed that the beneficial effects might have been even greater with different government policies. Spillovers were positive in advanced industrial economies and in some sectors substantial, whereas in the smaller developed and less developed countries results were mixed. A study by Young *et al.* (1994) suggest that dynamic gains from multinational activity are mainly confined to acquired companies and in the form of improved availability of investment funds, and improved management and marketing skills. In some cases, such as Scotland, inward FDI may have reduced subcontracting and corporate functions.

There are few direct analyses of the existence and significance of spillovers and most of these focus on the effects they have on the industrial structure. Early studies on Australia by Caves (1974), Canada by Globerman (1979) and Mexico by Blomström and Persson (1983) show that spillovers are significant at the industry level, but do not explain how they take place (Blomström and Kokko, 1998). A study by Kokko (1992) found that technology import and productivity levels of affiliates in Mexico appear to be positively related to the skills level of the host country's labour force, and the degree of competition from local firms, but negatively related to the existence of technology transfer and performance requirements. Blomström and Wolff (1994) found that spillovers increased productivity growth of local firms and led to a convergence of Mexican productivity towards US levels from 1970 to 1975. Nadiri (1991) reaches a similar conclusion for France, Germany, Japan and the UK. By contrast, a study of Moroccan manufacturing from 1985 to 1989 by Haddad and Harrison (1993) shows that spillovers did not increase productivity growth of local firms because it took place mainly in sectors with simpler technology and not in the more knowledge-intensive industries. Mixed results were also found for Venezuela by Aitken and Harrison (1999).

Several case studies from east Asia also support the existence of spillovers. Kim (1993) found that technology developed within electronic multinationals in Singapore and Malaysia spills over to their local suppliers and the labour market. Dahlman and Brimble (1990) show that foreign firms in Thailand have not developed significant linkages with local companies and have not generated positive spillover benefits in the areas of technical training or technology transfer to local firms. They offer limited technical assistance and quality control that normally accompany subcontracting arrangements. In addition, the training effect of foreign firms has been mainly felt at the level of direct shop-floor workers, with only isolated effects at the higher technical and management levels.

The evidence on spillovers reveals that individual country-, industry- and firm-specific factors influence the incidence of the spillovers. Bernstein (1991) analysed differences between Canadian-owned firms and affiliates and showed that there was a correlation between R&D activity and the spillover effects in different industries. In industries with high R&D propensity a complementary relationship exists between intra-industry spillovers and R&D capital for both groups. The more spillover benefits they receive, the more they invest in R&D. An empirical study by Kokko (1994) suggests that spillovers are industry-specific. He found that factors related to technology alone do not appear to inhibit spillovers, but large productivity gaps and large foreign market shares together appear to make up significant obstacles.

In industries where the productivity gap in relation to foreign affiliates is high and where their market share is also high, we may expect that foreign affiliates operate in enclaves, that is isolated segments of the market where technologies, products and plant sites are very different from those used by local firms. Spillovers are not an automatic consequence of foreign investment and depend on market structures and various inducements to the industry.

Finally, UNCTAD (1997) points to the technological capabilities of local firms relative to those of foreign affiliates, and how their market strategies have an important influence on the incidence of the spillovers. All of these individual country-, industry- and firm-specific factors may cause considerable difficulty in any empirical analysis, as Jenkins (1990) keenly observed.

The existence of spillovers suggests that FDI affects growth endogenously through increasing returns generated in interaction between local firms and foreign affiliates. Spillovers depend on the features of firms, industries, countries, technologies and markets. The causality among these factors and spillovers is context-specific and generalizations are limited. Three policy conclusions emerge from the literature. First, there is no general policy for maximizing spillovers. Spillovers are sector-specific, and general incentives to maximize the indirect benefits from the presence of foreign FIEs may be highly effective in some sectors but have no effect in others. The overall benefit is dependent on a country's industry and market structure and general technological level.

Second, the spillovers are less likely in sectors where product differentiation and scale economies are strong. In these sectors the advantages of FIEs are greater and they can easily take over the whole domestic market. Kokko (1994) suggests that backward countries should try to attract FDI in sectors where these factors are not dominant. This policy could be undermined, however, because FIEs are less present in sectors they cannot exploit ownership-specific advantages in differentiated products and scale economies.

Third, spillovers are more likely in sectors where the productivity gap between local and foreign firms is not too high (Kokko, 1994; Pack and Kamal, 1997; UNCTAD, 1997). If the productivity gap between them is too high, local firms are not able to capture the benefits of possible spillovers. This suggests that FDI may create large benefits only above a certain development threshold as suggested in the model of Verspagen (1991).

7   ECONOMIC RESTRUCTURING THROUGH TECHNOLOGY TRANSFER

Historical analyses show that technology transfer, complemented with domestic technology accumulation, is essential to the growth process (Mokyr, 1990). Successful catching-up is most often based on extensive technology acquisition from the leaders. The industrialization in the nineteenth century of Germany, France and the USA relied on the transfer of knowledge from the UK. The catching-up of Japan in the 1960s and 1970s, and South Korea in the 1980s, also relied initially on imported technology from the West. The reason for this is that the costs of imitation and technology import are lower for followers than the cost of innovation for the leaders. Freeman and Soete (1997) point out that the use of imported foreign technology is not a straightforward short cut to technical change and technological learning. Effective assimilation of foreign technology is actually difficult and complex. Access to imported technology is far from sufficient for catching-up and the import of technology does not of itself generate technological dynamism unless it is accompanied by an active building up of domestic technology capability (Sandberg, 1992).

There is great optimism in central Europe that FDI can speed up the process of economic transformation. Conformation of this optimism appears throughout this book, especially in the context of the direct effects of FDI on growth and restructuring. This chapter is much less optimistic that the indirect effects of FDI and technology spillovers can speed up the growth process. The reason is that FDI is both industry- and context-specific and there is no automatic mechanism to ensure a technology transfer. FDI affects growth endogenously and spillover effects cannot be understood out of a variety of country- and industry-specific factors. The chapters in this book show the variety of country- and industry-specific factors and the ways this may contribute to our understanding of how FDI can speed up the process of economic restructuring.

FDI is not the only channel of technology transfer into central Europe. The effects of FDI are complementary to various other forms of co-operation including trade, subcontracting and other types of alliance networks. Both the direct and indirect effects of FDI should be seen in the context of other technology transfer channels. This creates certain difficulties, however, since data on the technology composition of trade and subcontracting do not exist for central Europe. However, it is clear in the literature that there is no general policy for maximizing technology spillovers. The legislation in central Europe implicitly accepts this view in that it gives foreign enterprises the same status as domestic firms and provides certain incentives for FDI.

REFERENCES

Abramovitz, M. (1989), *Thinking About Growth*, Cambridge: Cambridge University Press.

Abramovitz, M. and P.A. David (1996), 'Convergence and deferred catch-up: productivity leadership and the waning of American exceptionalism', in R. Landau, R. Taylor and G. Wright (eds), *The Mosaic of Economic Growth*, Stanford: Stanford University Press, pp. 21–62.

Aghion, P. and P. Howitt (1992), 'A model of growth through creative destruction', *Econometrica*, **60**, pp. 323–51.

Aitken, B.J. and A.E. Harrison (1999), 'Do domestic firms benefit from direct investment. Evidence from Venezuela', *American Economic Review*, **89**, pp. 605–18.

Alam, G. and J. Langrish (1981), 'Non-multinational firms and transfer of technology to less developed countries', *World Development*, **4**.

Antonelli, C. and G. Perosino (1992), 'Technology transfer revisited', FAST Programme mimeo, June.

Arrow, K. (1962), 'Economic welfare and the allocation of resources for invention', in *The Rate and Directions of Inventive Activity: Economic and Social Factors*, Princeton: Princeton University Press, pp. 609–26.

Barro, R. and X. Sala-i-Martin (1995), *Economic Growth*, New York: McGraw-Hill.

Baumol, W.J. (1986), 'Productivity growth, convergence and welfare – what the long-run data show', *American Economic Review*, **76**, pp. 1072–85.

Bernstein, I.J. (1991), 'R&D capital, spillovers and foreign affiliates in Canada', in D. McFetridge (ed.), *Foreign Investment, Technology and Economic Growth*, Calgary: University of Alberta Press, pp. 111–32.

Bernstein, I.J. and M.I. Nadiri (1988), 'Interindustry R&D spillovers, rates of return, and production in high-tech industries', *American Economic Review*, **78**, pp. 429–34.

Blomström, M. and A. Kokko (1998), 'Multinational corporations and spillovers', *Journal of Economic Surveys*, **12**, pp. 247–77.

Blomström, M. and H. Persson (1983), 'Foreign investment and spillover efficiency in an underdeveloped economy: evidence from the Mexican manufacturing industry', *World Development*, **11**, pp. 493–501.

Blomström, M. and E. Wolff (1994), 'Foreign investment enterprises and productivity convergence in Mexico', in W. Baumol, R. Nelson and E. Wolff (eds), *Convergence of Productivity: Cross-national Studies and Historical Evidence*, Oxford: Oxford University Press, pp. 263–84.

Borensztein, E., J. De Gregorio, J-W. Lee (1998), 'How does foreign direct investment affect growth?', *Journal of International Economics*, **45**, pp. 115–35.

Caves, R.E. (1974), 'Multinational firms, competition and productivity in host-country markets', *Economica*, **41**, pp. 176–93.

Coe, T.D. and E. Helpman (1995), 'International R&D spillovers', *European Economic Review*, **39**, pp. 859–87.

Cohen, W.M. and D.A. Levinthal (1989), 'Innovation and learning: the two faces of R&D', *Economic Journal*, **99**, pp. 569–96.

Contractor, F.J. (1985), 'Licensing vs. direct foreign investment in US corporate strategy: an analysis of aggregate US data', in N. Rosenberg and C. Frischtak (eds), *International Technology Transfer: Concepts, Measures, and Comparisons*, New York: Prager, pp. 277–320.

Cortes, M. and P. Bocock (1984), *North–South Technology Transfer: a Case Study of Petrochemicals in Latin America*, Washington, DC: World Bank.

Dahlman, C.J. (1979), 'The problem of externality', *Journal of Law and Economics*, **22**, p. 141.

Dahlman, C.J. and P. Brimble (1990), 'Technology strategy and policy for industrial competitiveness: a case study in Thailand', *Industry and Energy Department Working Papers*, no. 24, Washington, DC: World Bank.

Dahlman, C.J., B. Ross-Larsonn and L. Westphal (1987), 'Managing technological development: lessons from the newly industrializing countries', *World Development*, **15**, pp. 759–75.

Davidson, W.H. and D. McFetridge, (1993), 'The choice of international technology transfer', in C.S. Nagpal and A.C. Mittal (eds), *International Technology Transfer*, New Delhi: Anmol Publications.

Dollar, D. and E. Wolff (1993), *Competitiveness, Convergence, and International Specialization*, Cambridge: MIT Press.

Dunning, J.H. (1985), *Multinational Enterprise, Economic Structure and International Competitiveness*, New York: Wiley.

Dunning, J.H. (1994), 'Re-evaluating the benefits of foreign direct investment', *Transnational Corporations*, **3**, pp. 23–51.

Edquist, C. (ed.) (1997), *Systems of Innovation, Technologies Institutions and Organizations*, London: Pinter.

Ernst, D. and D. O'Connor, (1990), *Technology and Global Competition: the Challenges for Newly Industrializing Economies, Development Centre*, Paris: OECD.

Freeman, C. and L. Soete (1997), *The Economics of Industrial Innovation*, 3rd edn, London: Pinter.

Gerschenkron, A. (1962), *Economic Backwardness in Historical Perspective*, Cambridge: Harvard University Press.

Globerman, S. (1979), 'Foreign direct investment and "spillover" efficiency benefits in Canadian manufacturing industries', *Canadian Journal of Economics*, **12**, pp. 42–56.

Griliches, Z. (1958), 'Research costs and social returns: hybrid corn and related innovations', *Journal of Political Economy*, **66**, pp. 919–31.

Griliches, Z. (1991), 'The Search for R&D Spillovers', *NBER Working Paper*, no. 3768.

Grossman, G. and E. Helpman (1991), *Innovation and Growth in the Global Economy*, Cambridge: MIT Press.

Grossman, G.M. and E. Helpman (1995), 'Technology and trade', in G. Grossman and K. Rogoff, *Handbook of International Economics*, vol. III, pp. 1279–337.

Helleiner, G.K. (1989), 'Transnational corporations and direct foreign investment', in H. Chenery and T.N. Srinivasan (eds), *Handbook of Development Economics II*, Amsterdam: North Holland, pp. 1442–80.

Hoffman, K. and N. Girvan (1990), 'Managing international technology transfer: a strategic approach for developing countries', mimeo MR 259e, IDRC, April.

Hollingsworth, R. (1993), 'Variation among nations in the logic of manufacturing sectors and international competitiveness', in D. Foray and C. Freeman (eds), *Technology and the Wealth of Nations: The Dynamics of Constructed Advantages*, London: Pinter.

Jenkins, R. (1990), 'Comparing foreign subsidiaries and local firms in LDCs: theoretical issues and empirical evidence', *The Journal of Development Studies*, **26**, pp. 205–28.

Jones, C.I. (1998), *Introduction to Economic Growth*, New York: W.W. Norton.

Karake, A.Z. (1990), 'Technology transfer and economic growth in the less-developed countries: a technology gap approach', in M. Chatterji (ed.), *Technology Transfer in Developing Countries*, London: Macmillan.

Keller, W. (1998), 'Are international R&D spillovers trade related? Analyzing spillovers among randomly matched trade partners', *European Economic Review*, **42**, pp. 1469–81.

Kim, Y.C.L. (1993), 'Technology policy and export development: the case of electronics industry in Singapore and Malaysia', mimeo.

Kokko, A. (1992), 'Foreign direct investment, host country characteristics and spillovers', Ph.D. thesis, Stockholm School of Economics.

Kokko, A. (1994), 'Technology, market characteristics, and spillovers', *Journal of Development Economics*, **43**, pp. 279–93.

Krugman, P. and A. Venables (1995), 'Globalization and the inequality of nations', *Quarterly Journal of Economics*, **110**, pp. 857–80.

Lucas, R.E. (1988), 'On the mechanics of economic development', *Journal of Monetary Economics*, **22**, pp. 3–42.

Lundvall, B.-A. (ed.) (1992), *National Systems of Innovation: Towards a Theory of Innovation and Interactive Learning*, London: Pinter.

Mansfield, E. and A. Romeo (1980), 'Technology transfer to overseas subsidiaries by US-based firms', *Quarterly Journal of Economics*, **95**, pp. 737–50.

Mohnen, P. (1990), 'New technology and interindustry spillovers', *STI Review*, **7**, pp. 131–47.

Mokyr, J. (1990), *The Lever of Riches: Technological Creativity and Economic Progress*, New York: Oxford University Press.

Mowery, D. and J.E. Oxley (1995), 'Inward technology transfer and competitiveness: the role of national innovation systems', *Cambridge Journal of Economics*, **19**, pp. 67–93.

Nadiri, M.I. (1991), 'Innovation and technological spillovers', mimeo, New York University.

Nelson, R.R. (1959), 'The simple economics of basic scientific research', *Journal of Political Economy*, **67**, pp. 297–306.

Nelson, R.R. (1993), *National Innovation Systems. A Comparative Analysis*, Oxford: Oxford University Press.

Pack, H. and S. Kamal (1997), 'Inflows of foreign technology and indigenous technological development', *Review of Development Economics*, **1**, pp. 81–98.

Parrinello, S. (1993), 'Non pure private goods in the economics of production processes', *Metroeconomica*, **44**, pp. 195–214.

Pavitt, K. (1984), 'Sectoral patterns of technological change: towards a taxonomy and a theory', *Research Policy*, **13**, pp. 343–73.

Radošević, S. (1997a), 'Technology transfer in global competition: the case of economies in transition', in D.A. Dyker (ed.), *The Technology of Transition: Science and Technology Policies for Transition Countries*, Budapest: Central European University Press, pp. 126–58.

Radošević, S. (1997b), 'The Baltic post-socialist enterprises and the development of organisational capabilities', in N. Hood *et al.* (ed.), *Micro-level Studies of the Transition in the Baltic States*, London: Macmillan, pp. 19–45.

Radošević, S. (1998), 'Defining systems of innovation: a methodological discussion', *Technology In Society*, **20**, pp. 75–86.

Rebello, S. (1991), 'Long-run policy analysis and long-run growth', *Journal of Political Economy*, **99**, pp. 500–21.

Reddy, N.M. and L. Zhao (1990), 'International technology transfer: a review', *Research Policy*, **19**, pp. 285–307.

Romer, P.M. (1986), 'Increasing returns and long-run growth', *Journal of Political Economy*, **94**, pp. 1002–37.

Romer, P.M. (1990), 'Endogenous technological change', *Journal of Political Economy*, **98**, S71–S102.

Sandberg, M. (1992), *Learning from Capitalists: a Study of Soviet Assimilation of Western Technology*, Göteborg: Almquist and Wirksell International.

Solow, R. (1956), 'A contribution to the theory of economic growth', *Quarterly Journal of Economics*, **70**, pp. 65–94.

Solvell, O. and I. Zander (1995), 'Organisation of the dynamic multinational enterprise: the home-based and the heterarchical MNE', *International Studies of Management and Organisation*, **25**, pp. 17–38.

Stewart, F. (1981), 'International technology transfer: issues and policy option', *World Development*, pp. 67–110.

UNCTAD (1975), *Major Issues Arising from the Transfer of Technology to Developing Countries*, New York: United Nations.

UNCTAD (1997), *World Investment Report 1997: Transnational Corporations, Market Structure and Competition Policy*, New York: United Nations.

Vernon, R. (1986), 'The curious character of the international technology market: an economic perspective', in J.R. McIntyre and D.S. Papp (eds), *The Political Economy of International Technology Transfer*, New York: Quorum Books, pp. 160–207.

Verspagen, B. (1991), 'A new empirical approach to catching up or falling behind', *Structural Change and Economic Dynamics*, **2**, pp. 359–80.

Young, S., N. Hood and E. Peters (1994), 'Multinational enterprise and regional economic development', *Regional Studies*, **28**, pp. 657–77.

4. The role of FDI in restructuring and modernization: an overview of literature

Miklós Szanyi

1 INTRODUCTION

A relatively large amount of literature deals with FDI in transition economies and much of it is written in the English language. However, many papers and studies are in local languages and hence inaccessible to a broad international readership. This chapter attempts to collect and summarize both the most important English and local language contributions to the problems of FDI in the CECs, the Czech Republic, Hungary, Slovakia and Slovenia.

This review of literature follows the principles laid down by Carlin *et al.* (1995) in their attempt to review literature on corporate adjustment in transition economies. Other scholars, such as Lankes and Venables (1996) and Szanyi (1996), also summarized some methodologically separable parts of the literature, most notably company samples of statistically meaningful size, but no attempt has been made to compile the case studies. This chapter analyses a substantial part of the CEC, especially Hungarian case study evidence, together with the major findings of sample surveys and papers based on nationwide data.[1]

The case study literature deals mainly with investments of large multinational corporations and usually disregards small international ventures. Another peculiarity of case studies is the fact that they are usually prepared for different purposes. Their structure and content is, therefore, far from identical. When summarizing their findings, we can rely only on the information they contain. The fact that some aspects were not analysed does not mean that they were irrelevant, but merely that the corresponding information is missing from the case study. Our summary obviously cannot replace thorough research of the companies; furthermore, we have not dared to risk hypotheses about them.

The second method is the sample survey of groups of companies. The drawbacks of this method are also fairly well-known. In terms of some aspects, samples are usually not representative. Moreover, the responding companies are most likely the more successful ones; therefore, such surveys display an inbuilt performance bias. More often than not, this problem is compounded by the subjective character of the companies' answers. Nobody wants to relate bad news. These constraints (especially subjective opinions) can be reduced to some extent by careful design of the questionnaires and interview itineraries.

Papers based on nationwide databases provided by the company register, the tax office and the customs office use sources which are not only confidential, but also subject to data protection, therefore, only aggregated figures can be obtained and no individual track records of companies can be drawn. This makes time comparisons extremely difficult, since no standard sample panel can be created. Nevertheless, the data are adequate for purposes of structural research. A wide range of indicators, especially financial indicators can be calculated and company groups created according to size, ownership and affiliation.

This chapter is structured according to the most interesting topics in research literature and merges the findings of the three different approaches. Section 2 deals with the motivations for FDI and we follow the criteria set up by Dunning differentiating between four major types of investment: market-oriented, resource-oriented, efficiency-oriented and strategic advantage-oriented. Although all four types have been observed in transition economies of central and eastern Europe, we focus on two in particular – resource-oriented (basically cheap labour) and market-oriented investments – because they feature prominently in current discussions.

In Section 3 we analyse the literature concerning the role of FDI in the overall activity of the investing company and the impact of FDI on the host company/country. First, we distinguish between the reasons and circumstances surrounding the creation or acquisition of new capacities (greenfield investments and privatization acquisitions). We cite answers to the basic question whether or to what extent FDI in central Europe is a relocation of capacities that would automatically mean reduction in production and employment in the donor country. As to the host company/host economy impact, a distinction is made between greenfield investments, privatization acquisitions and the establishment of JVs. We also test the relevance of a widespread observation concerning the shift from partial ownership and JVs to majority foreign ownership through capital increase or buy-outs. Opinions on the potential macroeconomic influence of the different types of FDI are collected. Here the major expectation is that the impact of greenfield investments is more substantial than that of acquisitions, unless the latter are hostile take-overs.

In Section 4 we focus on the specific characteristics of the division of labour in which the foreign-owned company participates. Distinctions are made between assemblers, sub-assembly producers and producers of complex finished goods. In this relationship special attention is paid to the degree of integration or independence of the subsidiaries. Two related topics are introduced at this juncture: subcontracting and local content. From the viewpoint of the host country the greater the value added locally, the greater the benefit enjoyed in the areas of employment, technological development, training and tax revenues. Less complex activities may yield a large turnover, but only little value added.

In Section 5 an analysis is made of different performance measures of FIEs. A comparison is made with other companies or with the national average. The common expectation of more efficient and, therefore, more profitable FIEs is tested through a series of different performance indicators that have been used in the literature. We also touch on the problem of transfer pricing and its impact on the trade balance (Section 6).

The most important features of the investment activity of FIEs are discussed in Section 7. The broad topic of restructuring companies and industries and the contribution of FIEs to the overall modernization of transition economies is covered in Section 8. The following topics are treated: labour and human resource management, changes in corporate functional activities, new marketing management, changes in markets and supplier networks, changes in product mix, introduction of new corporate management practices, downsizing of unwanted activities and assets. Section 9 presents research on the emergence and survival of monopolies, a possible negative impact of FDI. The chapter concludes with a summary in Section 10.

2   MOTIVATIONS FOR FDI

The emphasis on the different motivations and goals of investors has become ever more pronounced over the past 3–4 years. Lakatos and Papanek (1994) tried to identify the different interests and goals of certain groups of investors. They stressed the distinction between the different interests of those companies investing in order to capture or increase market share and those investing in order to establish strongly integrated processing facilities for sub-assemblies. Lankes and Venables (1996), Meyer (1996), Éltető and Sass (1997) also tried to draw up a useful typology of investors and used this typology in the analysis of their empirical tests. Common to their approach was the basic fact that empirical surveys of FDI could hardly identify the ultimate driving force

behind investments. The very same factors would be evaluated as determining factors by one respondent, but as negligible or even negative by
other respondents. Samples showed major standard deviations and there
was an obvious need to explain this phenomenon with endogenous factors. The explanations mainly offered were the different goals and
motivations governing the investments: market-oriented investments
versus factor cost-oriented investments.

The literature overview begins with the following sample surveys:
(A) Éltető and Sass (1997), (B) Meyer (1996), (C) Lankes and Venables
(1996) and (D) Konings and Janssens (1996). All these papers used a
sample of over 100 companies. In our view this is a statistical minimum
since contributions analysing less than 100 cases can be regarded more as
case studies. The samples of these surveys deal with investments in
Hungary and in other central and eastern European countries. Then,
under point (E), we turn to the case study evidence.

(A) Éltető and Sass (1997) placed the role of FIEs in the international
division of labour in the very centre of their research. Their survey sample
consisted of 124 companies that were Hungarian affiliates of foreign
investors. They distinguished between export-oriented (36 out of 124), non-
export-oriented companies (64) and those which could not be put into
these categories (25). Export orientation was further divided into assembly-
type activities (17) and host country supplier-based companies (19).

The major characteristics of the non-export-oriented firms were:
medium-sized companies with 40–45 per cent import share of production
inputs, over 40 per cent local content, less than 30 per cent intra-firm
trade and lower than average export profit margins. Many of the companies had been acquired through privatization.

Export-oriented assemblers were usually medium- or large-scale companies with 60–70 per cent imported input share and less than 20 per cent
local supplies. Over 80 per cent of their sales was intra-firm trade; the
most important trading partners were, therefore, countries in the EU.
They were typically 100 per cent foreign-owned greenfield investments,
half of them located in customs-free zones. Their export profit margins
were somewhat higher than average.

Host country supplier-based FIEs were typically medium- or large-scale
companies with a low share of imported inputs (below 20 per cent) and
local supply shares of over 40 per cent. Intra-firm sales were untypical; in
most cases they were JVs. In those cases where the companies had been
acquired in the course of the privatization process, the most probable co-
owners were State organs, but half of the companies in the sample were
greenfield investments. Export profit margins were usually average.

The sales and supply information of the sample yielded results of particular interest to the discussion about the impact of FIEs on trade. It transpired that only assemblers depended crucially on exports and imports, although the other two groups were also involved in trade. Domestic supplier-based exporters imported the least, while non-export-oriented firms had substantial imports, too. This fact supports the notion that FIEs tend to be more import-intensive than other firms.

The evidence here does not support the arguments on transfer pricing. Non-export-oriented companies tended to report low export profit margins; this may be a consequence of transfer pricing, but it may also be a result of forced exports. Since aggregate demand in Hungary was drastically cut in the year of observation (1995), companies were forced to seek new export opportunities despite their original intention. On the other hand, assemblers who enjoyed the closest integration ties and the most numerous possibilities to use diverted prices, reported significantly more cases of higher than average export profitability. With some exaggeration, we may even say that they diverted prices to the benefit of the Hungarian facility and siphoned off to Hungary profits generated elsewhere. Nethertheless, the most balanced evaluation of the results is that there is no clear evidence on the use of transfer prices.

The trade-related investor typology of Éltető and Sass also offers a good opportunity to distinguish between the most important motivations. The most important motive for non-export-oriented companies was acquisition of a share in the market, followed by good economic development prospects. Less pronounced were factors related to the quality and cost of labour or the quality of infrastructure services. Basic conditions governing the legal, economic and political stability of investments were also highly ranked.

By way of contrast, assemblers appreciated stability in the host country most, followed by labour-related qualities. The lack of trade barriers was also mentioned – obviously an important factor in the smooth operation of intra-firm deliveries. Domestic supply-based exporters chose factors similar to those of the assemblers. Stability was mentioned first, followed by labour-related issues, skills and flexibility, but not low wages. Good economic prospects also played a role in this respect.

(B) Meyer (1996) analysed the motives and behaviour of 267 British and German industrial enterprises. Of these 71 per cent already had some kind of business contact with central and eastern Europe (one-third having already invested). A further 20 per cent were considering the establishment of business linkages and could thus be considered potential investors.

The establishment of close (capital) contacts was usually preceded by commercial ties. In the establishment of JVs or purchase through privatization previous close commercial ties played a crucial role. From this aspect, the relatively liberal Hungarian trade regulations during the 1980s provided plenty of opportunities to enter into contract with Hungarian firms. British investors preferred greenfield investments and the acquisition of majority stakes in privatization in the CECs, while in the case of the Balkan countries and CIS countries greater preference was shown for the establishment of JVs. Access to local knowledge, need for connections and avoidance of restructuring burdens were cited as the most important reasons for collaborating with domestic firms in JVs.

As time went by, a shift in the investment mode was to be observed: away from JVs towards acquisitions and away from the purchase of existing capacities towards greenfield investments. This shift is clearly demonstrated by the increasing number of greenfield investments and the diminishing role of privatization deals in the CECs.

Meyer (1996) distinguished between three types of investments typical for FDI in transition economies. These groups were: (i) market orientation; (ii) production-cost orientation; and (iii) market- and production-cost orientation. His questionnaire survey showed that the investors' primary motive was to acquire market shares, while in most cases production-cost considerations were not at all important as independent determinants. They were only considered in cases where market opportunities were promising.

Investment motives and barriers were further investigated through the selection of the 5 most important factors out of 15 that determined investment motivation and barriers to investments. Market-oriented investors ranked the number of inhabitants of the target country highest, while production-cost oriented investors valued cheap labour most. Both types favoured political stability and good pre-investment contacts with local partners. The most important barrier to investment remained the high economic risk in the region, which is a barrier to all kinds of investment. A significant barrier to market-oriented investments was the low level of solvent local demand, the lack of solvent demand being partly caused by low wages. On the other hand, low labour costs were exactly what production-cost-oriented investors valued most. The two investor types proved to have conflicting preferences.

(C) In in-depth interviews, Lankes and Venables (1996) analysed 117 industrial companies with 145 investment projects in central and eastern Europe. The study differentiates between types of investor motivation that are similar, but not identical, to those used by Meyer (1996) and by Élteto and Sass (1997). Three groups of investors were identified according to the main purpose of the investment: distribution (investments to facilitate imports of goods) – 17 per cent of the companies; supply of the local and regional market – 51 per cent of the companies; and export from the CEE region (typically production-cost-oriented investments and processing) – 32 per cent of the companies.

A further distinction between intra- and inter-firm sales helped to identify different processing activities. Firms in the export supply category sold 43 per cent of their output within the corporation (88 per cent of which was sold to the parent company). Local suppliers, on the other hand, sold 97 per cent of their output outside the corporation. Sales patterns of distributors were similar to those of local suppliers.

The authors separated inputs and sales to the parent company (or its other affiliates) as well as inputs and sales bought or sold within central Europe or without. A detailed picture was thus drawn of the purchase and sales linkages of central and eastern European FIEs. The study found that export suppliers displayed a much higher proportion of both intra-firm and out-of-firm sales going outside the region than the other two types. Thus, sales orientation supported the logic of the classification. Export suppliers sold 43 per cent of the output on an intra-firm basis (88 per cent outside the region). Local suppliers sold 97 per cent of total output on an inter-firm basis (94 per cent within the region). The sales patterns of distributors were similar to those of local suppliers.

Production inputs were more decentralized. Distributors purchased 70 per cent of inputs intra-firm, whereas local and export suppliers purchased only 37 per cent each. Export suppliers tended to buy more from regional suppliers than from local firms. Local suppliers, on the other hand, purchased two-thirds of their production inputs locally. Thus, FIEs relied to some extent on local sources and developed commercial links to the host economy. Using the authors' data, our rough estimate is that the local supply content in the inputs of sample FIEs (including distributors) is 35 per cent.

Fears of the investors' home countries' exporting jobs are often voiced by governments and trade unions. The sample reveals that only 'exporters' tend to relocate production but not local market-oriented firms. Distributors and producers for the local market developed their activities in addition to the activities in the home country.

Among the main motivating factors, access to the local market determined investments in the case of distributors. For local-oriented FIEs, access to both the local and regional markets was most important. Somewhat surprisingly, the availability of low-cost local labour was not regarded as a significant determinant in the investment decision. Export-oriented FIEs, on the other hand, regarded low production costs as the single most important determinant. Access to the regional market ranked second, availability of skilled labour third. Interestingly, options such as access to EU markets and response to the one-off opportunity created by the transition (for example, privatization) was not selected as one of the motivation factors.

(D) Konings and Janssens (1996) also put the question of what motivated investment to a sample of 281 Belgian companies. Investors mentioned both labour costs and expansion arguments. Exploring new markets was chosen by 43 per cent, achieving strategic positions by 37 per cent and securing cheap labour by 26 per cent. This set of answers is in perfect corroboration with other (early) empirical surveys (that is Szanyi, 1995 or Pye, 1997a) where no distinction was made between market and factor-cost-motivated investments. Among the risk factors associated with investing in CEE countries the lack of clear legislation, political instability and uncertainty about the currency value were mentioned most frequently.

The Belgian respondents usually operated under increased competition that had forced them to invest abroad. They were most seriously hit by wage competition since wage costs are very high and stable in Belgium. Central European competitors played a minor, albeit growing role in the increased competition on the Belgian market. In response to the challenge of competition, most Belgian companies modernized their production process and/or cut their workforce. Outsourcing was chosen by only 16 per cent and relocation of production by 12 per cent. Forty six firms (16 per cent) established production, service or sales facilities in central and eastern Europe. Only 18 transferred production to the CEE region and only 2 admitted to this shift coinciding with a decrease in employment in the home country (p. 10).

Konings (1996) distinguished between two types of investment. The first was based on traditional comparative cost advantages (that is cheap skilled labour). These ventures are on a smaller scale and located in labour-intensive production; the investors most likely relocate facilities from the home country to the host country rather than set up a subsidiary plant. However, Konings cites a sample survey of the Belgian Planning Bureau that indicated out of 251 relocations surveyed, only 38 (15 per cent) went to central and eastern Europe. In addition, though restructuring (in 73 cases) and labour costs (in 59 cases) were the most frequent causes of relocation from Belgium, Konings concludes that 'most observed FDI in CECs is related to other reasons than wage costs'. He supports the view of other surveys, that the primary reason for FDI in CEE countries is the penetration of new markets (that also involves large sunk costs).

(E) Beyond the surveys, there are a number of case studies dealing with the issue of motivations for investing in CECs. Market-related motivations (capturing local and regional markets) proved an important factor (Aal, 1997; Antalóczy, 1997; Cseh, 1997; Havas, 1997; Kovács, 1996; Lakatos and Papanek, 1994; Legeza, 1997; Mike, 1996; Pye, 1997a; Szabó, 1997; Weiszburg, 1997). For countries with a very small domestic market, however, this motivation was definitely weak, as was recorded in the case of Slovenia by Rojec (1997a). The other major emphasis was placed on global strategy with market-share considerations once again playing a role together with expansion of capacities in low-cost locations. This motive was emphasized in a number of surveys, too (for example by Mikelka, 1996 for Slovakia; Kosta *et al.*, 1993 for the Czech Republic; Aal, 1997, Antalóczy, 1997, Csech, 1997, Halpern, 1997, Kovács, 1996, Legeza, 1997, Pye, 1997c for Czech Republic and Hungary). Since Hungarian privatization policy favoured sales to foreign investors, and there were also numerous cases of direct sales to foreign investors in the other countries, too, acquisition of local firms' assets also featured significantly in a large number of cases (Aal, 1997; Lakatos and Papanek, 1994; Mike, 1996; Pye, 1997c; Weiszburg, 1997). From this point of view, shares in local and regional markets were once again most important, but there were also cases (especially among small- and medium-sized investors) of special local knowledge or products being acquired.

Market considerations were not important for those investors who established assembly lines or component production facilities in customs-free zones especially in Hungary (Chapter 10). The motivation, however, was found to be activity-specific rather than company-specific. There were important cases of companies entering into affiliation with various activities, the motivations, and circumstances of which differed. Legeza (1997), for example, described the Opel (GM) investments in Hungary. The establishment of the engine factory in the customs-free area was clearly targeted towards cheap labour. The other part of the GM investment is vehicle assembly using imported components. It is meant for the Hungarian market, the size of which is so small that the facility cannot be run efficiently. Its losses are cross-financed by the engine plant's profits.

Legeza (1997) also found major differences in the motivation of different investors in the emerging Hungarian automotive industry. Audi and Ford established component production facilities. Audi processes sub-assemblies and assembles engines in Hungary that are then exported to other European facilities for installation. Ford's original investment was even more specialized: certain electrical appliances (fuel pumps, wiper engines, and so on) produced in the Hungarian plant in batches of several million pieces were then sold and used world-wide. On the other hand, Suzuki wished to establish a factory with a potential capacity to supply not only the Hungarian and regional markets, but the EU as well.

Lakatos and Papanek (1994) also discovered a wide variety of reasons and motivations for investing in Hungary. They also emphasized the role of acquiring regional market share and the market knowledge of sales-people in the companies purchased. This motivation lost much of its importance after 1992 with the breakup of the CMEA. Only very few major Hungarian companies were able to maintain or develop a presence in the markets of the former Soviet Union (FSU). One example is the pharmaceutical company Richter (Antalóczy, 1997) which applied the special market knowledge to exactly the opposite end to avoid merging with a large foreign multinational. This company endeavours to become an important niche player and offer its FSU sales network to MNCs.

Large pharmaceutical investors also had rather different motives. Some of them were young and rapidly expanding MNCs wishing to purchase both market opportunities, products and perhaps even R&D personnel. Others simply wished to increase sales by becoming a local firm and so bought up the shares of a smaller Hungarian privately established company on the stock exchange (Antalóczy, 1997).

The global strategy of MNCs can be detected perhaps most clearly in the case of companies in the food industry which almost exclusively supply the domestic market, for example, the Hungarian sugar industry (Kovács, 1996). Hungarian facilities are small and not really technologically efficient. There is excess capacity in the Hungarian sugar industry and profit margins are rather low. Nevertheless, this branch together with the breweries were among the first Hungarian industries to become 100 per cent foreign-owned. The investors obviously considered that they could increase their share and quota in the EU market once Hungary had joined the Union. One of the reasons why they have not invested much in modernizing their Hungarian facilities is the continuing uncertainty and speculation of when Hungary will join the EU. Similar tendencies can be detected in other countries, for example in the chemicals industry or in car production (see the Škoda–Volkswagen case study by Charap and Zemplínerová, 1993).

The case study evidence did not capture hostile take-overs but, in fact, there have been some cases where the motivation of the investor was not long term. For example 'Csepel F+K' was purchased by a German entrepreneur who wished to receive a discounted loan aimed at promoting FDI which he could then use to save his bankrupt company in Germany. The Szolnok paper-mill was purchased and subsequently closed down by the Austrian Prinzhorn Group. In that instance, business conditions changed so fundamentally that the foreign investor was no longer interested in running the facility (the largest and most modern of its kind in central Europe).

Rumours immediately surfaced claiming that the principal aim of the investment had been to shut down the nearby competitor. In some cases such rumours and bad feelings are fuelled by the incumbent management who wish to avoid being acquired by foreign investors. In fact, the management can effectively hinder privatization deals (Antalóczy, 1997). Possible negative effects of privatization to foreign investors were empha- sized also by Charap and Zemplínerová (1994) for the Czech Republic and by Brzica (1997) citing that ecologically damaging industries were deployed in Slovakia this way.

3   COMPARING THE MOTIVES OF INVESTORS AND HOSTS

Contribution to export expansion and economic growth, development of local supplier networks, job creation, transfer of modern technologies know-how and skills are the most frequently mentioned modernization needs that are expected to be satisfied through FDI. Expectations of host country firms, government and population are also very complex and sometimes differ substantially from the aims of investors.

Two of the expectations concerning FDI cited by CEE companies are the 'contribution to profitable export' and 'growing share of local content in the production'. In their sample, Lankes and Venables (1996) calculated that foreign-owned companies sold 27.3 per cent of total output in established market economies. A further substantial part was exported to CEE markets. This fact clearly demonstrates the export orientation of the companies. Furthermore, over one-third of the inputs was purchased locally, thus show- ing that industrial facilities had developed their local supplier network.

The use and development of local labour skills is another important factor in the modernization process. Foreign investors are interested in employing cheap skilled labour. They are not very interested in expanding wages and especially not via excess employment. An interesting finding derived from some sources was that FIEs tended to cream the local labour market. Salaries 20–30 per cent above local average proved to be an effective incentive for the best (most productive) labour force, the effi- ciency of which was perhaps not 20 per cent higher than average. Pye (1997b), Legeza (1997), Halpern (1997), as well as Benáček and Zemplínerová (1997), Zemplínerová (1997b) and Mikelka (1996) directly identified remuneration and employment policy as an important factor of competitiveness. Another important factor in labour issues was the policy of recruiting young (supposedly more flexible, perhaps less expensive) people (Aal, 1997; Legeza; 1997; Pye, 1997b).

The contribution of FIEs to income generation and increase in solvent demand is thus not very great. The paradox of employment hits different investors. Cheap labour is an important factor for local suppliers, especially for exporters. Lack of solvent demand (labour as consumer) hits distributors first, but also local suppliers, especially in branches producing consumer goods.

Modern technology, management and entrepreneurial skills play a crucial role in the modernization of companies which, through the network of suppliers, may also have a strong pull effect on domestically owned firms. The picture is rather fragmented in this respect. Some companies invest and use cutting-edge technologies (for example, greenfield investments), others only refine the local equipment to a minor degree. The deployment and improvement of information and data communication systems is more common. This is regarded as a precondition for efficient corporate management.

Discussion of technology transfer to transition economies had some past in the former Yugoslavia, where the establishment of JVs was first officially allowed. The conclusion of the debate of the 1980s was that the effect of technology development was rather limited because of the weak enforcement possibilities of property rights of potential foreign investors (Brada, 1979; Rojec, 1987). The complex modernization package that is needed in transition economies can only be provided if adequate level and quality of property right enforcement is granted (Štiblar, 1993; Svetličić and Rojec, 1994). Nevertheless, investors in Slovenia do not provide, in most cases, the latest technologies, but what they do is usually still superior to what Slovenian companies currently have. This technology supplemented with adequate know-how, sufficient working capital and new marketing methods may improve corporate performances considerably (Rojec, 1997a).

The role of central and east European subsidiaries in the international division of labour reveals the operational circumstances of FIEs. From the viewpoint of investors, new local facilities are an extension of capacity. None of the cases studied indicated major shifts in production or a relocation of activities to the new subsidiary (Antalóczy, 1997; Halpern, 1997; Havas, 1997; Kovács, 1996; Mike, 1996; Pye, 1997a, 1997b, 1997c; Szabó, 1997). This finding is identical with the general observation of both Konings (1996) and Meyer (1995). (Relocation is perhaps more typical for small companies than for large multinationals and the bias towards the latter peculiar to case studies may mask this.)

Similar to the multiplicity of motivations, subsidiaries may, however, play multiple roles in the operation of international networks. In fact, this can be regarded as typical. One important sign of this is the surveyed companies' indication of several types of simultaneous activity. Most typical is the acquisition of new capacity parallel with increasing exports (Antalóczy, 1997; Havas, 1997; Lakatos and Papanek, 1994; Szemlér, 1996; Weiszburg, 1997). Affiliates serve as both production bases and sales facilities at the same time. The combination of local and imported goods in the product range of FIEs in central and eastern Europe is in complete accordance with international practice. Companies supply complex solutions to specific demand, while components of the supply mix are produced at different locations.

Case studies reveal various ownership mixes in FIEs. In almost all cases of privatization, the foreign investors' initial share was less than 100 per cent, that is at least formally, they became owners of JVs with State authorities as co-owners. These quasi-JVs cannot be regarded as real JVs because the governance of these companies was usually executed by the foreign partners and the local co-owner was passive. Many greenfield investments were not exclusively 100 per cent foreign-owned either. A number of companies, especially in the early years of transition, were created as real JVs where local (insider) knowledge, infrastructure or other assets were provided by local companies, sometimes directly by the State. In other cases, privatization was deliberately shaped to incorporate a State 'security' stake in 'strategically important industries'. These minority shares were sold in Hungary *en masse* after 1994; this led to a general increase in the foreign share.

With time, foreign investors' interest veered more and more towards purchasing majority (even 100 per cent) stakes, because the reason for entering into JVs had ceased to exist. Local knowledge was rapidly learnt or acquired through experts or incumbent management; economic, political and legal frames became sufficiently stable; experiences with local production were gathered and evaluated as satisfactory. All these factors contributed to foreign investors aspiring to assume full control over their affiliates (Lakatos and Papanek, 1994; Kovács, 1996; Legeza, 1997; Szabó, 1997) Similar tendencies were observed in the Czech Republic; meanwhile JVs' importance was still more marked in Slovenia and Slovakia, two new and small countries, which 'first have to prove their viability' (Rojec, 1997a).

On the side of companies in transition economies numerous factors played a role in setting up JVs with foreign investors or in initiating a foreign take-over. They sought for a solution to their major shortcomings, such as the lack of capital (Antalóczy, 1997; Cseh, 1997; Pye, 1997a), up-to-date management and marketing knowledge (Lakatos and Papanek, 1994; Legeza, 1997) and an absence of competitive products and technology (Cseh, 1997; Havas, 1997; Szabó, 1997). Sometimes the reason was to gain market access, replacing former CMEA exports by new markets (Cseh, 1997; Lakatos and Papanek, 1994; Legeza, 1997). Case studies proved that all these factors were significant. Whether these expectations were met is, of course, another story. Becoming an integral part of a multinational company usually meant giving up much of your independence. The role of a local affiliate may have become different from the one it envisaged before the foreign take-over (Antalóczy, 1997; Cseh, 1997; Havas, 1997; Pye, 1997a).

The extent of independence of a subsidiary is a direct function of the role it plays in corporate networks. Component producers in the automotive industry are obviously very strictly managed and controlled: they are part of just-in-time (JIT) production systems. On the other hand, there are companies which have retained a certain degree of independence, such as pharmaceutical companies. Hungarian sugar factories were integrated in national, not international co-operation networks. In the ultimate analysis, the dominant change was a reduction of corporate independence.

Another typical and interesting feature concerns the development of the role of affiliates over time. Similar to the development of ownership structure, the activities of affiliates in central and eastern Europe are also changing. Good examples are once again to be found in the automotive industry. Audi started operations with engine assembly in 1994 in Győr. Operations were expanded in 1996 to include component production and there are plans to establish local production facilities for all main parts. Vehicle assembly started in 1998. The gradual settlement of Audi in Győr will result in 2000 new jobs and an investment of DM 1 billion by 1999 (Halpern, 1997).

A further important conclusion of the case study surveys is that most investments are preceded by looser co-operation links: regular partnership and co-operation, JVs and so forth (Kosta *et al.*, 1993; Lakatos and Papanek, 1994; Lankes and Venables, 1996; Legeza, 1997; Pye, 1997a; Rojec, 1997a). TDK established its first JV in Hungary in 1973. However, it was not until 1990 that direct investment was seriously considered. But then TDK decided to invest despite the fact that the Hungarian partner had gone bankrupt. Japanese investors were not discouraged by the financial failure of their partner and maintained their market presence, replacing the failed JV by establishing a new affiliate (Halpern, 1997).

4 THE ROLE OF FIES IN INTERNATIONAL TRADE FLOWS

With regard to the position of FIEs in the international division of labour and their impact on trade, Konings (1996) stresses that the most sizeable and affluent part of FDI is carried out by large MNCs. They typically operate on oligopolistic markets with a limited number of important players. FDI can no longer be seen as being simply based on interactions between agents taking comparative advantages as exogenously given. FDI must be considered an important part of the multinational companies' strategy aimed at keeping and increasing market power. Therefore, the 'sunk' character of FDI helps not only to utilize the internalization and ownership advantages of investors (distribution network, brand name, image, and so on), but it also creates threats to deter entry in the long run. The sunk (irreversible) character of direct investments also facilitates close integration with international networks.

The impact of FDI on trade flows caught the attention of Djankov and Hoekman (1996) and Naujoks and Schmidt (1995). Their major point of interest was whether the reorientation of CEE export and import flows from East to West contributed to an upgrading of facilities and an efficient integration of the economy in international production networks, or whether reorientation meant a degradation of export facilities and loss of value-added potentials. Intra-industry trade is regarded as a sign of close integration, whereas exports of raw materials, energy and simple processed goods are usually associated with inferior positions in international trade.

Djankov and Hoekman (1996) found that the export performance of CEE countries was strongly correlated to growth in vertical intra-industry trade with EU countries. They tried to explain changes in intra-industry trade and found that the only significant factor that explained the development of intra-industry trade was the level of FDI. Variables such as relative level of GDP and geographical distance were not significant. Similar results were reported by Naujoks and Schmidt (1995).

A possible interpretation of this finding is that the export performance of transition economies integrated into vertical intra-firm co-operation networks via FDI increased most. Evidences of international integration through FDI were put forward, for example, by Rojec (1997a, 1997b) and Myant (1997). In transition economies intra-industry trade mostly means intra-firm trade. This argument also holds in our view for complete integrated value chains of MNCs. Intra-industry trade in this sense may also mean trade among economically dependent, but legally distinct firms. This may be the case with the multinationals' traditional supplier networks, as well as with outward processing (for example subcontracting) by central European firms for multinational companies.

Naujoks and Schmidt (1995) draw attention to the increasing share of outward processing activities in intra-industry trade. Other authors also find outward processing highly relevant for central European countries (Chapter 10). They argue that a high share of tight, FDI-related intra-industry trade in total turnover is most likely to occur in the case of highly complex manufactures where transactions include intangible assets or R&D-intensive goods. For the most part, manufacturers of standardized goods do not enter into equity links but into an intra-industry type of trade via outward processing. Naujoks and Schmidt argue that both types of co-operation, FDI and outward processing, lead to a downgrading of the CEE partner's operations or at least 'flatten' them to a simple sub-delivery base or to the level of an assembly unit. Farkas (1997) and Benáček and Zemplínerová (1997) also provide some empirical evidence of the downgrading of activities in Hungarian and Czech companies privatized through FDI. In our view, this behaviour may be typical for FDI projects seeking factor cost advantages, but less so in the case of those seeking markets.

5 PERFORMANCE OF FIES

Papers using large databases usually focus on performance indicators of foreign affiliates and compare them with sample averages or indicators of other ownership groups. Performance is measured by a wide range of financial indicators such as gross and net profits per sales, operational profits compared to assets. Export performance is also used in some cases, as are investment outlays. All authors draw attention to the fact that balance sheet data should be viewed with special caution: they are likely to differ from real figures for a variety of different reasons. Companies calculate differently for different purposes: this is not a specifically central European practice, but one applied world-wide. It is expected that the errors induced by this practice do not change much over time, especially if taxation does not change much.

Another source of distortion may be the transfer-pricing practices of MNCs. This is a more difficult problem, since the motivating factors may differ in each individual case. Even the direction of distortion may differ depending on features peculiar not only to the local subsidiary, but also to the multinational network as a whole. Attempts, however, have been made to look at this problem more closely (Halpern, 1997; Matolcsy, 1997).

The third factor that detracts from the quality of balance sheet figures is the overall lack of discipline in the disclosure of data. While it had been in the best interest of State-owned companies to co-operate with State authorities in order to secure support in lobbying for State support, the private sector currently co-operates little with the authorities. The supply of company data is not only distorted, it is often incomplete or simply inaccurate. This means that random errors in the databases have increased substantially. Nevertheless, balance sheet data and customs declarations are the only available sources of complete data series that encompass the activities of all economic units.

Major (1996a, 1996b) calculated a wide range of financial, export and investment indicators in order to compare the performance of different ownership groups in the Hungarian economy in the period 1988–95. He did not find any striking differences up until 1994 in the financial efficiency of the groups of companies in the categories: 'majority foreign', 'Hungarian private' and 'State-owned' companies. They were all hit by recession, starting in 1991 and plunging deepest in 1992. Modest improvements were to be observed in 1994; this process continued and became stronger in 1995 by which time financial performance indicators had become generally positive in most economic branches and groups of ownership.

Major (1996b) found that over the entire period, returns on fixed assets were highest in State-owned enterprises and lowest in FIEs. By way of contrast, the operating profits of private (domestic and foreign) companies regularly exceeded those of SOEs. Unlike FIEs, domestic private firms enjoyed returns on fixed assets higher than those of SOEs in 1995. In our view, this discrepancy can be explained by the structure and age of the FIEs' assets and by the different patterns of investments that yielded higher asset values in FIEs compared to other companies. Major's conclusion is that the development of the private sector was slower than expected and the positive effects related to it did not develop very quickly.

Major (1996b, p. 214) also found that the net profits of FIEs were negative even in 1995, while their gross profits did not exceed 2 per cent of total turnover. At the same time their productivity in 1990 was already higher than that of SOEs and domestic private firms and this advantage continued to increase thereafter, that is in the case of FIEs productivity and financial efficiency did not develop in parallel. He also found that the export activities of FIEs were much more intensive than average throughout the entire period. However, during the early 1990s both the most and the least profitable companies tended to have the highest share of exports in their sales. One possible explanation of this 'anomaly' can be 'enforced exports' (Szanyi, 1996) that were maintained in order to ensure the minimum technical level of production necessary for survival. This in turn contributed to the deterioration of the companies' financial performance. Since 1994–95 higher exports usually coincided with higher profitability in FIEs.

The database used by Major (1996b) indicated one specific reason for higher efficiency in FIEs (Csányi, 1997). They operated with a lower share of wage costs (that is presumably at a lower level of employment per unit of sales), while wage costs in SOEs accounted for the highest share in total costs. The trend in FIEs towards swifter and more resolute downsizing, including dismissal of labour, was also proved by Novák and

Szanyi (1996). On the other hand, there is much evidence to indicate that FIEs pay measurably higher average wages than other companies. The higher wages offered by FIEs attract the cream of the labour force capable of above-average productivity. Thus, despite higher than average salaries, unit labour costs in FIEs may be lower than elsewhere. This fact grants FIEs greater licence in optimizing the level of employment.

Csányi (1997) also calculated the returns on financial investments. He found that the highest yields were achieved on short-term financial investments: greater risks associated with longer-term investment is 'rewarded' by lower returns. Returns on all kinds of investment lag far behind the return on financial investments and entail far greater risks. This was corroborated by Major (1996b). Csányi (1997) concluded, however, that highly efficient and profitable companies in all branches tended to invest less in financial assets and more in tangible assets. Others found financial investments more attractive.

Major (1996b) concludes that although ownership was an important factor in explaining differences in financial performance, exports and investments, those differences only started to appear in 1994–95. The primary explanatory factor was the companies' sectoral affiliation. This is by no means surprising; profit margins in trade and certain services are usually higher than in industry. Csányi (1997) also proved that SOEs tended to be concentrated in less efficient branches, while more attractive, more competitive branches were privatized and predominantly held by foreign investors. Major (1996b) evaluated developments after changes in ownership as substantial improvements in activity, but in no way as breakthroughs. Privatized companies still concentrated on short-term business goals; they did not risk much with substantial investments. The improvement in their performance was basically due to savings on operational costs (especially labour costs), not to increased returns on assets or new investments. FIEs are no exceptions in this regard either, even though their performance improved the most and their investment activity was the most vigorous.

Similar results were delivered by surveys in Slovenia and in the Czech Republic. The superior productivity of FIEs was proved by Outrata (1996) for Slovakia, Rojec (1997a), Rojec and Hocevar (1996) and Rems *et al.* (1997) for Slovenia or by Zemplínerová (1997a) for the Czech Republic. The existence of the productivity profitability gap was also evidenced. Using balance sheet data Zemplínerová (1997a) measured productivity levels twice as high for FIEs than for other companies; meanwhile, there were no significant differences in profitability. Rojec and Hocevar (1996) found very similar results for Slovenia. For both countries an important explanatory factor was the different branch structure

of FIEs than the national average. Besides, a number of important differences in operational characteristics (size, capital intensity, asset structure,
export intensity, structure of financial sources, liquidity level) were also
mentioned by the authors.

6   TRANSFER PRICING AND PROFIT REPATRIATION

The contradiction between superior productivity and efficiency and the
lack of profitability roused the interest of several scholars in the field of
FDI. Csányi (1997) lists a few explanations: tax strategy, a specific characteristic of early FIE operations, and macroeconomic developments. He
does not try to name which of these are the most important; he calls for a
closer look. A similarly cautious conclusion is drawn by Halpern (1997),
who analysed Hungarian balance sheet data and the evolution of export
and import prices in an attempt to find evidence on transfer pricing.
Export prices in FIEs increased at a much slower rate than import prices;
this was not the case with Hungarian exporters and importers.
Furthermore, import prices in FIEs proved to be higher than those of
Hungarian importers. Halpern (1997) concludes that these factors make
transfer pricing in FIEs, and thus the transfer of their profits abroad, likely.
   In fact, transfer pricing is a very widespread and well-known phenomenon. We should not think that FIEs operating in central and eastern
Europe would behave any differently than elsewhere in the world. It is
also no wonder that direct evidence can hardly be found, although international organizations undertook serious efforts in this direction during
the 1970s, albeit to no avail. Nonetheless, the rather obvious indirect evidence does not provide a basis for a general statement that FIEs do, in
fact, transfer their profits abroad via transfer pricing, as explicitly
expressed by Matolcsy (1997). There is case study evidence proving that
FIEs reinvest (at least partially) their profits in Hungary. The analysis of
the aggregated balance sheet data in 1996 also demonstrated that in that
particular year FIEs reinvested much of their profits (Pitti, 1997).
   Diczházy (1996) also evaluates the transfer of profits as a potential
danger to what he considers an already overburdened current account of
Hungary. At the same time, it is obvious that free profit transfer is an
absolute precondition for FDI and it is a prerequisite for membership in
both OECD and the EU. Diczházy cites another objection to FDI: the
high share of FDI in non-exporting branches. The transfer of profits
acquired on domestic markets may cause an exchange problem should
the Hungarian currency not be fully convertible. Besides, calculations by
Halpern (1997), IKIM (1996) and others have proved that FDI concen-

trated more on export-oriented industries. Diczházy's argument may be valid for the recently privatized Hungarian public utilities.

7 INVESTMENTS

Major (1996a) also investigated Hungarian investment data in the three ownership groups. He concluded that during the early 1990s domestic private firms invested least, SOEs scored an average figure and FIEs showed the highest investment activity. By the mid-1990s this picture had not changed much; the investment efforts of private domestic firms had strengthened somewhat and exceeded those of SOEs. On the whole, as much as 30 per cent of assets was invested in securities and other financial assets. The share of financial investments was substantial and increased in the case of FIEs, rising from 12.8 per cent to 29.2 per cent of the investment outlays during 1990 and 1994 (Major, 1996a, p. 95).

The weaker than expected investment performance of FIEs is also borne out by the survey of the Hungarian Ministry of Industry, Trade and Tourism, (IKIM, 1996). Though official statistics show that FIEs are responsible for an ever-increasing share of investments in Hungary (Hunya, 1997; Szanyi and Szemlér, 1997), the increase is largely due to their overall expansion in the economy. According to IKIM (1996) investment in FIEs was not higher than what was to be expected given their share in the nominal capital of firms. Of the nominal capital of all companies 28.3 per cent was in foreign ownership at the end of 1995. FIEs had an overall 40 per cent share in investments. Deducting the proportional share of the Hungarian owners, foreigners were responsible for only 27.6 per cent of the investments in that year. Thus, the investment intensity (outlays per nominal capital) of foreign capital was not greater than that of Hungarian capital. Since other authors who surveyed investment activity did not adjust for the ownership structure within FIEs, this interesting result cannot be supported by other (empirical) sources. The empirical evidence (Hunya, 1997; Szanyi and Szemlér, 1997; Szanyi, 1997b) indicates that foreign capital involvement acts as a catalyst and triggers off substantial investments in JVs. Hungarian owners (mostly State organs) are hardly active in any aspects of corporate governance; that was left to the foreign partner. Investments were often financed through capital increase on the part of the foreign partner and this was even included in the privatization agreement. Thus, we may conclude that, even in the case of JVs, investments were not only initiated but most probably also funded by the foreign owners.

For the manufacturing industries, even the Hungarian Ministry's calculations (IKIM, 1996) indicated an above-average investment intensity on the part of FIEs. Their share in manufacturing industry assets was 44.7 per cent in 1995; their proportional share in investments 57 per cent. The share of companies with foreign participation in fixed investment was as much as 80 per cent. In fact, there were industries where basically only FIEs invested: computers and business machines, road vehicles, electrical engineering and instruments. Strong investment activity of FIEs was recorded in the Czech Republic. Benáček and Zemplínerová found that the investment per unit of output ratio was much above the national average in FIEs. Zemplínerová (1997a) calculated that FIE's investment per capita of employees ratio was five times higher than that of domestic companies.

8   RESTRUCTURING

Modernization investments are the backbone of an enterprise's strategic restructuring. Carlin *et al.* (1995) surveyed the existing case study literature on enterprise restructuring in transition economies. A wealth of empirical evidence was found on vigorous restructuring activity in firms acquired by foreigners, especially in Hungary. Carlin found nine matching case studies in the literature, seven of which reported on major capital investment programmes. In those projects, investments had been coupled with the rationalization of management, introduction of new products and training of employees.

Éltető *et al.* (1995) argue that foreign firms tend to cut production and employment more than SOEs or domestically privatized firms. Carlin *et al.* (1995) also found case study evidence for plant closure and employment reduction. In our view, downsizing activities is a necessary step in the modernization of companies. Terminating certain activities creates space for the development of new activities. Market exit is a necessary precondition for market entry as former SOEs go through a process of reorganization.

Downsizing occurred in firms with different ownership structures: foreign firms, however, tended to be less hesitant than SOEs or domestic owners.[2] Consequently, it proved possible to reorganize foreign firms earlier and, in many cases, at a lower cost. Many domestic companies continued to make losses, thus causing serious financial difficulties. Carlin *et al.* (1995) and Rojec (1997a) found evidence of some companies being restructured prior to privatization. In order to attract foreign buyers, governments had been forced to engage in restructuring.

The case study evidence is strongest in the description of changes and the restructuring of acquired facilities, that is stakes acquired through privatization (Lakatos and Papanek, 1994; Mike, 1996). Since, in most cases, a general overhaul of corporate activities was necessary and access to investment financing was perhaps the most important local motive for initiating a foreign take-over, it is not surprising that most, but not all case studies, report significant investments (Halpern, 1997; Havas, 1997; Legeza, 1997; Mike, 1996; Szabó, 1997; Weiszburg, 1997). In a number of cases minor investments sufficed; in others such as the sugar industry, investments were postponed until important business conditions had been met (Kovács, 1996). In almost all cases, investments were combined with pronounced technology transfer and rapid improvements in quality. In many cases, one of the most important items of positive feedback that supported further investments was the very quick absorption of the latest technology. Employees were able and swift to learn and use up-to-date technologies efficiently.

One of the best-known examples is General Electric (GE), an early bird in central European FDI; it is the current owner of TUNGSRAM, once the fourth largest light bulb manufacturer in the world. Sceptical observers feared that this deal was a hostile take-over. Early outcomes of the deal were indeed rather disappointing: rationalization, lay-offs and poor financial performance. What really happened was that GE turned TUNGSRAM completely around and transformed it into the main business centre for its lighting activities throughout the world (Weiszburg, 1997). New products (compact lighting) and technology were transferred to Budapest. Even the main R&D facility of the company's lighting branch was set up in TUNGSRAM. GE is estimated to have invested an amount some 3–4 times higher than the original purchase price it paid for TUNGSRAM.

Particular emphasis was also placed on continuous training and education – human resource management was almost unknown and never applied previously in SOEs (Lakatos and Papanek, 1994; Mike, 1996; Weiszburg, 1997; Pye, 1997b; Szabó, 1997). In some cases employees were reluctant to accept certain types of aggressive training. A rather frequent source of conflict arises from the tendency of 'human resource developers' to disregard local conditions, to ignore the local emotional, cultural and behavioural characteristics and to force through educational methods and practices that were developed for employees with different characters. In other cases flexibility in human relations proved to be one of the strengths of co-operation (Aal, 1997). Dutch managers tried to get accustomed to the fact that 'fixing appointments may still include some delay, if there are important corporate matters to be settled before'. Foreign investors, in general, praised the quality of the labour force in central and eastern Europe, emphasizing the relatively high level of skills, flexibility and adaptivity (Szanyi, 1995; Mikelka, 1996).

Apart from investments, it was changes in organizational build-up and management practices that most companies undertook when they restructured newly acquired facilities. In fact, this type of change usually preceded any other restructuring activity. Effective control and management was the most important requirement for efficient corporate functions. The organizational structure was usually reshaped in order to match the established structure of the parent company. The hierarchical structure was also changed, decision-making levels reduced from 6–8 to 4–5 (Aal, 1997). Organizational and management changes were not bound to major changes in management personnel (Antalóczy, 1997; Filip *et al.*, 1997; Pye, 1997a; Rojec, 1997a). Local, in most cases incumbent, management took over the lead with the support of a few foreign experts, but they were also removed after local managers gained sufficient knowledge, skills and expertise.

Furthermore, the complete information network was reorganized and equipped with up-to-date data processing and communication appliances. The role of information had been neglected in SOEs since the most important sources of information were just beyond the company gates in the form of local party organs, ministries and local authorities. Decision making was based on these sources of information rather than on corporate internal sources that were hardly developed at the time.

Marketing was another important corporate function that usually underwent reshaping. In many cases, sales networks were created (also to facilitate imports from the parent company) and a marketing organization was set up. In some cases, new markets were opened for local companies (Lakatos and Papanek, 1994; Rojec, 1997a), but in other cases, the opposite was also true, when traditional markets were taken and occupied by the parent company's products. A precise division of market competencies was very typical (Lakatos and Papanek, 1994; Weiszburg, 1997; Havas, 1997).

However, not only were marketing competencies divided, but also those of production and the product range. In parallel with the introduction of new products, certain products were discontinued (Havas, 1997; Szabó, 1997). On the other hand, streamlining the product range was a normal adjustment step taken by all types of company as already shown by empirical tests (for example Szanyi, 1996). Streamlining production, however, also meant substantial product developments and a rapid improvement in quality. Many cases reported the introduction of quality controlling systems, some of them even introduced total quality management practices. Thus, downsizing ran parallel with changes in the product mix, and the overall competitiveness of the products usually increased to an appreciable extent. This product development was at least partially carried out by local R&D staff Although downsizing in most cases also meant closure of R&D facilities (Farkas, 1997), in some cases this did not happen (Havas, 1997; Lakatos and Papanek, 1994; Szabó, 1997; Weiszburg, 1997). There were also examples of R&D activities being streamlined to concentrate on specific areas (for example, in all pharmaceutical companies). There is some indication that multinationals make good use of the traditionally well-educated and also innovative local R&D personnel. Some of them also employ Hungarian staff in their foreign headquarters, others only locally. Ericsson and GE are even involved in large-scale development of local R&D facilities. There is the impression that, with time, the innovative value of central and east European engineers is being discovered by multinationals.

9   MONOPOLIES

As indicated earlier, the main motivation for foreign investment has been the acquisition of local markets. The widely held opinion is that, in many cases, market acquisition means the purchase of a monopolistic position which is even strengthened by the protection measures adopted by the Government. Obviously, the more secure the market position, the more attractive it is for investors. It is also clear that monopoly is not the most efficient market structure and decreasing competition ranks among the possible negative effects of FDI. A high degree of market concentration together with high entry barriers engender a situation in which companies do not face real and/or potential competition.

Monopolistic positions can be acquired and strengthened in several ways. Foreign investors may replace domestic products with their own standard products (albeit produced in the host country) and merely utilize the supply networks or distribution channels that they have purchased. Of course, it is always a problem to evaluate whether domestic products were obsolete and hence excluded from the market or whether the production of competitive products was discontinued, thus limiting product diversity. An increasing concentration of markets can also be interpreted both as a harmful process and as the early establishment of a degree of concentration that would have been inevitable in the long term. For example, the privatization of retail chains has been criticized for not giving adequate chances to small shopkeepers. The formation of retail chains would have occurred anyway, even if the shops had been sold individually.

Vissi (1994) assessed the highly concentrated Hungarian markets from three aspects: concentration ratio, entry barriers and strategic motivations. His conclusion was that only in a few cases had privatization through foreign investors led to protected or hardly contestable market structures. Product groups with over-concentrated production are: edible oil, aluminium, sugar, insurance, cement, paper, packaging and road construction. The total capital invested in these branches is only a small fraction of the total foreign investment stock in Hungary.

10   SUMMARY CONCLUSIONS

The main conclusions of the chapter are summarized in the following paragraphs:

(a) An overview of research results revealed a large diversity of FIEs in almost all possible respects. The fact that the sectoral affiliation of companies determined their performance and not their ownership pattern, the confusing results of sample surveys concerning FDI motivations and the extensive variation in the behaviour of FIEs – all these features stress the need for a better understanding of differences between FIEs. These differences can best be described by two characteristics: the original motivation for the investment and the actual role of the enterprise in the investor's global strategy. Three major types of investment can be identified: the domestic market-oriented (local supplier), the assembly-type export-oriented (greenfield investment with intra-firm trade dominance), and the export-oriented local supply-based company (usually privatized firms or JVs that also sell on the local market). The approximate share of these types has not been estimated.

(b) This typology could explain many of the differences experienced in the identification of major impediments to and advantages of FDI. For example, cheap labour may be of decisive importance to assemblers, but the lack of solvent demand (linked to low wages and low employment level) is a major impediment to domestic market-oriented firms.

(c) As investors may be involved in highly differentiated activities, the above typology can be used to characterize activities rather than companies. Moreover, activities follow a clear process of evolution, especially in greenfield projects and JVs. After an initial test project, further investments may follow with a shift in the major activity from assembly to more sophisticated production. In other cases, locally produced goods are coupled with imported products and together they provide full market supply.

(d) Many of the JVs were quasi-JVs with residual State ownership after privatization. In most cases, the State's share has, in most cases, not been used actively by the public owner and was gradually reduced by allowing the foreign partner to increase capital and buy out the company. Another tendency in the development of ownership patterns can be discerned: instead of JVs, 100 per cent foreign-owned companies are established. This development can be regarded as a clear sign of growing foreign confidence in Hungary and in the Czech Republic. Less so is the case of Slovakia and Slovenia.

(e) 'Assemblers' but also other foreign investors tend to fit their new affiliates into their international network. In many cases, this means incorporation into a global production and sales network. Of course, greenfield projects were planned and established according to this requirement. Acquisitions were followed by a streamlining of activities in order to fit the affiliate into the division of production within the multinational enterprise. In some cases, this means degrading activities, in others the opposite; in general, however, it resulted in the establishment of intra-firm trade links with the parent company. This was typical for almost all companies, regardless of type: distributors, global strategy-motivated investors, also tended to invest rather heavily. A possible explanation for this trend is the 'sunk' character of FDI. Investors do not solely pursue a primary goal, that is, utilizing cheap labour or penetrating the local market. FDI is also a tool in global competition because it heightens the barriers to competitors entering a specific market. The 'sunk' character of FDI is also underscored by the fact that it does not usually involve a relocation of existing capacities from other countries.

(f) Integration of new affiliates into global systems via 'sunk' investments do not exclude the potential role to be played by local supplies. The emergence of a local supplier network supplying items of adequate quality at competitive prices is of crucial importance to reducing production costs and gaining further competitive power. Research revealed the significant and expanding use of local supplier networks. This was certainly most widespread in FIEs created by the privatization of companies with inherited networks, but it also started in many greenfield investments. Local expectations as to the future development of local supplies are relatively high. Actual facts reveal a rather slow and cumbersome process of adjustment and integration among local firms.

(g) The sectoral orientation of FDI is strongly influenced by the development of alternative international co-operation networks. Textile, clothing, shoe production and branches of the chemical and engineering industries have been involved in outward processing activities for a long time. The most commonly used tool has been subcontracting: a co-operation agreement that can utilize fully the local cost advantages and make direct capital investment unnecessary. Trade turnover via subcontracting also continued to increase after 1990, although many subcontractors were targeted for privatization buy-outs and merged into a multinational company.

(h) A large part of the literature deals with efficiency and performance indicators in FIEs. Many scholars wished to verify their assumption concerning the generally superior performance of FIEs compared to domestic enterprises. They have not been very successful, except in the case of the manufacturing sector.

(i) There can be several reasons for the efficiency-profit trap described above. Efficiency improves more slowly than expected because of the time lag in correcting weaknesses inherited on account of sluggish investment. Profits may remain low because of the same time lag in adjustment efforts or the slow recovery of local demand. An important factor in the somewhat sluggish recovery of sales and investment may have been the exceptionally high return on financial investments. Financial investment opportunities crowded out a substantial part of the accumulation of physical assets. This behaviour has been more characteristic for companies whose performance was below average, that is for those companies with lower efficiency and profits that perpetuated their inferior position.

(j) Another possible explanation for the efficiency-profitability trap is the transfer-pricing activity of multinationals. Research in this direction indicates some suspicious circumstances, for example adverse price developments in exports and imports of FIEs; however, no direct evidence was found. On the other hand, there is extensive empirical evidence of companies reinvesting profits and expanding their activities on a massive scale.

(k) Many studies contained information on the investment activity of FIEs. Their increasing share in total investments was proven. This increment was fuelled basically by new greenfield investments and reinvested profits. The share of FIEs may also have increased on account of the continuing privatization process and the sale to foreign owners of minority State shares in quasi-JVs.

(l) Relatively little evidence was found for fundamental restructuring of companies acquired in the privatization process. It seems that under the given circumstances, only those SOEs could be sold to foreigners which could be run efficiently without a general overhaul of activities.

(m) Restructuring former SOEs was aimed at improving efficiency and product quality rather than at a complete change in activity. The most common restructuring steps included: reorganization of the organizational structure of the company; a take-over of key management positions by foreign experts; and an improvement in and rationalization of management decision-making systems. All companies invested in updating data and information communication systems so as to enhance the introduction of up-to-date corporate management systems. All these steps were also designed to fit the new facility into the international network. Streamlining activities as well as downsizing (shedding of labour) also contributed to this purpose. Strong emphasis was also placed on human resource development. Training and retraining were customary and many companies tried to recruit young, rather than older professionals. There was also a tendency to cream off the labour force: above-average salaries were offered to selected personnel who were also required to perform at above-average rates of productivity.

NOTES

1. For a more systematic overview of the literature on Hungary, see Szanyi (1997b).
2. Rojec (1997) gathered different experience. Surprisingly, FIEs operating in Slovenia did not do much downsizing, did not sell many facilities in non-core businesses and did not dismiss employees.

REFERENCES

Aal, E.B.W. (1997), 'Competitive strategy of Dutch companies in Hungary', mimeo, Budapest University of Economics, 'Competing the world' research project.
Antalóczy, K.(1997), 'A magyar gyógyszeripar versenyképessége – adatok, hipotézisek, töprengések' ('Competitiveness of the Hungarian pharmaceutical industry: data, hypotheses, considerations'), mimeo, Budapest University of Economics, 'Competing the world' research project.
Benáček, V. and A. Zemplínerová (1997), 'FDI in the Czech manufacturing sector', *Prague Economic Papers*, VI, June.
Brada, J. (1979), 'Markets, property rights and the economics of joint ventures in socialist countries', *Journal of Comparative Economics*, 1 (6), pp. 167–81.
Brzica, D. (1997), 'Review and lessons of FDI research papers', mimeo, Institute of Economics, Slovak Academy of Sciences.
Carlin, W., J. Van Reenen and T. Wolfe (1995), 'Enterprise restructuring in early transition: the case study evidence from central and eastern Europe', *Economics of Transition*, 3 (1), pp. 427–58.
Charap, J. and A. Zemplínerová (1993), 'A case study of the Škoda–Volkswagen joint venture', in *Methods of Privatising Large Enterprises*, Paris: OECD, CCEET.
Charap, J. and A. Zemplínerová (1994), 'FDI in the privatization and restructuring of the Czech economy', *Development and International Cooperation*, X (18), June.

Csányi, T. (1997), 'A versenyképesség egyedi cégadatok elemzése tükrében' ('Competitiveness in the mirror of individual firm data analysis'), mimeo, Budapest University of Economics, 'Competing the world' research project.

Cseh, J. (1997), 'A textil-és textilruházati ipar helyzete, a versenyképességét meghatározó tényezők' ('Situation of textile and apparel industry, and factors determining its competitiveness'), mimeo, Budapest University of Economics, 'Competing the world' research project.

Diczházy, B. (1996), 'Külföldi működőtőke-befektetések ösztönzéséről' ('On the promotion of foreign direct investments'), mimeo, Budapest.

Djankov, S. and B. Hoekman (1996), 'Intra-industry trade, foreign direct investment and the reorientation of east European exports', *CEPR Discussion Paper*, no. 7377.

Éltető, A., P. Gáspár and M. Sass (1995), 'Foreign direct investment in east-central Europe in comparative analysis with Spain and Portugal', *IWE Working Paper*, no. 51, May.

Éltető, A. and M. Sass (1997), 'A külföldi befektetők döntését és vállalati működését befolyásoló tényezők Magyarországon az exporttevékenység tükrében' ('Factors influencing decisions and activity of foreign investors in Hungary in the light of their export patterns'), *Közgazdasági Szemle*, 7, pp. 531–46.

Farkas, P. (1997), 'The effect of foreign direct investment on research, development and innovation in Hungary', *IWE Working Paper*, no. 85.

Filip, J., G. Slamecka, J. Spurry and K. Zigic (1997), 'Overview of Canadian Czech economic relationships in 1994–1996', mimeo, Prague.

Halpern, L. (ed.) (1997), 'A nemzetközi versenyképesség és a külföldi működőtőke-beruházások kapcsolatának vizsgálata' ('An analysis of the relationship of FDI and international competitiveness'), mimeo, Institute of Economics, HAS.

Havas, A. (1997), 'A távközlési ipar átalakulása' ('Changes in the telecommunication business') mimeo, Budapest University of Economics, 'Competing the world' research project.

Hunya, G. (1997), 'Foreign investment enterprises in the investment process of the Czech Republic, Hungary and Poland', mimeo, Budapest.

IKIM (Ministry of Industry, Trade and Tourism) (1996), 'Beruházások a változó tulajdonviszonyok között' ('Investments during changing ownership patterns'), mimeo, Budapest.

Konings, J. (1996), 'Foreign direct investment in transition economies', *Working Paper*, no. 56, Leuven Institute for Central and East European Studies.

Konings, J. and S. Janssens (1996), 'How do western companies respond to the opening of central and east European Countries? Survey evidence from a small open economy – Belgium', *Working Paper*, no. 60/1996, Leuven Institute for Central and East European Studies.

Kosta, J., J. Štouračová and M. Konstantinov (1993), 'Direct investment from Germany to the Czech Republic', mimeo, Prague.

Kovács, P. (1996), 'A Magyar Cukor Rt. stratégiája 1992–1996' ('Strategy of Hungarian Sugar Corporation 1992–1996'), mimeo, Budapest University of Economics, 'Competing the world' research project.

Lakatos B. and G. Papanek (1994), 'Azonos és eltérő érdekek a vegyes vállalatoknál' ('Identical and different interests in joint ventures'), *Strukturák, Szervezetek, Stratégiák*, 4, pp. 74–91.

Lankes, H.-P. and A.J. Venables (1996), 'Foreign direct investment in economic transition: the changing pattern of investments', *Economics of Transition*, 4 (2), pp. 331–47.

Legeza, E. (1997), 'A gépjármű- és gépjárműalkatrészgyártás versenyképességét befolyásoló tényezők' ('Determining factors of vehicle and parts production's competitiveness'), mimeo, Budapest University of Economics, 'Competing the world' research project.

Major, I. (1996a), 'A magángazdaság terjedése és a vállalatok beruházási és exportaktivitása' ('Expanding private business and the investment and export activity of companies'), mimeo, Institute of Economics, HAS.

Major, I. (1996b), 'A tulajdonosi szerkezet változásának hatása a versenyképességre' ('Impact of ownership change on competitiveness'), mimeo, Institute of Economics, HAS.

Matolcsy, Gy. (1997), 'Kiigazítás recesszióval. Kemény költségvetési és puha piaci korlát' ('Adjustment with recession: hard budget and soft market constrains'), *Közgazdasági Szemle*, **44** (9), pp. 782–98.

Meyer, K. (1995), 'Foreign direct investment in the early years of economic transition: a survey', *Economics of Transition*, **3** (3), pp. 301–20.

Meyer, K. (1996), 'Business operations of British and German companies with the economies in transition', *Discussion Paper Series*, no. 19, London Business School, Middle Europe Centre.

Mike, G. (1996), 'Hűtögépek a környezetvédelem szolgálatában?' ('Refrigerators in service of environmental protection?'), mimeo, Budapest University of Economics, 'Competing the world' research project.

Mikelka, W. (1996), 'Foreign direct investments in the Slovak Republic', Institute of Economics, Slovak Academy of Sciences, Bratislava.

Myant, M. (1997), 'Foreign direct investment and industrial restructuring in the Czech Republic', in *Central and Eastern Europe: Institutional Change and Industrial Development*, Tannishus, Denmark, 20–23 November, Aalborg University.

Naujoks, P. and K.-D. Schmidt (1995), 'Foreign direct investment and trade in transition countries: tracing links. A sequel', *Kiel Working Paper*, no. 704.

Novák, T. and M. Szanyi (1996), 'A tevékenységleépítés szerepe a magyar gazdaság átalakításában' ('The role of downsizing in the transformation of the Hungarian economy'), *Struktúrák, Szervezetek, Stratégiák (Ipargazdasági Szemle)*, **1–3**, pp. 110–19.

Outrata, R. (1996), 'Structural Changes and Competitiveness in Slovak Industry', Institute of Economics, Slovak Academy of Sciences, Bratislava.

Pitti, Z. (1997), 'A külföldi érdekeltségű vállalkozások működésének 1996. évi jellemzői Magyarországon' ('Operational characteristics of companies with foreign participation in Hungary, 1996'), mimeo, Budapest.

Pye, R. (1997a), 'Foreign direct investment in central Europe: results from a survey of major western investors', *Finance Working Paper*, no. A97/1, City University Business School, London.

Pye, R. (1997b), 'The A-B-Bs of the east: ABB Asea Brown Boveri in central Europe', *Finance Working Paper*, no. A97/2, City University Business School, London.

Pye, R. (1997c), 'The lion roars back into Budapest: the Generali Group in Hungary', *Finance Working Paper*, no. A.97/3, City University Business School, London.

Rems, M., M. Rojec and M. Simonetti (1997), 'Ownership structure and performance of Slovenian non-financial corporate sector', mimeo, Institute of Macro-Economic Analysis and Development, Ljubljana.

Rojec, M. (1987), 'Vlaganje tujega kapitala v jugoslavansko gospodarstvo' ('Investment of foreign capital in the Yugoslav Economy'), Center za mednarodno sodelovanje in razvoj, Ljubljana.

Rojec, M. (1997a), 'Lessons from foreign direct investment (FDI) research in Slovenia', mimeo, Vienna.

Rojec, M. (1997b), 'The development potential of foreign direct investment in the Slovenian economy', *WIIW Research Reports*, no. 245, The Vienna Institute for International Economic Studies, April.

Rojec, M. and M. Hocevar (1996), 'Allocative and industry efficiency of foreign investment enterprises in Slovenian manufacturing sector', in 'Innovation and International Business', *Proceedings of 22nd EWA Annual Conference*, Stockholm, 15–17 December 1996, Institute of International Business, Stockholm, pp. 639–63.

Štiblar, F. (1993), 'Pogled na tuje nalozbe v Slovenijo' ('A view on foreign investment in Slovenia'), Gospodarska gibanja, 235, Ljubljana, pp. 21–36.

Svetličić, M. and M. Rojec (1994), 'Foreign direct investment and the transformation of central European economies', *Management International Review*, **34** (4), pp. 293–312.

Szabó, M. (1997), 'A magyar tejipar versenyképességét befolyásoló tényezők' ('Determinants of competitiveness in the Hungarian diary industry'), mimeo, Budapest University of Economics, 'Competing the world' research project.

Szanyi, M. (1995), 'Experiences with foreign direct investment in Hungary', *Russian and East European Finance and Trade*, **31** (3), May–June, pp. 6/31.

Szanyi, M. (1996), 'Adaptive steps by Hungary's industries during the transition crisis', *Eastern European Economics*, **34** (5), September–October, pp. 59–77.

Szanyi, M. (1997a), 'Experiences of foreign direct investments in eastern Europe: advantages and disadvantages', *IWE Working Paper*, no. 85, November.

Szanyi, M. (1997b), 'Investment survey: Hungary', mimeo, Budapest.

Szanyi, M. and T. Szemlér (1997), 'Investment Patterns in Hungary', *IWE Working Paper*, no. 79, May.

Szemlér, T. (1996), 'Termelés vagy értékesítés? Esettanulmány az AL-KO Kft-ről' ('Production or sales? Case study about the AL-KO Ltd'), mimeo, Budapest University of Economics, 'Competing the world' research project.

Vissi, F. (1994), 'A külföldi mûködötöke-beruházások és a verseny' ('Foreign direct investments and competition'), *Közgazdasági Szemle*, **XLI** (4), pp. 349–59.

Weiszburg, J. (1997), 'General Electric Lighting – Tungsram', mimeo, Budapest University of Economics, 'Competing the world' research project.

Zemplínerová, A. (1997a), 'The role of foreign enterprises in the privatization and restructuring of the Czech economy', *WIIW Research Reports*, no. 238, The Vienna Institute for International Economic Studies, June.

Zemplínerová, A. (1997b), 'The role of foreign direct investment in restructuring and modernization of the Czech economy: an overview of the literature', mimeo, Vienna.

5. Austria – catching-up through inward FDI?

Christian Bellak

1 INTRODUCTION

This chapter focuses on the role of foreign MNCs and inward FDI in Austria.[1] Austria underwent a dramatic catching-up process after World War II. The stylized facts, as reviewed in Marin (1995), suggest that:

- among the small OECD countries Austria (and Finland) exhibit the fastest postwar convergence rate to OECD average;
- this catching-up process has come about through a low, though increasing share of R&D in GDP and a deficit in the technological balance of payments.

The speed with which the Austrian manufacturing sector moved up the technological ladder was slow compared to other Western industrialized countries, but its pace of GDP growth surpassed it. Despite a generally sceptical view of the role of foreign MNCs in Austria, there is widespread consensus that inward FDI did play an important role in the country's ability to catch-up. After World War II, catching-up started on a sound psychological basis determined by the experience of the State before 1938 and the separation from a larger entity (Austro-Hungarian monarchy) after World War I. 'The "normalized" Austria in the beginning of the 1950s found itself [being, C.B.] integrated into a growing Europe (West and East) and was able to utilize the positive impulses from these economies' (Rothschild, 1989, p. 117; translated by C.B.).

Why can Austria serve as a model of catching-up for the CECs? These more highly developed transition countries share a common border with Austria and some of them, like Austria, are also small in both geographical and economic terms. 'If one takes Austria's growth experience as a benchmark it will take CECs over 30 years to catch up with western Europe. This conclusion is not changed when the growth experience of Germany or Finland – the other two best performing countries – are taken as references.' (Marin, 1995, p. 38). Indeed, today, 'with the increased flow of people, capital and goods across the borders, they [the CECs, C.B.] come to see Germany and Austria as role-models for development.' (Wallace, 1997, p. 7).

The analysis below focuses on the restructuring and increased efficiency caused by inward FDI, and takes only a brief look at the macroeconomic effects. The former are very relevant for the role of FDI in CECs, while the latter are specific to a larger mix of policies on the macro-level.

This chapter is organized as follows. First, we present some stylized facts on catching-up and inward FDI of Austria and then assess the performance of FIEs and review the policy measures related to inward FDI. The chapter concludes with some remarks on the contribution of inward FDI to catching-up.

Table 5.1 Catching-up of Austria versus OECD

	Growth differentials to OECD percentage points, per annum			
	1950–70	1970–90	1990–97	1950–97
GDP per capita (at PPP)	1.5	0.7	0.6	1.0
Productivity (output per employee at PPP)	1.9	0.7	1.2	1.3
Manufacturing output growth	0.9	0.5	0.3	0.6
Share in OECD exports (+ = gain, – = loss) % p.a.	n.a.	1.4	–0.8	0.8 (1970–97)

Source: Kausel (1998), various tables.

2 STYLIZED FACTS ON AUSTRIA'S CATCHING-UP

The historical record of Austria's postwar recovery as shown in Table 5.1 is impressive. However, certain development gaps remain that bear examination.

Starting from per capita GDP of 84 per cent (relative to EU-12 = 100) in 1950, Austria surpassed EU-12 average in 1970 (101 per cent) and in 1994 reached a level of 113 per cent compared to EU-12. *Vis-à-vis* the USA, Austria showed the fastest gap closing during 1950–80 (measured by the reduction in per capita income gap over one decade), even before

Germany and Finland (Marin, 1995, p. 38). The average growth rate of Austrian real GDP per cent between 1960 and 1990 was 3.1 per cent as compared with an OECD average of 2.6 per cent.

The growth rate and consequent speed of catching-up are in most countries determined by productivity gains *vis-à-vis* competitors. Viewed from the single country, productivity growth means a more efficient use of inputs in the transformation into outputs. Catching-up occurs, if the increase in productivity in a certain country is higher than in others.[2] Analysing the growth rates of productivity for Austria reveals that it was higher than the average for developed countries during the whole postwar period. In the 1960s the gap was 1.0 (5.4 versus 4.4 average annual percentage change 1964/73; Bayer, 1983), in the 1970s 0.4 (2.9 versus 2.5); in the mid-1980s to mid-1990s 2.5 (Guger, 1996, p. 514) and almost twice as high as Germany's (5.4 versus 3.0 per cent). It is thus only comparable to growth rates achieved by Finland. Even in recent years, when productivity growth tended to slow down in many countries, Austria's growth rates were still outstanding.

Economic theory tells us that the impact of technology on growth is substantial in the course of a country's catching-up process. Technology can either be created or bought in the market, and by both means will be positively related to growth. Yet, while the first way creates indigenous capacity, the second way creates dependence, although we have to admit that the latter might be the basis for catching-up and a change in the trajectory followed. The first way may include R&D in domestic or foreign firms, while the second way refers to (a) technology import embodied in final goods and (b) technology transfer via FDI (that is, the transfer of a technological property right to a subsidiary). As Barell and Pain (1997) argue, it would be wrong to underestimate the effects of inward FDI in developed economies based on the fact that a relatively high proportion of investments consist of mergers and acquisitions rather than green-field investments. 'Take-overs and the associated reorganization of existing capacity and introduction of new ideas may raise the rate of technical progress and hence the long-run rate of economic growth' (p. 1777).

Austria's persistent technology gap is *inter alia* reflected in the trade structure (see below) and production structure. The bulk of manufacturing production in Austria is still concentrated within the resource-intensive and labour-intensive sectors (about 50 per cent). Science-related production was well below the OECD average in 1992 (3.8 versus 7.9 per cent; OECD (1996) Wirtschaftsbericht 1994–95, p. 71).

Surprisingly, the high growth of Austria's GDP and productivity has been achieved by a rather low R&D expenditure in GDP (for example, in 1995: 1.51 per cent; Germany 2.27 per cent). The growth of total R&D expenditure between 1981 and 1991 measured as a percentage of GDP was

0.33 (Germany: 0.57). Foreign MNCs contributed particularly to the closing of the technology gap and imported technology substituted local R&D.

Apart from foreign subsidiaries, technology import was the second tier to convergence. Marin (1988) provides empirical evidence:

> that the Austrian textile industry responded to massive foreign competition which mainly came from other industrialized countries, by introducing more efficient and advanced production techniques as well as by improving product design and quality. (pp. 562f.).

This technology transfer seems to be a success-model (which by the way was not discernible in other industries), because a significant part of productivity growth was achieved by the import of foreign best-practice technology, and 'the import of foreign process innovations has helped the industry to meet international price competition' (p. 563).

The trade gap is reflected in the following:

- the share of high-tech exports in Austria's total exports, which despite an increase between 1961 and 1991 from 1.3 to 6.8 per cent remains well below the OECD average of 8.3 and 15.9 per cent;
- a chronically 'negative' *balance of payments in technology,* that is the ratio of technology exports over imports even decreased from 1990 to 1994 from 0.32 to 0.29 (Germany: 0.91 to 0.77);
- the *market share* of the manufacturing sector's exports measured by different groups of goods. A catching-up process of a country is reflected by an increasing share of human capital-intensive and high-tech-intensive goods and (in a country where capital is the abundant resource) a decreasing share of labour- and real asset-intensive goods. During the 25 years between 1970 and 1994 Austria's OECD market share in manufacturing total increased from 1.39 to 1.89 per cent, showing the increasing competitiveness of Austrian exports and a measurable catching-up.
- though there is clear evidence of catching-up in trade, the structure of goods still reveals a potential to catch-up further. This becomes even more important at a time when the existing structure of manufacturing is put under cost and quality pressure from eastern Europe and Asia alike. Compared to other small countries the share of human capital-intensive and high-tech goods in total Austrian exports is generally lower, and considerably lower than the OECD average.
- also, a *unit-value comparison* points to unfavourable structural content of trade in the overall catching-up process (Hutschenreiter and Peneder, 1997, p. 109). First, the unit values in manufacturing

imports are still much higher than in exports (3.5 versus 2.7 US dollars/kilograms). Given Austria's small size, however, one expects some high-tech imports of intermediate and final goods and services primarily in sectors that are not present within the country. For example, among the smaller countries, only Switzerland and Sweden show higher export unit values than import unit values in high-tech goods. The other category, namely human capital-intensive goods, accounts for a much higher export share, yet earns only lower prices than human capital imports into Austria (5.2 versus 6.2 US dollars/kilograms).

Koman and Marin (1997) estimate the role of human capital for Austria's macroeconomic growth 1960–92. Using 1960 as the base year (= 100), the index of 'years of schooling' (used as a measure of the quality of 'human capital' inputs) increases to 106.3 for Austria and to 109.5 for Germany in 1992. The estimated contribution of 'human capital' to total factor productivity growth during this period is 9 per cent for Austria and 17 per cent for Germany (*ibid.*, Table 10). The convergence in income levels with Germany was achieved in Austria with a relatively low contribution of 'human capital' which is also reflected to some extent in the structure of exports (see trade gap above).

3   STYLIZED FACTS ON INWARD FDI TO AUSTRIA

Seen from the perspective of *capital transfer*, both inward and outward FDI have played a minor role in Austria's growth than in most other developed countries. This may sound somewhat surprising given the importance of inward FDI for the creation of employment. This subsection analyses the various indicators divided into three categories: stocks, flows and employment.

Early inward investments date back to 1878, when the first US investor set up production in Austria. After World War II, German capital moved in at a fast rate. Within three years of independence in 1955, annual inward FDI had reached about US\$ 10 million (1958 and 1959)[3] and the accumulated flows were about US\$ 40–60 million (at the then current price level). Between half and three-quarters of these flows came from Germany (Kursiv, 1960, p. 312). A labour shortage in Germany prompted FDI in Austria where manufacturing was characterized by a lower productivity but also by lower labour costs at that time.

Although the comparison of FDI stocks to GDP (as a *flow* measure) is somewhat problematic, it shows the capacity of the capital stock owned by foreigners relative to output. While overall inward FDI was between 5 and 6 per cent of GDP for the 1970s and 1980s, a 7 per cent share was reached in 1995 and may even hit 9 per cent in 1997. Manufacturing accounted for more than half of total FDI during most of the period (Tables 5.2 and 5.3). Compared to outward stocks, after a period of convergence, the gap to inward stocks again widened. Preliminary balance of payments data for 1997 suggest a continuation of this trend. Germany for the whole period after World War II developed a dominating position, accounting for about 60 per cent of all equity invested in Austria. Beer *et al.* (1991, p. 98) show the remarkable increases of German capital in foreign nominal capital over time: 1961: 9.5 per cent; 1969: 27.7 per cent; 1978: 35.8 per cent; 1989: 39.3 per cent.

Table 5.2   FDI stocks – total economy: ATS billion and ratio

Year	Book values		Book values/GDP	
	Outward	Inward	Outward	Inward
1970	n.v.	20.3	–	5.40
1980	7.3	43.7	0.73	4.39
1990	45.6	105.5	2.53	5.86
1995	118.1	176.9	5.10	7.60
1996	140.0	200.0	5.80	8.30
1997[a]	155.0	220.0	–	–
1997 US$ bn.	12.7	18.0	–	–

Note: [a] estimate.

Source: Oesterreichische Nationalbank (OeNB); own calculations.

Table 5.3   FDI stocks – manufacturing: ATS billion and ratio

Year	Book values		Book values/GDP	
	Outward	Inward	Outward	Inward
1975	2.485	16.374	0.38	2.50
1980	3.167	24.978	0.32	2.51
1990	28.069	61.096	1.56	3.39
1995	65.062	98.575	2.80	4.20

Source: OeNB; own calculations.

Table 5.4   Annual net FDI flows – total economy: ATS billion

Year	Outward FDI	Inward FDI	Balance
1980	1.3	3.1	–1.8
1985	1.5	3.5	–2.0
1990	18.9	7.4	11.6
1995	10.5	6.4	4.1
1996	14.9	40.2	–25.3
1997	18.0	21.0	–3.0

Source: OeNB; balance of payments.

The development of FDI flows is usually more difficult to interpret, since gross and net flows may differ unsystematically. This can be seen from a comparison of Table 5.4. Apart from some annual fluctuations, the EU membership in 1995 gave a new impetus to FDI in Austria. Even though there had been few restrictions left in trade and capital flows before accession, it seems that the decision to join the EU gave a positive signal to investors that the business location would also be attractive in the future. In the long term the 1990s brought a clear shift of flows to a persistently higher level, reflecting the overall internationalization.

In the manufacturing sector, strategic industries show the largest share of foreign MNCs by number of firms (in brackets): machine-tool industry (132), chemical industry (95), electronics (53) and metal industry (55). These also have the highest shares by market value and by the number of employees. The recent influx of foreign capital into the food industry is motivated by two mutual supporting factors: the exploitation of the MNC's brand names and the lack of international activities of Austrian firms. By incorporating these firms, which often produce high-quality goods, into large networks of MNCs like Unilever and Nestlé, the market size increases and allows access to niche markets at considerable economies of scale. Between 1994 and 1996 gross output of the food industry shrank by 2 per cent, the number of plants decreased by 100 to 450, and employment fell about 6 per cent annually. In such a situation, industry-wide accusations against foreign MNCs are frequently raised, yet it should be kept in mind that some Austrian firms would probably have been lost without foreign investments (Ehrlich, 1970).

As a real indicator, employment figures tell something about the direct effect of inward FDI on the domestic economy (Table 5.5). For the manufacturing sector, there is a clear trend discernible for the 1980s and

Table 5.5   Employment in outward and inward investment enterprises,
          unweighted, 1985–95, in 1000

	Total economy		Manufacturing	
	Outward FDI	Inward FDI	Outward FDI	Inward FDI
1985	60	241	31	157
1990	83	290	60	165
1995	166	249	102	137

Source: OeNB.

1990s: while overall employment in the manufacturing sector (and in the state-owned sector due to privatization) falls, the employment in the foreign-owned sector increased until the early 1990s and fell in 1995. Beer *et al.* (1991) show a reduction of employment in the manufacturing sector by 19 per cent during 1969–89 as opposed to an increase of employment in foreign-owned firms by 43 per cent.

Two conclusions emerge from this: (1) The relative importance of the foreign-owned sector increased as the employment growth was faster in the foreign-owned sector, while the reduction between 1990 and 1995 was relatively larger (almost 20 percentage points) than in total manufacturing (13 percentage points), taking into account the larger absolute number of employees in the latter sector. (2) There is an increasingly discernible de-linking between capital flows and the creation of jobs. Rising inward FDI does not automatically imply new jobs, in either manufacturing, or in services.

An examination of international figures shows clearly that Austria is among the countries with the highest share of employment in foreign subsidiaries. However, the share of employment of foreign-owned firms in the manufacturing sector increased only slightly (direct participations only) between 1975 and 1995 showing considerable industry differences (Table 5.6). Industries with shares above 30 per cent are electrical engineering, petroleum and construction.[4] When the catching-up process was discussed, we referred to Finland as a similar case, but what becomes clear is that the role of inward FDI is much less in Finland. This suggests that catching-up in Finland was to a larger extent based on the development of indigenous capacities than in Austria, a strategy which could be more successful in the long run.

Table 5.7 indicates the dramatic ownership change in the manufacturing sector during a period of 20 years. While the state-owned industrial sector ceased to exist, the private domestic and foreign sec-

Table 5.6   *Share of FIEs in employment in the manufacturing sector, per cent*

	1975	1980	1985	1990	1995
Metals, vehicles	17	16	19	26	24
Electrical engineering	44	58	54	57	46
Petroleum, chemicals	41	24	36	35	41
Paper, wood	25	20	19	16	17
Textiles, clothing, leather	24	29	25	25	22
Food, beverages, tobacco	20	27	25	14	22
Construction and allied industries	21	36	34	47	–
Other	n.a.	25	22	10	–
Total	25	26	27	30	29

Note: n.a. = not available

Source: Updated from Glatz and Moser, 1989, p. 87. (1995 = domestic industries: BS 68; FDI: ÖNACE) from Statistische Übersichten 7/96; OeNB FDI Survey.

Table 5.7   *Structure of employment by ownership categories in the manufacturing sector, in thousand and index in per cent, 1975–95, selected years*

	Total[a]		of which foreign[b]		of which state-owned[c]	
	Number	Index*	Number	Index	Number	Index
1975	627	100.0	153	100.0	117	100.0
1980	628	100.2	164	107.2	117	100.0
1985	562	89.6	157	102.6	102	87.2
1990	540	86.1	167	109.2	82	70.1
1995	460	73.4	137	89.5	0	0

Notes:
[a]   Industry minus construction, electricity, sawmills, 1990 and1995: Industriestatistik und Statistische Übersichten 7/96 and 10/93.
[b]   OeNB Survey; only direct participation; unweighted.
[c]   ÖIAG firms only.
*   1975 = 100

Source: Updated from Glatz and Moser, 1989b, p. 86 and OeNB Survey.

tors also reduced their employment but to different degrees.[5] A considerable share of employees of the state-owned sector were shifted to the other two sectors during the privatization process. As a result of these developments, the government has less control over a smaller amount of employment, but it is also evident that there is no foreign domination discernible.

The debate about the role of MNCs in the Austrian economy concerns the threat to Austrian sovereignty. The study of Beer *et al.* (1991) updates earlier surveys of the Chamber of Labour (1962, 1970) on foreign ownership. It also contrasts the dominance of German FDI in the manufacturing sector since the turn of the century with the weaknesses of domestic firms. It highlights, *inter alia,* a change in the structure of foreign investors, namely the increasing importance of medium-sized firms during the 1970s and 1980s as opposed to the large German MNCs of the earlier periods. The study also maintains that the relatively large share of the public and cooperative sector is a safeguard for strategic ownership and national interest. Currently, when public stakes in the major banks and in manufacturing enterprises have been sold, there is uncertainty about the strategic interests of owners. The ownership change may imply more volatile strategies in the future, so that the traditional long-term orientation may increasingly conflict with the strategy of other parts of the firm outside Austria, be it the mother company (that is, foreign-owned) or the subsidiary(ies) abroad in the case of a domestically owned firm. Foreign ownership is not just a relabelling of the firm, but changes the whole structure of the company and the industry as a whole. Barell and Pain (1997) quote several studies showing that the high level of inward investment in manufacturing activities has clearly been particularly important in the economic development of many smaller European economies.

4   PERFORMANCE INDICATORS OF FIES

The comparison of foreign and domestic firms involves several difficulties stemming from various sources:

- With all the comparisons it must be kept in mind that the FDI statistics use the firm (*Unternehmen*) as the unit of analysis while the statistics on the manufacturing sector refer to the plant (*Betrieb*). However, the relevant unit of analysis is, in fact, the firm as the decision-making organization.
- Austrian firms are not distinguished by ownership categories in the industrial statistics, therefore, the comparison is limited to foreign investment enterprises (OeNB) versus total manufacturing (statistical office).
- The two sources use different classifications of industries which can only partly be harmonized.

Various general arguments point to differences in the performance of foreign-owned subsidiaries and domestic firms. Most of them do not, however, relate to ownership.

- The comparisons of plants and firms: there are a number of reasons why a single plant may be much more efficient than a full firm, bearing all overhead costs and so on.
- The differences in the degree of internationalization: subsidiaries are typically less internationalized than their mother company, as their product range, market size and so on is limited.
- While the subsidiary's decision making depends on the objectives given by the mother company (that is local logic of decision making), the mother company employs a global logic in the decisions concerning the whole network.
- One particularly important aspect is the provision of technology by the mother company to the subsidiary (Fors, 1997), without charging the costs of development (positive externality), which then results in a higher profitability.
- Even if both groups of firms relate to the same industry, their value-added stages may be systematically different. For example, a foreign subsidiary engages in assembling while the domestic firm produces parts to be assembled. If foreign subsidiaries dominate a certain segment in an industry, performance comparisons do not make much sense.
- The financial strength of the companies differs, due to the dependence of the foreign subsidiary. There might be both positive (in the case of cross-subsidization) or negative (profit transfer abroad via transfer pricing) deviations from the industry average.

Given the limitations explained above, descriptive statistics (Table 5.8) show a similar picture of indicators for the total manufacturing sector (MS) and FIEs. Further testing would have to show if the small differences are systematic and if they are significant. Assuming they are significant (that is, FIEs are 'better' performers than MS) the follow-up question would be, if and how does it matter? Any conclusion as to a preferential treatment of FIEs versus DEs would certainly contradict existing and future competition laws (EU, World Trade Organization (WTO), OECD).

The tables reveal that not every indicator shows a superior performance of foreign-owned firms. Their equity-ratio is lower (Table 5.8), their size is partly smaller (for example textile industry, Table 5.9), their rentability is lower (Table 5.8), yet their productivity is higher in all the comparisons (Tables 5.8 and 5.1). It should be emphasized, however, that indicators including profit figures are difficult to comment on. For example, foreign firms have more possibilities to influence profits via transfer pricing.[6]

*Table 5.8   Indicators of FIEs compared to the MS total – selected years
            (ATS and per cent) – median values*

	FIEs (1)		MS (2)		(1)/(2)	
	1992	1993	1992	1993	1992	1993
1. Equity – ratio[a] (equity/total assets)	23.9	22.5	25.62	25.73	0.93	0.87
2. Rentability[a] (net-profit/turnover)	1.2	1.2	2.25	1.74	0.53	0.69
3. Productivity (turnover/employee)[a] ATS mn	1.6	1.7	1.41	1.45	1.13	1.17
4. Equity per firm[b] ATS mn	94.6	101.5	152.28	154.0	0.62	0.659
5. Employees per firm[c]	207	194	60.03	56.7	3.45	3.42
6. Number of firms	563	543	8204	8110	–	–

Sources: [a] FIEs Neudorfer, 1995, Manufacturing Sector (MS): OeNB: Jahresabschluβ–kennzahlen, Statistisches Monatsheft, 12/96, p. 9. [b] FIEs: FDI Survey of OeNB; Manufacturing Sector: Equity per firm provided by OeNB. [c] FDIs: FDI Survey of OeNB; Manufacturing Sector: Industriestatistik 1994.

The fact that foreign-owned firms show a superior performance in CECs is no surprise. The fact that this also applies to a highly developed country like Austria as well is somewhat surprising. Since we find a higher share of intra-industry FDI (and trade) in the latter than in the former, this points to more similar competitors of differentiated goods.

Table 5.10 introduces turnover and from this a crude measure for productivity is derived. The figures for FIEs and DEs refer to different years, follow a different classification and were partly reclassified, therefore, this comparison is also to be treated with caution. Yet, given that productivity changes only gradually from one year to the next, the productivity of FIEs is higher, particularly in those industries with a high share of foreign capital. This is apparent in the food, wood, electronics, transport equipment, chemicals and petroleum industries. Industries with a share of employment in FIEs larger than 30 per cent all show a productivity level above the manufacturing sector total.

A wide variety of literature deals with the comparison of foreign-owned and domestic firms in Austria revealing a significant influence of ownership on the long-term performance 1980–94, for example, equity ratio, value added per employee.

Table 5.9 Size of the companies by equity and employment: comparison of FIEs and the MS

	1992		1993		1994		1995	
	FIEs	MS	FIEs	MS	FIEs	MS	FIEs	MS
Equity, ATS billion	68.9	220.8	73.1	234.7	76.46	244.8	59.96	242.2
Number of firms	729	1538	720	1610	946	1593	647	1080
Employment th.	151.0	431.9	139.9	439.0	144.0	426.1	138.8	322.3
Number of firms	729	1538	720	1610	719	1593	689	1080
(excluding mining)		(1508)		(1580)		(1568)		(1063)
Equity/firm	0.095	0.146	0.101	0.149	0.81	0.156	0.093	0.228
Employment/firm	207	281	194	273	200	267	202	298
Selected industries								
Electro(nics)								
Equity/firm	0.140	0.198	0.153	0.218	0.160	0.232	0.174	0.344
Employment/firm	603	572	628	558	603	553	527	459
Pulp and Paper								
Equity/firm	0.062	0.313	0.030	0.125	0.25	0.173	0.076	0.241
Employment/firm	234	105	154	107	151	132	100	149
Textile and Clothing								
Equity/firm	0.036	0.061	0.026	0.061	0.27	0.067	0.027	0.084
Employment/firm	187	265	175	243	165	236	140	259
Food								
Equity/firm	0.056	0.153	0.062	0.169	0.066	0.180	0.112	0.264
Employment/firm	132	214	145	202	167	215	145	230

Sources: FIEs: FDI Survey of OeNB; employment = unweighted, direct stakeholding only. Manufacturing sector: number of firms and employment from Statistisches Monatsheft, 12/96, p. 11, ÖNACE adjusted to classification used by FDI survey of OeNB.

Table 5.10 Share of FIEs in employment and turnover of the MS by NACE industries, 1994–95, in per cent

Industry		Employment	Turnover
DA	Food products, beverages, tobacco	20.9	28.6
DB	Textiles and textile products	17.4	22.4
DC	Leather and leather products	42.0	43.1
DD	Wood and wood products	4.9	10.5
DE	Pulp, paper, publishing, printing	30.4	33.1
DF	Coke and petroleum	–	–
DG	Chemicals	21.3	27.6
DH	Rubber and plastic	–	–
DI	Other non-metallic minerals	27.3	32.8
DJ	Basic metals	17.5	19.5
DK	Machinery and equipment n.e.c.[a]	22.2	39.6
DL	Electrical and optical equipment	46.1	84.6
DM	Transport equipment	37.3	64.7
DN	Manufacturing n.e.c. (including construction)	–	–
D	Manufacturing	31.4	51.4

Note: [a] n.e.c. = not elsewhere classified.

Sources: FIEs: data provided by OeNB for 1995; manufacturing sector: Industriestatistik 1994. Partially different industrial classifications recalculated.

Gugler (1998) compares a sample of the 214 largest Austrian non-manufacturing firms by ownership, foreign firms, state-owned companies and family businesses. Among others, the foreign firms are larger (average sales ATS 3973 million versus ATS 2680 million) than the total sample; their R&D intensity is higher (2.6 versus 1.7 per cent on average) and their 'cash flow/equity ratio' is higher (34 versus 29). From a subsample of 94 Austrian firms between 1975 and 1994 he concludes that 'foreign-controlled firms obtained the highest returns (mean 16.2 per cent), and nearly three quarters of foreign-owned firms are high profitability companies' (*ibid.*, p. 28); on the whole foreign control raises profitability of ventures.

Although there has been no systematic research on a broad level so far, a recent study by AMC and IHS (1997) shows clear differences in the R&D ratio between a sample of foreign-owned and domestically owned manufacturing firms (Table 5.11). Not only is the R&D expenditure in absolute terms much higher for foreign firms, their ratio is also increasing substantially, while it is decreasing with domestic firms. Although some firms may have also included licensing fees to the mother company in their R&D expenditures this was generally excluded in the study. The study concludes that there is no coherent pattern of ownership-specific innovation and R&D. Yet, if one adds additional factors (for example, technology intensity) a significant heterogeneity of the role of innovation and technology transfer can be seen.

Table 5.11 R&D ratio (R&D expenditure/turnover) by ownership structure, MS

	All firms	Foreign firms	Austrian firms
1990	3.3	3.9	2.9
1995	3.6	4.4	2.7

Source: AMC and IHS (1997).

5 THE ROLE OF POLICY ON INWARD FDI

The contribution of FIEs to employment creation and regional development was recognized by industrial policy makers in Austria soon after World War II. Quantitative criteria were important relative to qualitative criteria. During the 1970s and 1980s, the role of FIEs for enhancing structural change became important. It is clear from the policy decisions that Austrian politicians were convinced that DEs, because of their financial and technological weaknesses, could not cope with structural change. According to Glatz and Moser (1989, p. 190) FIEs should step in to help overcome these problems. By the 1990s, however, under the pressure of intensified competition from EU membership and the opening of eastern Europe, the hopes of policy makers shifted again towards an optimization of the international division of labour. With the aggravation of regional and employment problems, quantitative aspects became again important. The fact that there is little choice for host countries ('you must take what you get') was widely recognized, as 'competitor locations' emerged in CECs for certain types of inward FDI.

Austria's experience of policy measures to attract FDI is remarkably limited given the important role of FDI. Most FDI has been attracted through the general location advantages rather than by specific policy measures and problems concerning foreign subsidiaries were limited. One of the rare cases was in 1989 when the Advisory Committee of the Social Partners to the Government (*Beirat für Wirtschafts- und Sozialfragen*) mentioned the high remittances abroad (50 to 80 per cent of annual inward FDI) in the form of management fees and licensing fees paid back to the foreign parent, a situation attributed to unfavourable tax laws causing 'hidden' profit transfer.

Apart from general tax policy, which is always very important, several tax incentives and investment- and export-promotion measures apply to all companies located in Austria. These incentives have varied over time and have recently been reduced in general under the recent budget reductions of the Austrian government. The following sections provide a brief overview of the incentive structure.

5.1 Monetary and exchange rate policy

Austria's hard currency policy – the schilling was pegged to the German mark appreciating against most other currencies – implied that the purchase of assets by foreign investors in Austria became more and more expensive. On the other hand, once a company was established, the importing of intermediate goods became relatively cheap. In addition, the stability of the exchange rate was a major positive location factor. Export prices did not matter much as long as exports were intra-firm, that is components, parts to be assembled in another subsidiary abroad. Otherwise, exports to third parties would have been affected negatively.

5.2 Fiscal incentives

Austria employs a range of measures to all (foreign and domestic investors), like tax holidays, corporate tax and VAT relief, accelerated depreciation, customs duties exemption and deductions of the re-invested profit from the taxable base. According to the Austrian Business Agency (ABA) of the government, 'taxation of companies in Austria is competitive in international comparison'. In 1994 Austria implemented a tax reform that won international recognition. Taxes on property, such as capital tax and inheritance tax equivalent, were abolished, and as trade taxes have also been phased out, there is one effective rate of tax on earnings of 34 per cent (as compared to the previous rate of 39 per cent). The rate at which companies in Austria are taxed is now one of the lowest in Europe (EU average 52.5 per cent). In addition to this, the general environment in Austria (including a variety of double taxation agreements) makes it particularly suitable as a location for holding companies.

5.3   Non-fiscal incentives

Foreign MNCs have access to incentives provided with no discrimination both to foreign and domestic owned companies: R&D grants, subsidies for employment, government equity participation, risk-sharing models, export guarantees ensured by the government, subsidized dedicated infrastructure are sometimes related to a particular large project. Financial subsidies are also granted for *innovative* projects: for example, in Styria: 5 to 20 per cent of eligible project costs; for *R&D* projects up to 60 per cent for industrial basic research and up to 35 per cent for applied research with a maximum amount of ATS 10 million in 1997 are subsidized. For *environment* projects, for human capital *training* and for producer-related *services* other subsidies are granted in Styria. Inward FDI in Austria has had technology-related benefits to the economy through demonstration, observation, imitation and application of advanced technologies (Mowery and Oxley, 1997, p. 152).

5.4   Industrial parks and regional policy

Several business parks have been established over the years, two of them are 'cross-border' business parks with the Czech Republic and Hungary. Competition between business parks on the national level has been limited, rather they seek to specialize. For example, Upper Austria presents itself as a 'logistics location'. Often they are used as measures of regional and sectoral policy in order to compensate for the loss of uncompetitive 'old' industries there.

5.5   Sectoral policy: example of automotive industry

Currently the Austrian car industry consists of a lot of small-and medium-sized suppliers (manufacturing and services), primarily for the German automobile industry, and larger subsidiaries of major foreign car producers. The government introduced subsidies in 1976 and 1977 to support the Austrian automotive supplier industry in order to balance car imports. This measure proved to be very successful. The coverage ratio (defined as exports over imports) was about 11 per cent in 1977, 24.2 per cent in 1980 and 90 per cent in 1992 with automotive exports growing tenfold from 1980. In 1996, output of the automotive supplier industry was ATS 51.3 billion (1977: ATS 2.3 billion; 1990: ATS 37.3 billion), the coverage of auto imports was 106 per cent, not including the 100 000 passenger cars and a number of trucks produced in Austria in foreign affiliates. 12.8 per cent of total employment is related to the automotive sector (that is approximately 55 000–60 000 jobs). Locations for the larger inward FDI are Steyr (BMW, MAN) and Graz (Chrysler, Jeep, Puch, Mercedes). BMW invested ATS 20 billion since 1979 and employs about 200 people in its R&D centre. The province of Styria more or less has managed to create an automobile cluster with the participation of foreign MNCs, which helped to overcome some of the negative effects of structural change in other industries (iron, textile, paper and so on).[7] The cluster provides information and initiates exchange of information between firms; supports upgrading of firms by establishing co-operation with university and non-university research institutions; and helps to reap synergies between firms on various levels of the value-added chain. The cluster activities are coordinated by a cluster council.

This example shows clearly that there is room for interventionist measures with a certain chance of success. However, no cost-benefit analysis has so far been commissioned by the government to evaluate the effectiveness of the subsidies granted.

Competition policy has not been very effective in Austria in the past. Only under the pressure before EU membership and, of course, since then competition-policy has led to privatization and opening of sheltered sectors. Foreign MNCs moved rather quickly into these sectors, for example, when state-owned industries were sold to the public. The lack of an effective competition policy in earlier periods also meant that the beneficial effects of inward FDI by stimulating competition with indigenous firms could have been much stronger.

The experience with direct subsidies of greenfield investments was mixed. Even before Austria's membership, the granting of large subsidies (for example, an approximate ATS 1 billion subsidy for Chrysler) was rejected by the EU Commission and several cases were discussed in the EU competition policy report. The reason for this was that most output produced by the subsidiaries in question was intended for re-exporting from Austria to EU markets and thus the subsidy would have led to a competitive disadvantage for EU suppliers.

5.6   Institution building

Austria's effective social partnership has been and will continue to be the country's strongest general location advantage. The co-operation between employer and employee representative organizations manifests itself in low strike rates and a favourable relative unit labour cost position which is very important for exports under the hard currency regime.

Another factor has been the streamlining of administrative procedures. For example, in the province of Vorarlberg, the average length of the procedures to set up a subsidiary has been reduced considerably, although there is still a comparative disadvantage *vis-à-vis* Germany, as the share of procedures over one year there is 28 per cent while it is 48 per cent in Austria. The length and structure of procedures may create unnecessary impediments to new FDI and thus is an important element of a differentiation strategy for a national or regional authority.

5.7 Non-financial incentives

Among others, the provision of monopoly or preferential treatment, exemptions for foreign MNCs from certain social standards, provision of land, participation in national R&D programmes, special treatment on the repatriation of earnings and capital proved successful in the past. Most of these incentives cannot be applied under EU competition laws.

5.8 Evaluation

The evaluation of policy measures consists of bits and pieces of information, since there is no recent systematic evaluation (except Bayer and Blaas, 1986) of the effects of incentives available. An evaluation of the past policy in 1989 showed the following results (update based on Beer, 1989, mimeo; and Beirat für Wirtschafts- und Sozialfragen, 1989):

- Apart from the general conclusion that technology transfer within foreign MNCs to their subsidiaries in Austria benefited Austria, there is no direct measurable result available (*cf* Buchinger *et al.*, 1994 for case studies).
- The former Industrial Corporate Development (ICD), now Austrian Business Agency (ABA), a government agency to promote Austria's location advantages and to co-ordinate the regional agencies, has about 20 employees. Between 1984 and 1992, they attracted 53 projects (subsidiaries) with about 5000 employees and a total investment volume of ATS 6.2 billion Between 1984 and 1996 the figures increased to 7112 employees and an investment volume of ATS 9.38 billion. Hence, between 1992 and 1996 more than 2000 jobs have been secured and/or created. For example, in the province of Upper Austria, there were about 60 investment projects, of which 30 were foreign, thereof 25 German between 1994 and 1997, including many take-overs.

- A list of projects realized by the ABA between 1984 and 1996 shows the wide range of industries involved. Unfortunately, there is neither information about the share of take-overs and greenfield investments, nor about the specific services of ABA in the projects. No details about specific companies are available to the public.
- Besides the ABA, regional agencies (80–100 employees in total) exist which sometimes compete against each other, thus possibly creating an overall loss for the economy. Overall, the Austrian experience concerning the incentive system and the behaviour of foreign firms has been positive. It must be emphasized that exceptions are rare[8] and negative behaviour can also be seen in the case of Austrian firms.

5.9   Future strategy

The economic environment of Austria as a location for manufacturing activities changed at the end of the 1980s when (primarily German) investors turned their attention towards eastern Europe and the former GDR and when efficiency-seeking foreign subsidiaries started to relocate part of their activities there. So far, several studies suggest the effects of relocation to eastern Europe have been positive for Austria, mainly on the basis of additional exports. Austria's EU membership has brought a new wave of inward FDI, albeit mostly by take-overs. The main task for the future is to attract new investments in order to facilitate the creation of *additional* jobs.

In the past Austria was a location that favoured 'screw-driver factories' or assembling plants with a mass production of specific products via comparatively low production-cost, high increases of productivity and so on. This kind of production activity tends to be subject to a substantial pressure to relocate (partly but not exclusively to eastern Europe). In such an environment, a growing inflow of foreign capital may have negative consequences for the business location in the long run. It implies an increased possibility for relocation by large MNCs which concentrate certain value-added functions in certain locations, possibly abroad.

It is argued that international competition has two specific features with regard to the role of foreign capital and that these features are a basis for the improvement of the business location. First, the deepening economic integration of states, by reducing transaction costs, opens new possibilities for internalizing transactions into the firm internationally ('globally integrated production') and thus favours large MNCs. Second, it gives impetus to an increased mobility of firms optimizing their international portfolio via (easier) relocation. Both features imply that firms have several immobile elements in the value-added chain, which cannot be separated easily from the business location (for example, localized learning, the national innovation system, institutional environment, human capital). Only financial capital is footloose, while real capital has a high degree of location specificity. The potential for a business location lies in the fact that the location-specific elements often are the high value-added elements.

This problem approached from a policy view can be defined as the necessity of bridging a 'structural gap', which has arisen because the business environment has not been transformed in accordance with the structural transformation of the firms. The 'screw-driver firm' location has become obsolete, but has not yet been reshaped as a location for immobile firm activities mentioned above. The Austrian government needs to understand the changing nature of Austria's location advantages. Those advantages which were relevant for initial entry of MNCs after World War II and during the *Wirtschaftswunder* have became obsolescent.

Regional innovation premia and other measures have been discussed as means to locate R&D-facilities in Austria. Yet, as with other fields of policy, the general quality of human capital available regionally is a much stronger determinant of inward FDI than financial subsidies. Also, a cluster-oriented location policy has been frequently proposed, in order to support complementary investment, which may then accumulate know-how and networks between suppliers and customers and competition between cluster firms. Among the various general location policies, the optimization of the national innovation system has priority. This should ensure not only technology transfer and technology creation in foreign subsidiaries but also attract *additional* investment. A steady process of upgrading human capital is also seen as a necessary condition to ensure inward FDI. As Mowery and Oxley (1997, p. 157) emphasize, 'the fact remains that an economy's system for training workers at all levels is one of the most distinctively "national" components of systems of innovation'.

6   REMARKS ON THE CONTRIBUTION OF INWARD FDI TO CATCHING-UP

This subsection reviews empirical evidence on the effects of inward FDI.[9] Economic theory analyses the effects of FDI at the macro- and micro level. At the macro-level, trade theory and the macro-type marginal productivity theory assess effects on trade, capital flow, knowledge and the resulting income distribution. On the micro-level, several models exist on the effects of FDI on exports in different markets (substituting or com-

plementing exports), as well as the internalization of intermediate product markets. Effects of FDI are usually defined and measured by the
difference between the actual outcome and what would have happened if
the FDI had not been carried out (counterfactual hypothesis). Yet, the
fact that mostly *input indicators*, such as capital invested, R&D expenditure and so on, are covered by the data does not permit the empirical
consideration of efficiency in the possible outcome. For example, Austria
has maintained high levels of employment in terms of inward FDI capital transferred as well as a strong record of R&D intensity of foreign
MNCs etc.[10] The crucial question then is, does the economy and not only
the MNC itself benefit from inward FDI? The results of the most important studies are presented below.

Ehrlich (1970) surveyed US investments in Austria and showed that
most of them were market-driven. After take-over, small- and medium-
sized Austrian firms began to grow rapidly and expanded into new
markets. Ehrlich concluded that the effect of US investment on Austria
had overall been positive and, contrary to contemporary studies, the linkages with Austrian firms had also been extensive and successful.

Since the 1970s the internationalization strategy of MNCs has
changed substantially from simple horizontal and vertical integration
towards a functional specialization of subsidiaries. Also, the main competitors of foreign subsidiaries are no longer Austrian firms but are other
foreign companies which means that few dynamic effects of competition
have emerged.

Haschek (1982) contrasts positive and negative effects of inward FDI
and their changes over time, stating 'that direct foreign investment had a
positive effect on the Austrian balance of payments only until 1970 and
1971, and that the situation changed thereafter to Austria's disadvantage'.
In particular, foreign subsidiaries started producing relatively import-
intensive goods and 'were often, at least informally, bound through
world-wide company guidelines to export restrictions'. The balance of
payments 'has gradually eroded because of increases in the amount of
yearly remittances of profits, licensing and management fees' (Peischer,
1981). Haschek also found, 'in several cases that a larger share of the
production-palette could have been transferred to Austria. This includes
finished-goods production with a high value-added component generally
reserved for the mother company'. Among the positive effects Haschek
mentions the employment effect, contributing to Austria's low unemployment rate, and the structural change of output leading to efficient import
substitution in the food, textile and electric industries in Austria.

The only large-scale survey on effects of foreign investment in
Austria so far has been conducted by Glatz and Moser (1989). They

examined all larger investments (36) in the manufacturing sector since 1970 which were attracted by the state agency ICD and which received subsidies. They found that the *employment* growth of foreign subsidiaries in Austria was higher than that of Austrian firms. (Annual average employment growth between 1980 and 1986: +7.7 per cent for subsidiaries; –1.9 per cent for Austrian firms.) The investment/turnover ratio was also significantly higher in the former (10.6 per cent) than in the latter group.[11] Buchinger *et al.* (1994, p. 20) analysed employment growth in foreign R&D units since the year of foundation and showed substantial increases, for example, for Siemens 1960–90 from 10 to 2500 employees; ALCATEL 1986–93 from 20 to 120.

Glatz and Moser found that the *balance-of-payments* effect, in particular the direct effect on the trade balance, was positive because of the high export ratio of foreign subsidiaries (85 per cent in the first half of the 1980s). It was, however, reduced if the share of imported intermediate services (75 per cent) was taken into account. They stated that in the long run, capital outflow would exceed capital inflows but that the rentability and profitability of foreign MNCs is higher than that of domestic enterprises. The *value-added* effect of FDI was highly positive, value added per employee in foreign subsidiaries being 25 per cent above the average of the Austrian manufacturing sector. The higher efficiency could be an effect of a few but highly specialized activities of foreign subsidiaries, at least some of them being only assembly lines. The parent company applies steady pressure to restructure and improve performance. One management strategy that shows the dependence of the subsidiary on the mother company has been to shift less production than originally planned to a particular location, creating additional pressure to perform well (Flecker *et al.*, 1990).

Foreign MNCs have often been accused of having a negative impact on *industrial relations* by undermining the established relationship of capital and labour on the national level. The widespread expectation is that industrial relations can deteriorate following a foreign take-over, mainly because the previously independent firm is turned into a foreign subsidiary. Case study evidence (Flecker *et al.*, 1990) shows that the foreign owners and the new management generally try to make use of the positive relations existing between management and workers. Yet, the driving force behind this is not altruism, but rather to include the works councils in the responsibility of the management *vis-à-vis* the workforce. Complicated or unwelcome decisions can thus be implemented more easily and this may help the subsidiary to overcome competition between subsidiaries in different locations.

Karlhofer's (1985) study was motivated by a number of strikes in Austrian subsidiaries of foreign MNCs in the 1970s although strike rates in Austria traditionally have been among the lowest in Europe. In the public debate, the immediate reaction was to accuse foreign firms of not fitting in to the 'social partnership'-type industrial relations in Austria. This study shows, however, that the opposite was the case. First, the number of strikes has actually not been as high as in domestically-owned firms. Second, the strikes in foreign-owned firms were the expression of an adjustment process of a foreign management after a new take-over, trying to get the most out of the productivity–labour cost gap between Austria and Germany. After an initial phase, industrial relations tended to normalize.

An important question for a small destination country is whether or not *technology* is transferred to and R&D conducted in the subsidiary of the foreign MNCs. In general, Austria has done well in this respect as most, if not all, foreign firms transferred know-how into their subsidiaries and their R&D ratio (5.12 per cent in 1986) is more than twice as high for manufacturing as a whole. However, the external effect for Austria has been quite small since know-how is used primarily intra-firm and in some cases even involved the transfer of human capital abroad.

The Ehrlich study (1970) was the first evaluation of inward FDI in Austria after World War II. It analyses technology transfer (i) from a foreign parent to its Austrian subsidiary; (ii) from an Austrian firm to a new foreign parent (acquisition); (iii) transfer of management know-how; and (iv) brain drain effects. For example, he mentions two cases of foreign takeovers that were prompted by a desire to benefit from the superior technological know-how of Austrian firms (plastic ski and extrusion machines) and one to gain a specific type of engineering skill. The survey suggests that the gap in organizational and management skills compared to international standards may have been even larger than in technology.[12]

All the 17 US subsidiaries performed sophisticated production functions and all of them had full access to all technologies developed by the parent company. (Although not all actually used this technology in the production process, none was confined to simple assembly.) The degree of technological dependence increased with the degree of specialization in earlier stages of the investment, but may have led to greater independence when the investment matures. On average, US firms spent 46 per cent more on R&D per employee than the manufacturing sector's average (which was partly due to the fact that they invest in technology-intensive sectors) (Ehrlich, 1970, p. 14). Ehrlich concludes that 'the majority of American firms invested in areas where Austrian firms could also be successful' (*ibid.*, p. 18). The lack of venture capital may – according to Ehrlich – have been the cause for the take-over in many cases.

Buchinger *et al.* (1994, p. 14) surveyed several R&D subsidiaries of foreign firms in Austria. Especially in science-based industries the electronics or chemical industry, where transfer sciences are important, Austria lacks certain preconditions for successful co-operation between universities and the business community.

The (vertical and horizontal) relationship of foreign subsidiaries with Austrian firms is seen as problematic since there is only one additional job created per three employees in a foreign subsidiary in Austria. State subsidies to attract foreign firms are thus not as efficient as they could have been. Overall, Glatz and Moser conclude that the quantitative effects have outweighed the qualitative effects of foreign subsidiaries and that future subsidies should be concentrated on the latter.

The findings of Glatz and Moser (1989, p. 154) point to an increasing technological gap for Austrian-owned companies *vis-à-vis* foreign subsidiaries since the 1960s. The logic of the MNC, namely to economize on transaction costs by internalizing certain value-added stages, is clearly at work in foreign subsidiaries in Austria: 50 per cent of subsidiaries stated the use of first-class technology and imported most investment goods. Ninety per cent of output was then re-exported to the mother company, reflecting a high degree of specialization. The fact that this technology is used internally implies that spillovers are not automatically created and thus the economy may profit little from the high R&D ratio of foreign MNCs, which is about 2.5 times higher than the manufacturing sector's average.

According to Mayerhofer and Palme (1997), the situation in Austria is characterized by two general aspects: Austrian industry has received important growth stimuli through technology transfer from abroad. 'Relatively few firms [foreign subsidiaries in Vienna, C.B.] do their own R&D, as most of them receive an important part of their technological knowhow from abroad' (pp. 123f., translated C.B.). Therefore, in a small country, foreign MNCs determine to a large extent the specialization of regions, and internal diffusion of know-how within these MNCs are an important part of overall R&D activity. The limited competition on the small domestic market hampers the propensity to innovations in both DEs and FIEs. For example, empirical estimations for Vienna (Mayerhofer and Palme, 1997, pp. 494–5) reveal that a large share of FIEs reduces the innovation intensity over time and market-related FDI and rent-seeking in protected markets remain responsible for the largest share of inward FDI. Foreign MNCs direct their technological development from abroad. According to Mayerhofer and Palme '40 per cent of all innovations introduced were actually only imitations' (*ibid.*, pp. 495f, translated C.B.).

As a small country, Austria's development critically depends on spillovers from technology developed abroad. To the extent innovations are internalized in MNCs, technology is turned from a public into a private good. A small country then is in danger of lagging behind or being pushed into less technology-intensive sectors. Another factor is human capital, which may compensate for the smaller rate of innovation, if the small country's endowment of high-skilled labour is greater than in the large country. Integration then opens the possibility for the small country to benefit from the knowledge stock of the larger country. According to Marin 'these cross-country knowledge flows have been clearly at work between Austria and Germany' (Marin, 1995, p. 28).

There is only one major study on the impact of the second tier of technology import, namely via finished goods. The empirical study by Marin (1988) provides positive evidence on the textile industry.[13] Import-led innovation – including findings up to 1980 – could, however, not prevent the textile industry from a subsequent sharp restructuring and shrinking process. During the decade 1984–95 employment in the textile industry decreased from 14 730 to 8880 and turnover from ATS 11 billion to ATS 9.9 billion, with an increase in productivity from ATS 0.75 million turnover per employee in 1984 to ATS 1.11 million in 1995 (translated by C.B.).

Conclusions: The weaknesses of inward FDI in Austria are several. First, the limited forward and backward linkages and spillovers. Both vertical and horizontal relationships of foreign subsidiaries with Austrian firms can be seen as problematic since there is only one additional job created per three employees in a foreign subsidiary in Austria. State subsidies to attract foreign firms are thus not as efficient as they could have been. Second, there is a *danger* that regional specialization creates 'lock-in', a too big dependence on selected industries. Third, plans of MNCs for a certain level of output were *not fulfilled* in some cases. Fourth, expansionary effects from take-overs have been limited. Fifth, high value-added activities, while their effect has been highly positive, have been limited. The value added per employee in foreign subsidiaries is generally about 25 per cent above the average of the Austrian manufacturing sector, but the higher efficiency may be an effect of the aggregation of a few, but highly specialized activities of foreign subsidiaries, including some assembly-line plants.

Among the main *benefits* of inward FDI in Austria are:

1. technology-importing via FDI that is then embedded in final goods;
2. the clustering of MNCs, which in turn attracted additional investment;
3. efficient import substitution in some industries (e.g. food, electric industries);
4. a direct employment effect;

5. good industrial relations and no evidence of deterioration in the course of foreign takeovers;
6. inward FDI has technology-related benefits to the economy through demonstration, observation, imitation and application of advanced technologies.

It should be emphasized that the limits to welfare effects of inward FDI do not suggest that Austria would have been better off without inward FDI, particularly regarding the employment effect which would have been lower. Rather, public funds could probably have been used more effectively in some cases.

NOTES

1. The study focuses on the manufacturing sector, since (i) these industries are the main problem areas in restructuring and (ii) they are relatively well covered by empirical studies as compared to the service sector. Overall, the study concludes that the results of inward FDI in Austria have been positive and no legitimate case can be made against FIEs.
2. Similarly, the level of the wage rates is also a determining factor in overall competitiveness.
3. This amounted to about 1 per cent of gross fixed capital formation, about 2 per cent of private savings and about 10 per cent of capital imports.
4. The low share in the paper and wood sector is attributed to the large number of domestic employees. If the wood sector were removed, we would probably see a larger foreign employment share.
5. *Note*: it is not possible to calculate the employment figures for the domestic private sector as the balance between the foreign, the state-owned and the total, since the foreign sector includes only direct participations.
6. Note that in Table 5.9 the sample of firms used for equity and employment is the same for 1992 and 1993, but differs slightly in 1994 and 1995. In order to show this clearly, the number of firms is given twice. Table 5.9, similar to Table 5.8, also refers to the manufacturing sector, yet figures are taken from a different source, which allows us to also consider 1994 and 1995 and particular industries. While the size of DEs is larger than that of FIEs on the level of the manufacturing sector, the opposite applies to the selected industries shown here. Again, the question remains open if these differences are significant.
7. See Steuer and Hartmann (1998) and Bergman and Lehner (1998) for an illustration.
8. Some exceptions, reviewed in Bellak (1996, pp. 28f.), are as follows:

   • The Japanese spinning mill TNS (Tsuzuki) closed its plant after a short period (1991–96), despite receiving exemptions from labour regulations to keep up three shifts a day.
   • Several subsidiaries had to close their R&D laboratories (for example, Hafslund/Nycomed, Norway; Semperit/Conti, Germany), which is often only the first step towards further reductions of activity.
   • Substantial reductions in employment after foreign take-overs (for example, Leobersdorfer Maschinenfabrik, which cut 250 employees; Aeterna, which cut 370 employees) occurred.
   • In some firms (for example, Tandon, US) the mother company led its subsidiary into bankruptcy via transfer pricing or by strict regulations of its supply and

output. In most cases subsidiaries have no room for discretion and 'entrepreneurial' decisions – and the government subsidies are lost.

9. See, for example, Belderbos (1992) for a survey of recent literature and Hatzichronoglou (1997) for a general discussion. While, in principle, one should distinguish between vertical and horizontal FDI and related effects, empirical studies seldom address these issues for Austria.

10. It would be preferable to see more econometric studies on this subject, yet data constraints are severe in this area.

11. *Note*: the comparison of foreign subsidiaries and domestic firms is problematic because the firm structure (range of activities and so on) might be totally different.

12. This meets another result, namely the motive for the sale of the Austrian firm to a foreign firm in most cases was inefficient management (p. 15).

13. The results of this study were subject to widespread criticism which drew primarily on the possibility of a long-term 'free-rider position' on technology created abroad. Apart from the fact that firms have to pay for the technology, so they are not free-riding, it should be mentioned that today the reliance on foreign technology is seen as a viable strategy for catching-up only for countries of a low level of development. The creation of long-term competitive advantages, however, can only be achieved by tapping into the networks of MNCs, which are technological leaders in many industries. If technology is the main factor behind growth, there seems to be no alternative to owning R&D of any type and the creation of national systems of innovation as part of the policy to attract FDI. A similar argument is put forward by Meyer (1997) concerning catching-up via technology import, which is the restriction stemming from the generation of new innovation inside MNCs, trying to prevent leakages and positive externalities.

REFERENCES

AMC and IHS (1997), 'Der Einfluβ von Auslandseigentum in der österreichischen Industrie auf das FTE-Potential' *Executive Summary*, *Study for GBI*, Vienna.

Arbeiterkammer Wien (ed.) (1962), *Das Eigentum an den österreichischen Kapitalgesellschaften*, Vienna: Arbeiterkammer.

Barell, R. and N. Pain (1997), 'Foreign direct investment, technological change, and economic growth within Europe', *The Economic Journal*, 107 (November), pp. 1770–86.

Bayer, K. (1983), 'Produktivitätswachstum österreichischer Industriebranchen im internationalen Vergleich', *WIFO Monatsberichte*, **10**, pp. 630–39.

Bayer, K. and W. Blaas (1986), 'Volkswirtschaftliche und finanzwirtschaftliche Rentabilität von Ansiedlungssubventionen', mimeo, Vienna.

Beer, E. (1989), Passive Direktinvestitionen in Österreich, Vienna: mimeo.

Beer, E., B. Ederer, W. Goldmann, R. Lang, M. Passweg and R. Reitzner (1991), *Wem gehört Österreichs Wirtschaft wirklich?*, Vienna: Orac.

Beirat für Wirtschafts- und Sozialfragen (ed.) (1989), *Internationalisierung*, Vienna.

Belderbos, R.A. (1992), 'Large multinational enterprises based in a small economy: effects on domestic investment', *World Economic Review*, **128** (3), pp. 543–57.

Bellak, C. (1996), *Ausverkauf der Industrie: Entwicklung und Konsequenzen für die Interessenvertretung*, Vienna: Studie im Auftrag der Vereinigung Österreichischer Industrieller.

Bellak, C. and J.A. Cantwell (1998), 'Globalisation tendencies relevant for latecomers: some conceptual issues', in L. Tsipouri, M. Storper and S. Thomadakis (eds), *Industrial Policies for Latecomers*, London and New York: Routledge, pp. 40–74.

Bergman, E.M. and P. Lehner (1998), 'Industrial cluster formation in European regions: U.S. cluster templates and Austrian evidence', paper presented at the 38th Congress of the European Regional Science Association, August, September, Vienna.

Buchinger, E., E. Schiebel and P. Gheybi (1994), *F&E-Ansiedlung in Österreich*, OEFZS- 4706, Seibersdorf.

Ehrlich, R. (1970), 'Amerikanische Direktinvestitionen in Österreich', *WIF0 Monatsberichte*, Beilage 89, December.

Flecker, J., J. Hofbauer, M. Krenn, and U. Pastner (1990), Betriebsübernahmen, Beschäftigung und industrielle Arbeitsbeziehungen, Endbericht, Dezember, *Studie im Auftrag des Bundesministeriums für Wissenschaft und Forschung und der Kammer für Arbeiter und Angestellte*, IHS: Vienna.

Fors, G. (1997), Utilization of R&D results in the home and foreign plants of multinationals, *The Journal of Industrial Economics*, XLV (2), June, pp. 341–58.

Glatz, H. and H. Moser, (1989), *Auswirkungen ausländischer Direktinvestitionen in der österreichischen Industrie*, Vienna, Frankfurt/Main and New York: Campus.

Guger, A. (1996), Internationale Lohnstückkostenposition 1995 deutlich verschlechtert, *WIFO Monatsberichte*, **8**, pp. 511–17.

Gugler, K. (1998), 'Corporate ownership structure in Austria', mimeo, Vienna.

Haschek, H.H. (1982), 'Trade, trade finance, and capital movements', in S.W. Arndt (ed.) *The Political Economy of Austria*, Washington and London: American Enterprise Institute, pp. 176–208.

Hatzichronoglou, T. (1997), 'The impact of foreign investment on domestic manufacturing industry of OECD countries', in P.J. Buckley and J.-L. Mucchielli (eds), *Multinational Firms and International Relocation*, Cheltenham: Edward Elgar, UK, pp. 123–60.

Hutschenreiter, G. and M. Peneder (1997), Österreichs 'Technologielücke' im Außenhandel, *WIFO Monatsberichte*, **2**, pp. 103–14.

Karlhofer, F. (1985) 'Multis in Österreich – Konsens auf Abruf, Wie Konzerne agieren und Belegschaftsvertreter reagieren', *IMK*, **3**, pp. 6ff.

Kausel, A. (1998), 'Ein halbes Jahrhundert des Erfolges: der ökonomische Aufstieg Österreichs im OECD Raum', Vienna.

Koman, R. and D. Marin (1997), 'Human capital and macroeconomic growth: Austria and Germany 1960–92', *CEPR Discussion Papers*, no. 1551, London.

Kursiv (1960), 'Ausländische Direktinvestitionen in Österreich', *WIFO Monatsberichte*, **7**, pp. 310–15.

Marin, D. (1988), 'Import-led innovation: the case of the Austrian textile industry', *Weltwirtschaftliches Archiv*, **124** (3), pp. 550–65.

Marin, D. (1995), 'Learning and dynamic comparative advantage: lessons from Austria's post- war pattern of growth for eastern Europe', *CEPR Working Papers*, no. 1116, London.

Meyer, K.E. (1997), 'Enterprise transformation and foreign investment in eastern Europe', draft, mimeo, Copenhagen Business School, Copenhagen.

Mowery, D.C. and J. Oxley (1997), 'Inward technology transfer and competitiveness: the role of national innovation systems', in D. Archibugi and J. Michie (eds), *Technology, Globalisation and Economic Performance*, Cambridge University Press, pp. 138–171.

Neudorfer, P. (1995), 'Indikatoren zu den Direktinvestitionen', *Berichte und Studien der OeNB*, **4**, Vienna, pp. 69–84.

OECD (1996), Wirtschaftsbericht 1994–95, OECD; Paris.

Peischer, J. (1981), 'Multinationale Konzerne in Österreich: Auswirkungen auf die Zahlungsbilanz und Finanzierungsgewohnheiten', *Quartalshefte*, **16** (1), pp. 69–89.

Rothschild, KW. (1989) 'Ziele, Ereignisse und Reaktionen: Reflexionen über die österreichische Wirtschaftspolitik', in H. Abel, E. Nowotny, S. Schleicher and G. Winkler (eds), *Handbuch der österreichischen Wirtschaftspolitik*, Vienna: Manz, pp. 113–24.

Steuer, M. and C. Hartmann (1998), 'Interfirm co-operation and learning within SME networks – two cases from the Styrian Automotive cluster', paper presented at the 38th Congress of the European Regional Science Association, August, September, Vienna.

Wallace, C. (1997) 'Austria at the Centre of a new Euro-Region', *IHS Newsletter*, **1**, pp. 6f.

Zemplínerová, A. (1997), 'The role of foreign enterprises in the privatisation and restructuring of the Czech economy', *WIIW Research Reports*, no. 238, June, Vienna.

6. Foreign penetration in central European manufacturing

Gábor Hunya

---

1 THE DATABASE ON FOREIGN INVESTMENT ENTERPRISES

The foreign penetration in manufacturing in the CECs can be expressed as the share of foreign affiliates in the economy as a whole by various indicators. Data are available for a somewhat larger group of companies than truly foreign-controlled affiliates. Companies with some foreign share in their nominal or equity capital, FIEs were sorted out from national databases which contain data of the income statements of companies. The remaining companies are classified as DEs.[1] Including minority foreign ownership may not distort the picture significantly, because even in such affiliates the foreign investor usually has control over the management and the trend of foreign investment is to go in for majority or exclusive ownership. In the case of Hungary (for the years 1995 and 1996) and Slovenia the coverage could be limited to companies with at least 10 per cent foreign ownership which corresponds to the internationally accepted definition of FDI. For the other countries, companies with even lower foreign share had to be included.

The database on FIEs is biased towards large companies. While in Hungary, Slovenia and Austria only very small ventures fall out, most of the data for the Czech Republic cover only companies with 100 or more employees, and for Slovakia companies with 25 or more employees.

Most of the problems emerged with the compilation of the database for Austria. There is no systematic match between the FIE data and overall industrial data, not even the industrial classification of the two sets is identical. The computation efforts led to a more or less acceptable result in the case of output and employment, but no further indicators are available for individual industries.

Due to the above limitations in coverage, the number of manufacturing FIEs in the database in 1996 is the following: 284 for the Czech Republic,

4312 for Hungary, 272 for Slovakia and 286 for Slovenia. The relatively small numbers in the Czech Republic and Slovakia are due to the size limit. In Austria 647 FIEs were found for 1995 which is 82 less than it was five years earlier due to mergers in the foreign sector and very few new entries. The coverage in terms of the FDI stocks is much larger, about 70 per cent to 90 per cent of the invested foreign capital appears in this database.

Table 6.1   Number of companies, share of FIEs in the total, per cent

	1993	1994	1995	1996	1996/94	Number of FIEs 1996
Czech Republic	5.2	6.5	9.4	12.5	191.7	284
Hungary	24.0	23.4	21.4	21.6	92.4	4312
Slovakia	8.2	12.3	14.7	15.5	126.4	272
Slovenia	–	4.9	4.1	4.9	98.8	286

FIEs do not have a big share in the number of manufacturing enterprises. The maximum set by Hungary is about one-fifth (Table 6.1). Slovenia stands out with a very low share, below 5 per cent of FIEs. The circumstances in which to establish a new foreign venture or acquire a domestic company are not favourable here so the foreign sector is confined to a small number of companies. There is an increase in the number of FIEs in the Czech Republic and Slovakia which may partly be due to the fact that there is a minimum size above which companies were included in the database (100 and 25 employees) and the growth of employment in FIEs has shifted smaller enterprises into the survey sample. Employment in DEs has generally been on the decrease which, if it reduces employment below the threshold, makes companies fall out from the sample. The two countries, which do not have this minimum size problem, Hungary and Slovenia, show a fairly constant share of FIEs by number. In Hungary the lower FIE numbers in 1995 and 1996 compared to the previous two years are due to the newly introduced 10 per cent foreign threshold. All these limitations suggest that the database has certain weaknesses to show changes in time.

2   BASIC FEATURES OF FOREIGN PENETRATION IN CEC MANUFACTURING

The relative size of the foreign sector compared to the domestic sector is larger by all other indicators than by the number of enterprises. This is because the size of FIEs is generally larger than that of domestic companies in terms of employees per company and even more so in terms of nominal capital or assets per company (Table 6.2).

Table 6.2 Equity capital per company, FIEs per DE, per cent

	1993	1994	1995	1996	1996/94
Czech Republic[a]	–	204.9	192.0	190.4	92.9
Hungary[b]	259.8	506.4	639.4	748.5	147.8
Slovakia	–	–	120.1	131.1	–
Slovenia	–	218.4	294.3	330.3	151.2

Notes:
[a] Own capital
[b] Nominal capital.

The size of the foreign penetration is shown by the share of FIEs in nominal capital, assets, value added, employment, sales, export sales, investment outlays and profits. The indicators, equity capital, sales or output, employment and investment outlays are available for all the four countries (Table 6.3). An increasing role of FIEs has been present for all the countries and by all indicators over the period 1993–96. This is partly due to the change in company coverage described earlier, but an expansion of the foreign sector in comparison with the domestic one is quite apparent.

Table 6.3 Share of FIEs in main indicators of manufacturing companies, 1996, per cent

	Equity capital	Employ-ment	Invest-ments	Sales/output	Export sales
Czech Republic	21.51[a]	13.1	33.5	22.6	–
Czech Republic 1997[b]	–	16.0	31.2	26.3	42.0
Hungary	67.4[c]	36.1	82.5	61.4	77.5
Slovakia	19.4	13.0	24.7	21.6	–
Slovenia	15.6	10.1	20.3	19.6	25.8
Austria[d]	24.8	32.9	–	51.4	–

Notes:
[a] Own capital.
[b] Companies with 25 and more employees.
[c] Nominal capital in cash.
[d] 1995.

Source: 1997 data for the Czech Republic: Zemplínerová (1998).

Table 6.4   Share of FIEs in the manufacturing sector, per cent

	1993	1994	1995	1996	1996/94
Equity capital					
Czech Republic[a]	–	12.5	16.7	21.5	171.0
Hungary[b]	45.1	60.8	63.5	67.4	110.9
Slovakia	–	–	17.2	19.4	–
Slovenia	–	10.2	11.2	14.5	142.2
Value added					
Czech Republic	8.6	9.2	16.1	21.7	236.6
Hungary	–	–	–	–	–
Slovakia	10.1	13.0	18.6	19.1	146.7
Slovenia	–	12.1	12.5	13.4	110.2
Total assets					
Czech Republic	–	10.3	14.8	19.5	188.5
Hungary	–	–	–	–	–
Slovakia	8.9	9.4	13.6	16.0	170.0
Slovenia	–	12.6	12.5	14.8	117.7
Number of employees					
Czech Republic	5.9	7.1	9.6	13.1	183.6
Hungary	31.7	37.2	37.2	36.1[c]	96.9
Slovakia	8.0	9.3	11.8	13.0	139.8
Slovenia	–	7.8	8.5	10.1	129.7
Sales					
Czech Republic	11.5	12.5	16.8	22.6	180.5
Hungary	41.3	55.4	56.1	61.4	110.9
Slovakia[d]	11.1	13.6	19.6	21.6	159.1
Slovenia	–	16.9	17.6	19.6	116.3
Export sales					
Czech Republic	14.9	15.9	–	42.0[e]	–
Hungary	52.2	65.5	68.3	73.9	112.8
Slovakia	–	15.7	–	–	–
Slovenia (exports)	–	21.1	23.2	25.8	122.4
Investment outlays					
Czech Republic	25.3	26.9	27.4	33.5	124.8
Hungary	58.9	79.0	79.9	82.5	104.5
Slovakia	24.4	34.3	29.3	24.7	84.3
Slovenia	–	–	14.0	20.3	–

Notes:
[a]   Own capital.
[b]   Nominal capital.
[c]   Change of methodology.
[d]   Output.
[e]   1997, exports of companies with 25 and more employees.

The highest share of FIEs by all indicators has been reached by Hungary. This is on average three times higher than the penetration rate in the Czech Republic, the two others having somewhat less. The foreign penetration in Austria is between that of Hungary and the Czech Republic. It is of much earlier origin and, therefore, does not change much over time. The most dynamic increase has been recorded in the Czech Republic. There is a steady but relatively slow increase of foreign penetration in Slovenia. In Slovakia there was a more dynamic period until 1995, and less increase of FIE shares in the following year.

Comparison of the development of foreign penetration over time can be made for 1993–96 keeping in mind the distortions caused by shifts from the domestic to the foreign sector (Table 6.4). The upswing of foreign penetration in Hungary's manufacturing took place before 1994, when the FIEs' share in nominal capital reached 60 per cent, and has only slightly increased since then. The same refers to the employment share of FIEs which has stagnated at 37 per cent since 1994, partly due to the changes of computing the number of employees. The investment share of FIEs came close to 80 per cent in 1994 and increased only slightly in the following two years. It seems that the foreign penetration in Hungarian manufacturing has already reached a level where further increase cannot be very dynamic. There is nevertheless still very intensive FDI activity in the form of capital increase in existing FIEs and the number of important greenfield projects growing. Sales and especially export sales were the indicators by which the share of FIEs increased fastest between 1994 and 1996. This indicates that the intensive investment activity of the first half of the 1990s established competitive production capacities which can increase sales both in Hungary and abroad more rapidly than Hungarian-owned companies lagging behind in terms of restructuring.

Foreign penetration in the Czech Republic almost doubled between 1994 and 1996 by most indicators. The foreign sector shows rapid expansion not only in terms of capital and sales but also in terms of employment. Fifty thousand new manufacturing jobs were created in, or shifted to the foreign sector, while the domestic sector lost 85 000. The sales shares of FIEs increased in a period of overall recovery in the Czech manufacturing industry following the transformation recession. Sales of FIEs increased by 130 per cent, while DEs increased by 14 per cent (in current US dollar terms). Although ownership shifts cannot be sorted out, it seems that the foreign sector was an important driving force of the recovery in the mid-1990s. The upswing of car sales due to the success of the car manufacturer Škoda, after being acquired by Volkswagen, has been the most important single case.

Slovakia had in 1993 and 1994 somewhat more intensive foreign penetration than the Czech Republic, but in 1996 the situation changed. Due to the worsening climate for FDI (increasing political risk, new privatization policy) in Slovakia, foreign penetration lost momentum. Slovenia has never had a foreign-investment-friendly policy and the privatization policy of the last few years did not allow foreign take-overs. Most of the larger FIEs of 1996 were established several years earlier. Increasing shares of FIEs are thus due mostly to their better performance and more dynamic growth in comparison to the domestic sector.

Table 6.5   Labour productivity and capital endowment, FIEs per DEs, per cent

	1993	1994	1995	1996	1996/94
Sales per employee					
Czech Republic	209.1	186.3	190.5	193.7	104.0
Hungary	151.4	209.0	216.4	281.8	134.8
Slovakia	145.2	153.5	181.6	184.9	120.5
Slovenia	–	240.9	228.0	217.8	90.4
Assets per employee					
Czech Republic	–	149.8	163.9	160.2	107.0
Hungary	–	–	–	–	–
Slovakia	–	–	125.8	145.7	–
Slovenia	–	170.8	152.2	155.1	90.8

Labour productivity in FIEs is on average as much as two times higher than in DEs. In this respect there is no significant difference between the CECs in 1996 (Table 6.5). The gap between FIEs and DEs does not increase over time in the Czech Republic, decreases in Slovenia and increases in Hungary (further information is contained in Chapter 9). The high and increasing productivity gap in Hungary shows on the one hand the gain foreign ownership means to the economy, on the other hand it demonstrates an unhealthy duality between the booming foreign sector and the stagnating domestic sector. The generally weak perfor- mance of the domestic sector is all the more problematic as it employs almost two-thirds of the manufacturing labour force producing less than 40 per cent of output. The success indicators of FIEs reflect the failures of the domestic sector which has not been able to restructure rapidly enough and was less successful on foreign markets. Thus it was also more severely hit by the 1995 stabilization package.

As endowment with capital and also labour productivity are higher in the FIE sector than in the domestic-owned enterprises the expectation is confirmed that the foreign investors use more recent, capital-intensive and labour-saving technology. It also reflects the concentration of FDI in manufacturing branches with high capital intensity. FIEs pay on average higher wages than domestic companies. They can afford to employ the younger and better trained part of the workforce which contributes to their high productivity.

The lead of FIEs in terms of capital intensity is especially pronounced in Hungary where capital-intensive industries (for example, steel industry, oil refineries) were more accessible to foreign investors than in the others. The relative capital intensity of FIEs, measured by the amount of nominal capital per employee, grows over time in Hungary and Slovenia and declines in the Czech Republic measured by own capital. As to the difference in the amount of assets per employee, there has been an increase in the Czech Republic and Slovakia and decline in Slovenia.

Despite high capital intensity, capital productivity (sales per assets) is higher in FIEs than in DEs in the Czech Republic, Slovakia and Slovenia. There are no data for assets in Hungary, the usually lower figure for nominal capital was applied instead. Relatively low capital productivity in Hungarian FIEs is mostly due to the presence of the oil refining sector among the FIEs and its absence from the domestic sector. This industry with very high capital intensity and low capital productivity distorts the average.

The outstanding export performance relative to output indicates that FIEs are more export-oriented than domestic firms (Table 6.6). This is confirmed by 1996 data in Hungary and Slovenia and by 1994 data also for the Czech Republic and Slovakia. Contrary to most survey results indicating that FDI in CECs was mainly motivated by local market penetration, the activity of FIEs turns out to be somewhat different. In Hungary FIEs account for more than three-quarters of manufacturing exports and the distance of export intensity between the domestic and the foreign sector has been growing.

FIEs contribute more than proportionately to fixed investment outlays. This is a confirmation of the positive effect of FDI on economic growth and restructuring. Investment data also suggest that foreign investors rapidly restructure the acquired manufacturing firms. Rationalization of production is generally connected with lay-off. Foreign penetration thus may increase unemployment in the short run, but establish more new jobs later. Stepped up investment activities of FIEs was confirmed by recent company surveys in CECs, too. Investments of FIEs are mostly financed by retained profits, which thus may not be repatriated on a massive scale. Although the current account shows an increasing profit transfer of FIEs, their profit-reinvestment is also growing. As long as CECs remain favourable locations for FDI in terms of expected profit, there is no reason why most profits should be repatriated. Internationally competitive corporate tax rates such as the 18 per cent practised in Hungary are certainly of advantage to keep profits in the country.

Table 6.6 Export and investment intensity, FIEs per DEs, per cent

	1993	1994	1995	1996	1996/94
Exports per employee					
Czech Republic	280.2	246.4	–	–	–
Hungary	235.1	319.7	364.9	500.9	156.7
Slovakia	–	–	–	–	–
Slovenia	–	317.3	323.1	310.3	97.8
Exports per sales					
Czech Republic	134.0	132.3	–	–	–
Hungary	155.3	152.9	168.6	177.8	116.2
Slovakia	–	–	–	–	–
Slovenia	–	131.7	141.7	142.5	108.2
Investment outlays per assets					
Czech Republic	–	318.9	218.2	208.6	65.4
Hungary	–	–	–	–	–
Slovakia	328.1	501.3	263.8	171.7	34.3
Slovenia	–	–	114.4	146.2	–
Investment outlays per sales					
Czech Republic	260.3	256.4	187.5	172.5	67.3
Hungary	204.0	302.6	311.6	297.4	98.3
Slovakia	256.9	331.8	169.8	118.8	35.8
Slovenia	–	–	76.4	104.1	–

The rate of profit is much higher in FIEs than in DEs, as loss-making is hardly tolerated by foreign owners albeit in the starting period of a project. Of the profit in Czech manufacturing in 1996 92 per cent was earned by FIEs and 90 per cent in Hungary. In Slovakia DEs made losses, while FIEs earned profits.

Based on the evidence derived from case studies, central European countries do benefit from the transfer of advanced technology, management and marketing knowledge. Macroeconomic developments suggest that FDI has contributed to the upgrading of production and export structures. The positive effects of FDI are far from uniform, a number of negative cases can be quoted. Also short-term problems emerge due to fast restructuring in terms of capacity destruction and the lay-off of the workforce. These may generate social and regional inequality in the host country and a surge of foreign trade deficits.

3 COMPARISON WITH FOREIGN PENETRATION IN OECD COUNTRIES

A wider international comparison of FDI penetration can be made based on a 1996 OECD survey concerning the share of FIEs in production and employment (Table 6.7). The comparison cannot be accurate as the data for OECD countries refer to various years in the 1988–92 period, to years before the recent upswing of world-wide FDI, and there are also a number of methodological differences between countries. It is also unfortunate that the foreign penetration in the south European and south-east Asian countries cannot be included in the comparison. Keeping all this in mind, some general conclusions can be drawn.

There is a distinct group of countries, comprised of Hungary, Ireland, Canada and Austria, which have significantly higher penetration rates than the rest of the countries surveyed. In these countries the share of

Table 6.7 *Share of FIEs in manufacturing production and employment in OECD countries in about 1990, CECs in 1996, Austria in 1995, per cent*

	Production	Employment
HUNGARY	**61.4**	**36.1**
Ireland	55.1	44.2
AUSTRIA	**51.4**	**37.1**
Canada	49.0	38.0
Australia	32.0	23.8
France	26.9	22.1
United Kingdom	25.5	17.2
CZECH REPUBLIC	**22.6**	**13.1**
Italy	22.3	17.2
SLOVAKIA	**21.6**	**13.0**
SLOVENIA	**19.6**	**10.1**
Sweden	18.0	16.9
Denmark	14.2	12.4
Germany	13.7	7.3
Finland	6.7	6.2
Turkey	5.9	4.4

Source: OECD (1996); WIIW.

FIEs in manufacturing production is around or above 50 per cent, and in employment about 35 per cent. These are all relatively small economies, especially in comparison to a dominant neighbour. The three OECD countries are examples for catching-up by FDI: they have been net importers of FDI capital and have had rates of economic growth above the OECD average. It is too early to say if Hungary will be able to follow their example.

In a second group of countries with medium intensity of foreign penetration (20 per cent to 25 per cent FIE share in production) we find large, advanced OECD countries, like France, the United Kingdom and Italy. These have large amounts of both inward and outward FDI. Also the remaining three of the CECs are in this group in terms of FDI penetration, but not in terms of capital exports.

The group of countries with low intensity of foreign penetration is very heterogeneous. Germany is in this group, a type of country usually found in the second group. There are also advanced small open economies like Denmark and Finland which may also be in the first group. They are different from group 1 countries concerning the strength of the local companies which were big enough to avoid a foreign take-over. There had also been restrictions for foreign take-over.

Seeing the characteristics of OECD countries on the whole, there is no correlation between FDI penetration and GDP growth. Countries have been successful with both foreign and domestic ownership. Similar differences of patterns are also present in Asia (Korea versus Malaysia) and among the CECs (Slovenia versus Hungary). FDI has a positive growth impact but it is not absolutely necessary for sustained economic growth. Its role can be different depending on historical, geographical and institutional circumstances. Recently there has been a general trend for more openness towards FDI world-wide.

The comparison of FIE penetration rates by production and employment in OECD countries' manufacturing confirms that FIEs have higher than average productivity in each country and this is because of several reasons. Those companies which invest in another advanced country are the top companies of their branch with superior productivity compared to host country firms. Making use of the international division of labour can increase overall productivity and also the productivity of each subsidiary. Another factor can be the general specialization of the foreign sector in industries using advanced, labour-saving technologies. High labour productivity is often matched by lower capital productivity but not in FIEs. In addition, subsidiaries may lack some of the labour-intensive departments connected to management and research which are present in fully-fledged domestic companies.

The lead of FIEs in terms of labour productivity is thus not specific to CECs, but the size of the productivity gap is especially large in their case. In OECD countries the productivity advantage of FIEs compared to the average productivity of the manufacturing industry is 30 per cent, in the CECs 70 per cent to 90 per cent. (The smaller and more specialized the FIE sector, the larger its lead over the average productivity in the country.)

In addition to the general factors contributing to higher productivity of subsidiaries, there are some peculiarities in FIEs operating in CECs. In transition economies FIEs usually represent a special quality in technology, management and marketing, more developed than in domestic, especially State-owned enterprises. The productivity advantage exists both in technical terms and in terms of higher output value due to higher sales prices. Higher prices can be achieved by better marketing, Western brand names and so on. If the FIE sector is very different from the domestic, the two segments of the economy may find it difficult to co-operate and the foreign sector functions as an enclave. In this case direct spillover effects do not exist, only through the income and knowledge of individual employees. At the same time, there is a learning process going on in domestic owned companies which may with time lead to narrower FIE/DE gaps.

4 CHARACTERISTICS OF FIES BY MANUFACTURING INDUSTRIES

The presence of foreign capital in CECs' manufacturing industries is very uneven. FIEs' allocation across industries is very different from DEs (see Figures 6.1–6.4). The concentration of FIEs' capital in the first three most important branches in 1996 made up about half of the capital controlled by foreign investors: 67.3 per cent for the Czech Republic (own capital), 47.7 per cent for Hungary (nominal capital), 44.5 per cent for Slovakia (equity capital) and 54.4 per cent for Slovenia (nominal capital). 1996 shares were lower than for 1994 pointing to a deconcentration of foreign investments. In all four countries it was mainly the dominance of the leading industry which diminished. It did not lose its leading position in the Czech Republic (motor vehicles 26.8 per cent); in Hungary (food, beverage, tobacco 22.5 per cent). It lost its position in Slovakia (chemicals from 18 per cent to 13 per cent), and in Slovenia (transport equipment from 21 per cent to 16 per cent) The new leading industries in Slovakia in 1996 are the food, beverages, tobacco industry and metals, fabricated metals, both with 15.7 per cent of the equity capital. In Slovenia the new leader is the paper industry with 20 per cent of the nominal capital.

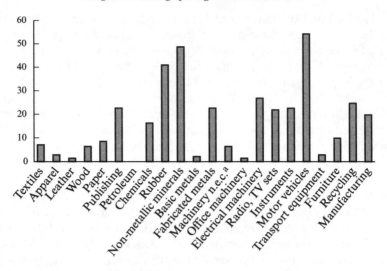

Note: ᵃ n.e.c. = not elsewhere classified.

Figure 6.1   Czech Republic: share of FIEs in assets, 1996 (per cent)

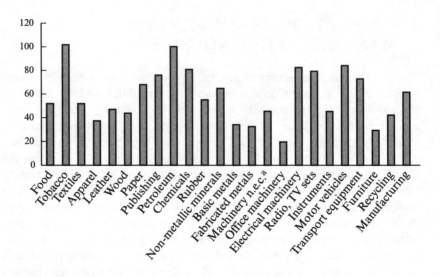

Note: ᵃ n.e.c. = not elsewhere classified.

Figure 6.2   Hungary: share of FIEs in nominal capital 1996 (per cent)

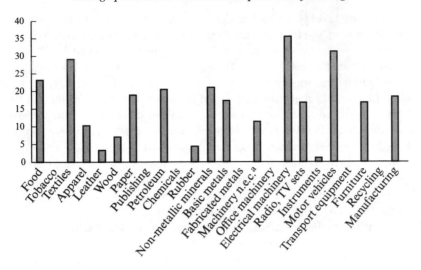

Note: ᵃ not elsewhere classified.

Figure 6.3 Slovakia: share of FIEs in assets, 1996 (per cent)

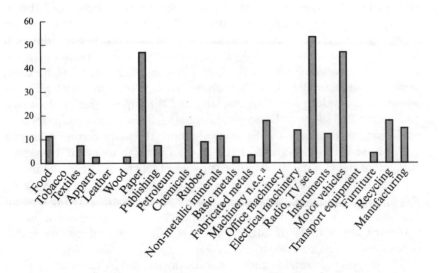

Note: ᵃ not elsewhere classified.

Figure 6.4 Slovenia: share of FIEs in assets, 1996 (per cent)

The most evenly spread is the foreign capital in Slovakia with the lowest share of the first and the first three most important industries. The highest concentration is in the Czech Republic followed by Slovenia. These figures can be linked to the privatization policy. In Slovakia most larger, quasi-monopoly companies were privatized to insiders and foreigners got only medium-size companies not the leading ones in their branches. (In addition, the higher aggregation of the data also smoothes out differences.) In the Czech Republic foreign privatization was concentrated to a few showcases, large companies with leading positions in their branches. Privatization to foreigners was also very selective in Slovenia but took place at an earlier stage of transformation.

Industries where FIE capital concentrates are usually those branches where FIEs have also attained a dominant position. The share of FIEs in the nominal capital of a branch points out the activities with high foreign penetration, even foreign dominance. As to the capital controlled by FIEs, industries with above-average penetration were sorted out with special reference to those where this penetration is over 50 per cent.

In the Czech Republic, the average FIE penetration measured by own capital is 21.5 per cent. In 1996 there were five industries out of twenty above this rate, with two of them, the car and non-metallic minerals' industries exceeding 50 per cent. In Hungary the average itself was above 50 per cent, namely 67.4 per cent. In this country six branches had above-average foreign penetration and only eight out of twenty-two had no foreign dominance. In Slovakia four out of seventeen activities had penetration rates above the 19.4 per cent country average and not even the car industry reached 50 per cent. As to Slovenia where the database comprises eighteen branches, six had above-average foreign penetration of which the car industry had the majority and the paper industry close to a 50 per cent FIE share in the nominal capital of the respective industry.

Turning to the role of FIEs in production, the main common branch with above-average share of FIEs is the manufacturing of transport equipment, most notably of motor vehicles (Table 6.8). This is the industry with the highest FIE shares in sales except for Hungary. In the Czech Republic and Slovakia the share is above 60 per cent, in Hungary and Slovenia over 80 per cent. The new or rapidly modernizing car industry was attracted both by unsatisfied domestic demand and by favourable conditions for low cost production.

The second industrial branch generally dominated by the sales of FIEs is the manufacturing of electrical machinery and equipment. It is above

Table 6.8   Share of manufacturing sales/output in FIEs by industries, 1996, per cent

ISIC Industries Code		Czech Republic	Hungary	Slovak Republic	Slovenia
15	Food products, beverages	24.7	49.5	16.5	10.0
16	Tobacco	in 15	98.7	in 15	*
17	Textiles	9.2	49.6	26.4	8.4
18	Wearing apparel, dressing	5.5	35.2	9.4	1.4
19	Tanning and dressing of leather	3.9	46.1	6.9	*
20	Wood	11.5	42.6	9.4	0.9
21	Paper and paper products	16.9	66.9	25.6	35.4
22	Publishing, printing	29.0	73.7	in 21	5.9
23	Coke and petroleum	0.0	99.2	15.2	*
24	Chemicals	11.3	78.7	in 23	17.4
25	Rubber and plastic	43.8	54.6	5.7	16.0
26	Other non-metallic minerals	45.6	63.5	14.2	13.3
27	Basic metals	3.1	34.7	16.7	5.0
28	Fabricated metals	26.5	33.2	in 27	4.4
29	Machinery and equipment n.e.c.[a]	8.1	45.1	17.2	21.3
30	Office machinery	9.3	19.1	in 29	*
31	Electrical machinery and appliances	32.0	82.7	50.0	14.4
32	Radio, TV sets	35.9	79.0	47.8	40.4
33	Medical, precision, optical instruments	21.6	45.8	1.6	10.9
34	Motor vehicles, trailers	66.9	84.8	61.4	82.3
35	Other transport equipment	1.9	71.8	in 34	*
36	Furniture, manufacturing n.e.c.	26.5	29.6	20.5	5.6
37	Recycling	36.8	42.4	0.0	*
*	Industries with less than 3 FIEs	–	–	–	12.9
D	Manufacturing	22.6	61.4	21.6	19.6

Note: [a] n.e.c. = not elsewhere classified.

average in three of the countries and has a foreign majority in two. There is no other industry outside Hungary in which the share of FIEs in sales would be above 50 per cent, but the production of drinks and tobacco, if they could be separately identified in the industrial classification, would also have high foreign penetration. The tobacco industry is almost totally foreign-owned in the Czech Republic, Hungary and Slovenia. The production of radio and TV sets has above-average shares in all countries but Slovenia and the paper industry in all but the Czech Republic.

Above-average shares of FIEs in output appear both in domestic-oriented branches like beverage and tobacco and in export-oriented industries like the car and the electric machinery industries.

In the Czech Republic the most intensive foreign presence, with two-thirds of the sales supplied by FIEs, can be found in the car industry, followed with over 40 per cent by the production of non-metallic minerals and the rubber and plastics industry. FIEs in electrical machinery, radio and TV sets, printing and publishing, fabricated metals, food products and beverages, tobacco, medical/precision/optical instruments, and furniture and other industries also have shares over the 22.6 per cent average in sales. Fabricated metals and furniture are unique for this country. Foreign penetration intensified between 1994 and 1996. The share of FIEs increased in all activities, in some of them very significantly: radio, TV sets and fabricated metals. None of the shares became higher than in the case of Hungary, but some of them have come close it: rubber and plastics, non-metallic minerals and motor vehicles. The distribution of foreign presence remained uneven; there are still eight industries where the share of FIEs remains below 10 per cent.

In Hungary FIEs have high shares in most manufacturing activities. The highest foreign penetration is in the petroleum branch which is dominated by one single company. The tobacco industry was totally privatized to competing multinationals. In some export-oriented activities of machine-building FIEs control four-fifths or more of output: electrical machinery, motor vehicles and more than 70 per cent of the industries: other transport equipment, radio and TV sets. The latter applies also to chemicals and printing and publishing. Only chemicals is a Hungary-specific branch with above-average foreign share in sales, which is most probably due to the well-developed pharmaceutical industry. With regard to other branches, foreign ownership may be less than average, but still significant in an international comparison such as the 50 per cent in the food and the textile industry. The share of FIEs in the sales of textiles, apparel and leather industry is about 45 per cent in Hungary, which is rather high in international comparison. In other CECs trade and co-operation agreements are usually more common than take-overs to integrate manufacturers of the light industries into multinational networks. The reason may be that in the early 1990s most Hungarian companies were in financial difficulties. The only hope for survival was a foreign take-over. The crisis-hit steel and metal industries were still mainly in domestic, that is public hands, in 1996. The pace of change concerning the industry composition of FIEs in Hungary is relatively small. There was some intensification of foreign penetration in the chemical industry and the production of machinery and transport equipment in recent years.

In Slovakia the general trend of high foreign penetration refers to the car industry, electric machinery and the production of radio and TV sets. Country-specific is the above-average rate for the textile industry with more than a quarter of the output given by FIEs, a rate surpassed only by Hungary. In Slovenia the general trend applies to the car industry, paper and TV production. A specific feature is the high FIE rate for other machinery.

Summing up the above-mentioned characteristics, the size of foreign penetration in the CECs depends on industry-specific features and on the characteristics of the privatization policy. FDI in CECs follows worldwide characteristics in the corporate integration of industries; technology-intensive electrical machinery and car production are the main targets. Foreign capital also penetrated activities with relatively stable domestic markets, for example, in the food, beverage and tobacco industries. Privatization by sales attracted FDI to all industries in Hungary, but only to few in other countries. The foreign presence remained relatively small in branches with great structural difficulties and oversized capacities, such as the steel industry.

FDI helped CECs to shift their product structure to resemble more developed EU countries. This may give further impulses to economic growth and narrow the development gap between the more advanced eastern countries and the EU. Some results are already at hand. The CECs plus Poland and Estonia are those central and east European countries that have been able to expand their exports to the EU in reaction to fast-growing demand there.

The FIE sector of Austria's manufacturing is more concentrated on specific industries than in the CECs. In the two leading branches, electric machinery with 85 per cent and transport equipment with 65 per cent of sales FIEs dominate the economy. There are no other activities among the 14 NACE industries with rates above the average of 51 per cent. There are three industries with about 40 per cent: leather, other machines and chemicals. More detailed surveys point out a high foreign presence in the pharmaceuticals industry, too. The major common characteristic of most foreign dominated industries in Austria is that they are more technology- and R&D-intensive than other activities.

The labour productivity gap between FIEs and DEs discovered at the aggregate level is present in most industries. Among the few outliers are the office machinery in the Czech Republic and Hungary as well as the production of medical and other instruments in Slovakia and Slovenia. Low productivity occurs in industries and countries with lower than average foreign penetration, when foreign presence is marginal, with no major multinational enterprises (MNE) present. If the labour productivity gap of an industry is compared to the average of the country, only a few industries stand out. The car industry is the first in all the four countries. In Slovenia there is no other industry with an above-average productivity lead of FIEs over DEs. In the other three CECs the production of radio and TV sets are also common. Country-specific outliers are: non-metallic minerals and furniture in the Czech Republic, other machinery in Slovakia and printing and publishing in Hungary. The highest productivity gap can be associated with above-average foreign penetration in a branch. This must reflect the presence of a larger MNE which transferred especially superior knowledge and technology.

Capital productivity is on the average higher in FIEs than in DEs with the exception in Hungary. The lead of FIEs is 21 per cent in the Czech Republic but in 5 out of 20 industries, DEs have higher sales per assets than FIEs. The latter number 5 out of 17 in Slovakia and 7 out of 19 in Slovenia. FIEs generally have a leading position in highly foreign-penetrated industries, while they lag behind where foreign presence is small. In Hungary, in all the machinery industries as well as in paper and publishing, FIEs have higher capital productivity. In all other industries, including the most capital-intensive ones, the DEs have higher capital productivity.

In all countries FIEs have especially high investment intensity in industries with high foreign penetration. The importance of FDI in these branches increases via new and restructuring investments. In addition there are some industries emerging as new targets of foreign penetration with still low FIE sales but very high investment outlays. In Hungary the production of office machinery, which recovered from a depression in a 1995 by a foreign take-over, was followed by very intensive investment activities. Further such activities in 1996 were the wood industry and electric machinery. In the Czech Republic the highest gap of investment intensity between FIEs and DEs appears in the production of instruments as well as radio and TV sets. These are relatively recent penetrated industries. In Slovakia, FIEs in the production of vehicles and machines had exceptionally low investment intensity in 1996. It was more intensive in the less sophisticated industries such as food, garment and metals. It would be premature to conclude an adverse tendency in restructuring as investment activities usually have high volatility year to year.

In 1994–96 there were rapidly growing economies with small amounts of FDI (Slovakia and Poland) and slowly growing Hungary with a massive inflow of FDI. In the former group economic growth could be stimulated by domestic demand and financed from domestic earnings. In Hungary, the inflow of foreign capital could only mitigate the 1995–96 recession, but the investment activity of foreign affiliates has contributed to overcoming the crisis. The recent upswing of economic development in Hungary (also in Poland) can be associated with the results of earlier foreign capital inflows. Slower economic growth in the Czech Republic and Slovenia and the coming crisis in Slovakia can be associated with a slow pace of economic restructuring in the absence of less than necessary foreign capital.

NOTE

1. Data for this database were collected at the national statistical offices by Bellak (1998), Austria; Zemplínerová (1997), Czech Republic; Éltetö (1998), Hungary; Brzica (1998), Slovakia; and Rojec (1997), Slovenia. For their publications see the list of references. For the publication with the database, which is the source of all data and tables in this chapter, see Hunya, 1998.

REFERENCES

Bellak, C. (1998), 'Lessons from Austria's post-war pattern of inward FDI for CEECs', The Vienna Institute for International Economic Studies (WIIW), *WIIW Research Reports*, no. 251, November.

Brzica, D. (1998), 'Foreign direct investment in the Slovak Republic: theory, policy, facts and future', final report, Institute of Slovak and International Economic Studies, mimeo.

Éltetö, A. (1998), 'The Economic Performance of firms with foreign investment in Hungary', *Working Papers*, no. 94, Institute for World Economics, Budapest, July.

Hunya, G. (ed.) (1998), 'Database on foreign investment enterprises in central European manufacturing', WIIW, Vienna, September.

OECD (1996), *Globalisation of Industry: Overview and Sector Reports*, Paris: OECD.

Rojec, M. (1997), 'The development potential of foreign direct investment in the Slovenian economy', The Vienna Institute for International Economic Studies (WIIW), *WIIW Research Reports*, no. 235, Vienna.

Zemplínerová, A. (1997), 'Policies and climate for FDI', paper written in the framework of the Phare-ACE project P96-6183-R, mimeo.

Zemplínerová, A. (1998), 'Key determinants of restructuring: evidence from the Czech manufacturing output, trade and foreign direct investment', paper presented at the workshop 'Trade Between the European Union and the Associated States: Prospects for the future', Paris, 26 November.

7. Restructuring and efficiency upgrading with FDI

Matija Rojec

1 THE CONCEPT OF ALLOCATIVE AND TECHNICAL EFFICIENCY

When analysing the impact of FDI on a host economy, the differentiation between allocative efficiency impact and industry (or technical) efficiency impact proves to be convenient, from an analytical as well as a methodological point of view. Allocative efficiency relates to macroeconomic restructuring and industry (technical) efficiency to microeconomic restructuring. As pointed out by Koo (1993, p. 303), FIEs may affect allocative efficiency of an economy through altering the distribution of industrial investment, and technical or industry efficiency[1] by increasing productivity through FIEs' own activities and through their spillover effects on DEs.

The issue of allocative and industry efficiency of FDI is closely related to the notion of a comparative-advantage augmenting type of FDI introduced by Ozawa (1992a) in his paradigm of TNC-assisted (transnational corporation) development, and denotes FDI which 'fosters and fully maximizes existing or potential comparative advantage of (host) developing countries'. According to Ozawa, in the framework of outward-looking, export-based development in a host country, MNEs – which have a global perspective – will structure their FDI in accordance with the pattern of relative factor endowments of each particular country; that is, FDI will be oriented to the activities which intensively use factor(s) which is (are) relatively abundant in a particular host country. This kind of inward FDI will foster structural upgrading in accordance with the existing and potential pattern of relative factor endowment of a host country and will, consequently, help develop its comparative advantages.

A very similar concept – that of structural change FDI – has been introduced by Meyer (1995) in his attempt to explain the role of FDI in a host country's structural change and development. In the manner of the product life-cycle theory, he sees cost pressure in an investor's home country as the major push behind the structural change of FDI. Because of the cost pressure, enterprises in industries which are threatened by a loss of competitiveness are faced with a need to restructure. One possible way of restructuring is to move production facilities abroad. By doing this, enterprises continue to utilize their existing industry-specific assets, but swap the home country labour force with the cheaper one in a host country. In this way, the investing enterprise is combining its own owner-ship-specific advantages with location-specific advantages of a host economy. 'Thus, structural change FDI is – by its motivation – compara-tive advantage augmenting, i.e. its complementarity to the domestic human and capital resources makes its externalities particularly useful' (Meyer, 1995, p. 7).

When a host country follows an outward-looking, export-oriented devel-opment policy, factor-cost advantages seeking FDI will go into those manufacturing industries where a particular host country has superior factor endowments. In this way, FDI will foster upgrading of a host country's com-parative advantages by increasing allocative efficiency (macroeconomic restructuring). According to Ozawa's (1992b) model of Japan's four-phase development, the future development course of the CECs lies in shifting from supply-push to demand-pull orientation. More precisely:

> given the high level of human capital accumulation and technological sophisti-cation, though unevenly distributed both sectorally and geographically, the region has an excellent capacity to absorb advanced technology from the West and initiate commercial R&D, thereby fostering . . . the development of con-sumer-oriented assembly-based industries (Phase III: Differentiated Smithian industries) and the growth of Schumpeterian innovation-based industries (Phase IV) (pp. 23–5).

In Meyer's (1995) concept of structural change FDI, certain activities will be relocated through FDI from more to less developed countries, in accordance with the changing pattern of relative factor endowments in a foreign investor's home country. Typically, this FDI comes from indus-tries that are labour-intensive by the standards of the home country, but technologically intensive by the host economy standards.

Theoretical background for the industry efficiency (microeconomic restructuring) impact of FDI in a host country, that is for the impact of FDI on the increasing efficiency on a company (in the first instance in FIEs but then through spillover effects also in DEs) level, is obvious. It relates to the concept of ownership-specific advantages of foreign investors as a precondition to invest abroad, and to the concept of inter-nalization advantages originating from being a part of a MNE network

(Buckley and Casson, 1985; Dunning, 1993a). This is even more pertinent for factor-cost advantages motivated (export-oriented) FDI where the efficiency of a FIE affects the efficiency of other FIEs in a MNE system, and of a parent company itself. As Dunning (1993b) pointed out:

> because they (foreign firms) are the repository of much of the world's techno-logical capability, managerial capabilities and organizational competencies, MNEs are ideal vehicles for spearheading industrial restructuring through their ability to transfer technology and management skills; through their intro-duction of up-to-date industrial practices and quality control techniques, through their example and spill-over effects on local entrepreneurship, suppli-ers and competitors; and through their network of international linkages – with both large and small firms, they can provide much of the competencies and initiatives for economic growth (p. 30).

According to Willmore, who compared the performance of FIEs and DEs in Brazil, the finding that FIEs differ from DEs should not come as a surprise, since the size and the fact that a FIE is a part of a much larger organization 'give the foreign firm its advantage over local firms in export markets, enable it to attract and retain highly-skilled employees, and may explain its preference for capital and skill intensive techniques of produc-tion' (Willmore, 1993, p. 269).

Both concepts, of comparative-advantage-augmenting and the struc-tural change FDI, basically relate to factor-cost-oriented FDI, in which an important share of FIEs' production goes to exports. (Local) market-seeking FDI does not fit into the two concepts. The explanation of FDI's role in a host country's development in Ozawa's TNC-assisted develop-ment and Meyer's structural change and development with FDI is, thus, confined to pro-trade or trade-creating FDI,[2] based on comparative advantages in factor costs. They can provide a basis for the analysis of FDI role in the restructuring of former socialist countries of CEE – in terms of increasing allocative and industry efficiency – to the extent in which FDI in these countries is motivated by factor-cost differentials; that is, to the extent in which FDI in CECs is export-oriented.

For more than four decades, CECs basically practised an inward-looking, import-substituting development concept with rather limited co-operation and specialization in the framework of the council for mutual economic aid (CMEA), which was backed by an extremely high protection from competition from developed market economies. In principle, the structure of individual country's manufacturing sectors, which developed in these circumstances, reflected only to a limited extent the actual pattern of their relative factor endowments. In other words, the development was only partly based on individual country's actual comparative advantages. Ozawa (1992a) would say that CECs were developing manufacturing industries that were typical for different than their actual patterns of relative factor endowments, that is for a higher stage of development than that enabled by their actual patterns of relative factor endowments. The major consequence of this kind of development was that competitiveness of CECs' exports was to a considerable extent based on exporting at lower than cost prices, which was compensated for by much higher prices on the protected domestic markets.

A collapse of communist regimes also saw the collapse of the inward-looking, import-substituting development concept and of the CMEA. The dissolution of countries like Czechoslovakia, the Soviet Union and Yugoslavia severely reduced the size of protected domestic markets for a number of successor states, while the collapse of CMEA severely reduced export demand. Large protected markets, as the basic backing of an inward-looking, import-substituting development concept, disappeared. CECs became aware of the necessary reorientation to an outward-looking, export-oriented development concept and soon initiated a process of reducing the level of economic protection. The effective rates of protection were reduced and the share of exports (of goods and non-factor services) in GDP increased. A parallel process was a radical restructuring of the regional structure of CECs' exports, as a result of which developed market economies, notably the EU, have become the major export market. The structures of CEE economies, notably their manufacturing sectors, were largely inadequate since they had evolved in circumstances of protected domestic and CMEA markets. As a consequence, a number of CE enterprises got into trouble; they not only lost their highly protected markets but also the grounds for exports at lower than cost covering prices. The other part of enterprises, whose development and export competitiveness had been hindered by the import-substitution policies including administrative restrictions (especially administrative prices favouring some and disfavouring other industries, and administratively set foreign exchange rates), really began to prosper only with the initiation of an export-oriented development policy.

In any case, with the collapse of large protected markets and the application of an outward-looking, export-oriented development concept, CEE economies were faced with an absolute necessity (i) for major macro-economic restructuring of their manufacturing sectors in accordance with the actual pattern of their relative factor endowments (that is, increase of allocative efficiency) and (ii) for increasing efficiency on a company level (that is, increase of industry efficiency).

By definition, greenfield FDI changes the industrial structure of a host country by adding facilities to a particular industry. When FDI is effectuated as a foreign privatization[3] its restructuring and development impact depends on the utilization of proceeds by a host government as a major beneficiary. CEE governments have not always spent such funds very productively; social networks and subsidization of non-privatized loss-making companies absorbed a considerable proportion of proceeds from foreign privatizations. In all these cases FDI has brought about significantly lower macroeconomic restructuring impact than the amount of FDI would suggest.

Early analysis of foreign investors' motivation in CECs offers ample evidence that host country markets have been the most important motivation of foreign investors in CECs (Business International and Creditanstalt, 1993; EBRD, 1994). EBRD analysed a number of country studies on FDI in CECs and, as far as the motivation of foreign investors is concerned, the 'most striking perhaps is the predominance of market access . . . (while) factor-cost advantages are clearly related as less important than market access in all the surveys' (EBRD, 1994, p. 132). On the other hand, more recent analysis suggests that factor-cost advantages are becoming an increasingly important motivation of foreign investors in CECs. According to Szanyi (1997, pp. 4–11), who analysed six relevant recent sample surveys dealing with foreign investors' motivation in CECs, results are not clearly in favour of market-seeking motivation, and do not give a unanimous answer regarding the importance of individual motives. What is unanimous is that 'three major types of investments could be identified: the domestic-market-oriented, the assembly-type export-oriented, and the export-oriented local-supply-based company'. The increase in importance of factor-cost advantages and export-oriented FDI is linked to an accelerated integration of CEE enterprises into MNEs' corporate networks and of CEE economies in the single market of the EU.

In this chapter we hypothesize that manufacturing FDI in the CECs contribute to both (i) allocative-efficiency or macroeconomic restructuring of the manufacturing sector in accordance with individual country's comparative advantages and to (ii) industry efficiency or the increasing productivity on the company level in general. The first part of the hypothesis is based on the presumption that the analysed CECs, namely the Czech Republic, Hungary, Slovakia and Slovenia, are all relatively small and open economies. The former reduces, to a certain extent, the rationale for (local) market-seeking FDI, while the latter eliminates administrative obstacles (protection policy) which would distort the resource allocation according to the existing and future comparative advantages. We suppose that industrial distribution of FIEs in the manufacturing sectors of the four CECs is different and more in accordance with individual country's comparative advantages than the industrial distribution of DEs. This is due to the fact that the industrial structure of DEs was, to a great extent, created in the phase of the import-substituting development concept and that restructuring is still only half-way through, while most FDI projects started after the opening up of the economy and after the intensive export activities began, that is, after the initiation of outward-looking, export-oriented development concept.

The second part of the hypothesis – the positive contribution of FDI to efficiency (productivity) on the enterprise level in general – is based on theoretical and empirical evidence on superior efficiency of MNEs, and on the presumption that FIE's production in the four countries is importantly export-oriented, which, by definition, asks for high efficiency (productivity). This is even more so if FIEs' exports are inputs for other subsidiaries/associated enterprises of a MNE.

In testing the two hypothesis, we will try to establish whether the presumed superior performance of FIEs is more a result of FIEs' industrial structure (in a sense that they are relatively more than DEs engaged in manufacturing industries with better performance indicators), or more a result of higher FIEs' efficiency on a company level. In other words, is the transformation impact of FDI more important in its allocative efficiency (macroeconomic restructuring) component, or in its industry efficiency (microeconomic restructuring) component?

Methodological approaches to analysing allocative and industry efficiency impact on a host economy range from statistical comparison of performance indicators for FIEs and DEs in general and/or by industries, to questionnaire surveys, case and industry studies. In the research of FDI in CECs, questionnaire surveys and case studies which mostly also encompass some industry studies approach have been the most typical approaches. What FDI and transition research in CECs lacks is a statistical analysis. World-wide, more approaches have been used in the framework of statistical analysis. The first is to collect information for pairs of firms (one foreign and one local), carefully matched by industry and size (Willmore, 1993), which enables us to distinguish the size and industry effect on company performance from that of foreign ownership itself. This method has a rather limited applicability for the four sample countries since, due to their relatively small size, one can rarely find adequately matched pairs of FIEs and DEs.

The second approach (Blomström, 1993; Shimada, 1996) is to specify and estimate a regression model in which ownership characteristics are included as one of the explanatory variables. The problem with this approach is that it usually entails some time series which are not available in the countries in question. The available database in the Czech Republic, Hungary, Slovakia and Slovenia currently allows only comparison of a number of performance indicators for FIEs and DEs in general and by industries, similar to that of Koo (1993) for Korea. It also partly enables us to estimate the influence of different industry distribution of FIEs and DEs on their performance indicators, and in such a way to distinguish between allocative (macroeconomic) and industry (microeconomic) efficiency of FDI.

2 RESTRUCTURING OF THE MANUFACTURING SECTOR WITH FDI – ALLOCATIVE EFFICIENCY OF FDI IN CECS

2.1 The Extent of the Efficiency-seeking Versus Market-oriented FDI

Theory suggests that FDI in the manufacturing sector will foster macroeconomic restructuring in accordance with host country comparative advantages (predominantly) by factor-cost advantages, that is, export-oriented FDI. The question is to what extent FDI in the Czech Republic, Hungary, Slovakia and Slovenia is of factor-cost advantages-seeking type and to what extent of (local) market-seeking type? Although gaining access to or enlarging market share locally has been put forward as traditionally the most important motive of foreign investors in CECs, more recent research seems to indicate an increasing importance of factor-cost advantages' related motives and export-oriented FDI. We can guess that this is especially the case in smaller countries such as the Czech Republic, Hungary, Slovakia, Slovenia, which are the subject of our analysis.

To indicate the extent in which FIEs (and DEs for the sake of comparison) are of a (local) market-seeking versus factor-cost-seeking character, we use exports to sales ratios of manufacturing FIEs and DEs in the analysed countries. The ratios show that, with the exception of Slovenia, local markets are the most important destination of FIEs sales, but on the other hand, FIEs exhibit much higher export orientation than DEs. Thus, in the Czech Republic, manufacturing FIEs export 41.3 per cent of their sales, while manufacturing DEs export only 31.2 per cent (1994 data); in the Hungarian manufacturing sector export to sales ratio is 39.7 per cent for FIEs and 22.3 per cent for DEs (1996 data), while in the Slovenian manufacturing sector as much as 65.3 per cent is for FIEs and 46.0 per cent is for DEs. Also, export to sales ratio is increasing faster in the case of FIEs than DEs. In the 1994–96 period, export to sales ratios in the Hungarian manufacturing sector increased by 9.6 percentage points in the case of FIEs and only by 2.6 percentage points in the case of DEs, while in the Slovenian manufacturing sector it increased by 2.4 percentage points in the case of FIEs and decreased by 1.7 percentage points in the case of DEs (Chapter 6).

All in all, although the available research and statistical data indicating the extent of market versus factor-cost seeking FDI in four countries show that the first motivation is more important than the second, there is no doubt that factor-cost seeking FDI is becoming increasingly important, and in Slovenia already outweighs market-seeking FDI. We can guess that with the accession of the CEE applicant countries to the EU this trend will further strengthen, therefore, the testing of our two hypothesis (especially the first one on allocative efficiency) is relevant.

2.2 Industrial Distribution of FIEs and DEs

Although an intensive restructuring process is under way in the CECs, the structure of the manufacturing sector (that is of DEs), as it is today, has been formed mostly in the framework of the pre-transition import-substituting policy. On the other hand, industrial structure of FIEs has been, with few exceptions, created mostly in the transition period when outward-looking, export-oriented development concept has already made its way. This situation leads to the expectation that the structure of FIEs and of DEs in the CECs' manufacturing sector is rather different.

In 1996, in the Czech Republic, motor vehicles and trailers, other non-metallic minerals, food products and tobacco, and rubber and plastic absorbed 63.8 per cent of all manufacturing FIEs' assets and only 22.9 per cent of all manufacturing DEs' assets; in Hungary, chemicals, coke and petroleum, electrical machinery and apparatus, motor vehicles and trailers, and other non-metallic minerals absorbed 47.3 per cent of all manufacturing FIEs' nominal capital and only 14.6 per cent of all manufacturing DEs' nominal capital; in Slovakia, coke and petroleum, chemicals, food products and beverages, tobacco, transport equipment, electrical machinery and apparatus, and textiles absorbed 53.4 per cent of all manufacturing FIEs' assets and only 37.3 per cent of all manufacturing DEs' assets; in Slovenia motor vehicles and trailers, paper and paper products, machinery and equipment, and radio and TV sets absorbed 47.4 per cent of all manufacturing FIEs' assets and only 14.9 per cent of all manufacturing DEs' asset (Chapter 6).

FIEs are the most 'over-represented' in motor vehicles and trailers (in all four countries), food products, beverages and tobacco (in Czech Republic and Slovenia), other non-metallic minerals (in Czech Republic and Hungary), coke and petroleum (in Hungary and Slovakia), chemicals (in Hungary and Slovakia), electrical machinery and apparatus (in Hungary and Slovakia), in the Czech Republic also in rubber and plastic, in Slovakia in textiles, and in Slovenia in paper and paper products, machinery and equipment, and radio and TV sets. Considerable differences in industrial distribution of FIEs and DEs suggest that a relevant restructuring of the four countries' manufacturing sectors is going on through FDI.

If FIEs' distribution in the framework of the manufacturing sector is basically different than that of DEs, the issue is as to what the specifities of manufacturing industries 'over- represented' by FIEs are. To describe individual manufacturing industries, a series of performance/operating indicators was calculated for each manufacturing industry (Table 7.1). Next, a ratio which we call allocation diversity ratio (AD) was calculated for all the indicators included, according to the following formula:

$$AD = \sum_{i=1}^{23} \left(\frac{p_i}{P} \cdot \frac{a_i}{A} \right); \text{ in \%}; i = 1 \dots 23$$

where: i = individual manufacturing industry; total number of manufacturing industries according to the NACE classification of activities is 23 (15–37):

p_i = performance indicator p in industry i;
P = average performance indicator p for the manufacturing sector;
a_i = assets in industry i;
A = total manufacturing sector assets.

AD ratio above 100 per cent means that FIEs (and DEs, for the sake of comparison) tend to be located in industries (manufacturing sector) with above-average value of a particular indicator, and in industries with below-average value of a particular indicator if AD ratio is less than 100 per cent.

The picture drawn by AD ratios in Table 7.1 basically confirms the hypothesis that FIEs' allocation efficiency, that is, the efficiency due to their different industrial distribution across the manufacturing sector, is superior to DEs' allocation efficiency. FIEs in all four analysed countries tend to be located in the manufacturing industries with (much) above-average profitability, while DEs in those with below-average profitability. Compared to DEs, FIEs also tend to be located in more capital-intensive (all four countries) and export-oriented industries (Slovenia and Hungary but not the Czech Republic) than DEs.

To conclude, by allocation of investment different from the existing distribution of assets in the manufacturing sectors of the analysed coun-

Table 7.1 *Allocation diversity (AD ratios) of FIEs and DEs in the Czech, Hungarian, Slovak and Slovenian manufacturing industries in view of selected indicators; 1995–96 average in per cent*

Indicator	FIEs	DEs
Czech Republic		
Profit per nominal capital	124	75
Value added per employee	118	111
Nominal capital per company	180	212
Assets per employee	124	117
Exports as a share of sales (1994 data)	104	108
Hungary		
Profit per nominal capital	108	86
Value added per employee	n.a.	n.a.
Nominal capital per company	5527[a]	182[a]
Nominal capital per employee	157	113
Exports as a share of sales	102	98
Slovakia		
Profit per equity	2482[b]	–484[b]
Value added per employee	131	122
Equity per company	222	190
Assets per employee	134	126
Exports as a share of sales	n.a.[c]	n.a.[c]
Slovenia		
Operating profit per equity	107	98
Value added per employee	112	112
Equity per company	212	209
Assets per employee	123	118
Exports as a share of sales	109	99

Notes:
[a] If one excludes coke and petroleum, AD for FIEs is 204 and for DEs 168.
[b] This ratio should be interpreted with caution because P is close to zero that makes p/P for individual industries extremely high/low.
[c] n.a.: not applicable.

Source: WIIW Database.

tries, FDI fosters macroeconomic restructuring of these manufacturing sectors. By tending to be located in manufacturing industries with above-average profitability, assets per employee (as a proxy for technical sophistication) and also export orientation, FDI seems to foster the restructuring in an allocative efficient way.

2.3 Comparative Advantages of CECs Manufacturing Sectors and Industrial Distribution of FIEs and DEs

FIEs' and DEs' industrial distribution is, thus, considerably different and FIEs' distribution seem to tend to more 'efficient' manufacturing industries. The issue now is whether different industrial distribution of FIEs is such as to foster the restructuring of CECs' manufacturing sectors in accordance with their comparative advantages. Does FDI, therefore, foster shifts from those manufacturing industries where CECs have no or little comparative advantages towards industries where CECs have some or considerable comparative advantages? To test comparative advantages in host countries' manufacturing sectors, revealed comparative advantage (RCA) method could be used with the following formula of RCA ratio in industry i:

$$RCA_i = \left(\frac{x_i}{X} \frac{m_i}{M}\right); i = 1 \ldots 23$$

where: i = individual manufacturing industry; total number of manufacturing industries according to the NACE classification of activities is 23 (15–37):

x_i = exports of industry i to EU countries;
m_i = imports of industry i from EU countries;
X = total manufacturing sector exports to EU countries;
M = total manufacturing sector imports from EU countries.

According to the above formula, if RCA ratio for a particular industry is above 1, this industry possesses comparative advantage *vis-à-vis* the same industry in EU countries, and vice versa if RCA ratio for a particular industry is below 1.

To get a synthetic indicator of FIEs' (and, for comparison, of DEs') industrial distribution in accordance with comparative advantages of a particular host country manufacturing sector, synthetic RCA ratio (SRCA) could be calculated according to the following formula:

$$SRCA = \sum_{i=1}^{23} \left(RCA_i \cdot \frac{a_i}{A}\right); \text{in } \%; i = 1 \ldots 23$$

where: i = individual manufacturing industry; total number of manufacturing industries according to the NACE classification of activities is 23 (15–37):

a_i = assets in industry i;
A = total manufacturing sector assets.

SRCA ratio higher than 100 per cent means that industrial distribution of assets of a particular category of enterprises (FIEs or DEs) tends to be oriented/concentrated in manufacturing industries with revealed comparative advantages *vis-à-vis* the EU, and vice versa for the ratio lower than 100 per cent.

The results presented in Table 7.2 confirm the hypothesis that FDI fosters shifts from those manufacturing industries where the analysed countries' manufacturing sectors have no or little comparative advantages *vis-à-vis* the EU, towards industries where they have some or substantial comparative advantages. In other countries, with the exception of Slovenia, distribution of FIEs' manufacturing assets is very much in line with the pattern of comparative advantages *vis-à-vis* the EU.[4] However, the data does not support the hypothesis that FIEs' industrial distribution is superior to that of DEs; DEs in Hungary, Slovakia and Slovenia exhibit superior industrial distribution to that of FIEs as far as revealed comparative advantages *vis-à-vis* the EU is concerned. This suggests that (i) because of its allocative efficiency, FDI is a powerful vehicle of manufacturing restructuring in host CEE economies, but also that (ii) manufacturing DEs have already undergone a process of restructuring which increased allocative efficiency of manufacturing DEs' assets, by putting forward industries with comparative advantages *vis-à-vis* the EU.

Table 7.2   SRCA ratios for manufacturing FIEs and DEs in Czech Republic, Hungary, Slovakia and Slovenia in 1996; in per cent

	FIEs	DEs
Czech Republic	122	121
Hungary	193	217
Slovakia	206	222
Slovenia	42	104

Source: WIIW Database.

In the Czech Republic, high SRCA ratio for FIEs is to a major extent a consequence of foreign involvement in manufacturing of other non-metallic minerals, and motor vehicles and trailers; in Hungary, it is predominantly the foreign involvement in food products' and beverages' manufacturing, while in Slovakia in heavy industries, such as manufacturing of basic metals and fabricated metal products, other non-metallic minerals, coke and petroleum and chemicals, and paper. Inferior industrial distribution of FIEs in the Slovenian manufacturing sector in RCA terms seems to have a lot to do with the fact that FIEs are heavily 'under-represented' in relatively more labour-intensive industries and 'over-represented' in relatively more capital-intensive ones. Slovenia has the highest RCA ratios in the above-average labour-intensive industries, such as wearing apparel and dressing fur and wood products. Manufacturing DEs engage a considerable share of their assets in these industries (higher than in the other three analysed countries) while FIEs are almost non-existent in them. Foreign investors' perception of Slovenian manufacturing sector comparative advantages seems to be different – in relatively more capital-intensive industries – than the actual structure of Slovenian foreign trade flows suggests. Taking into account the increasing problems of labour-intensive industries in Slovenia and increasing wage rates, their view might be more accurate.[5]

3 EFFICIENCY (PRODUCTIVITY) OF ENTERPRISES AND FDI – INDUSTRY EFFICIENCY OF FDI IN CECS

The performance comparison of FIEs and DEs (Chapter 6) does not leave much doubt that FIEs perform much better (measured by FIEs/DEs indexes for the major performance indicators). As far as return on equity (net profit per nominal capital or equity) is concerned, manufacturing FIEs in all four countries achieve results which are more than considerably better than those of DEs. In Slovenia, in each individual year of 1994–96 period, FIEs realized a net operating profit (operating profit minus operating loss), while DEs a net operating loss, the operating profit per equity being constantly more than 50 per cent higher in FIEs than in DEs. In Slovakia, in 1995 and 1996, and in the Czech Republic and Hungary in 1996, the difference in net profit per nominal capital in favour of FIEs was even higher than in Slovenia. Interestingly, profitability in Hungarian FIEs has become better than that of DEs only in 1996, while in the Czech case in 1995. The major trend is that differences between FIEs and DEs are increasing as far as return on equity is concerned.

The indicator of profitability (profit per equity or nominal capital) has been further disaggregated into three indicators: profit margin (profit to sales ratio), total assets turnover (sales to assets ratio) and assets to equity ratio. We can see that higher profitability of FIEs is due to their higher profit margin, which means that they are more successful in costs control, and due to higher total assets turnover which means that they use their assets more efficiently. On the other hand, FIEs on average have lower assets per equity/nominal capital ratio which means that they operate with lower assets to equity, or with lower external sources of financing.

The data do not allow an exact conclusion as to what extent FIEs' superior performance is due to their higher allocative efficiency and to what extent is due to their higher industry efficiency. AD ratios for profit per equity/nominal capital and value added per employee seem to indicate that quite a considerable portion of FIEs' superior performance is due to their higher allocative efficiency. However, detailed analysis shows that the industry efficiency component is probably even more important; FIEs do not have higher profitability only in manufacturing total, but also in the vast majority of individual manufacturing industries in which they are involved: in the Czech Republic, FIEs have higher profitability than DEs in 15 out of 21 manufacturing industries in which they are engaged; in Hungary, in 19 out of 23; in Slovakia, in 13 out of 16; and in Slovenia, in 12 out of 18.

Theoretically, the reasons for FIEs' superior efficiency in its industry component should be traced in MNEs' ownership-specific and internalization advantages, which are transferred in the form of technology and management skills, up-to-date industrial practices and quality control techniques, network of international linkages and so on to a FIE in a host country. A thorough approach to the analysis of reasons for FIEs' superior performance in CECs' manufacturing sectors would require a detailed regression analysis which would tell to what extent 'does the relative performance of firms within an industry vary systematically with the presence of foreign subsidiaries' (Blomström, 1993, p. 273). This, however, is beyond the reach of the present database. In part, the second best solution is to analyse distinctive features of FIEs as compared to DEs as they are reflected in the income statements and balance sheet data. This gives a flavour of some of the probable areas that might explain the superior performance of FIEs.

The results presented are very much in line with the existing research on the subject in other countries (Blomström: 1993; Koo, 1993; Willmore, 1993; Shimada, 1996). There are four major areas in which FIEs show distinctively different operating indicators that might explain their superior performance (Chapter 6). These areas are company size, level of capital intensity, investment activity and level of export orientation. Compared to DEs, FIEs are much larger in size, more capital-intensive, much more active investment-wise and more export-oriented.[6] Of these four areas, one – distinctive differences in export orientation – can be by definition attributed to 'foreign ownership', that is, to the fact that FIEs are a part of larger MNEs' systems. The other three distinctive features – larger company size, higher level of capital intensity and more intensive investment activity – are not necessarily correlated to 'foreign ownership', but statistically are characteristic for the world of MNEs.

One of the most distinctive feature of FIEs in the manufacturing sectors of the CECs, as compared to DEs, is their superior size measured by any indicator (nominal capital/equity, assets, employment, net sales, exports). According to Willmore (1993, pp. 256–7), size determines a number of company characteristics (for example, production techniques, type of products, skill intensity, salary level and so on) and only by size can an important part of differences among companies be explained. We do not know to what extent the superior size of FIEs is responsible for their superior performance; the larger this extent is the less FIEs' superior performance can be attributed to the factor of 'foreign ownership' itself Nevertheless, it is certain that in the manufacturing sectors of the CECs, company size and 'foreign ownership' are related.

The second distinctive feature of FIEs is their superior capital intensity. FIEs in the analysed CECs not only tend to invest in more capital-intensive manufacturing industries, but in addition they use considerably more capital-intensive techniques than DEs.[7] In this regard, it should be borne in mind that all the efficiency indicators which include number of employees are influenced by a superior capital intensity of FIEs. That is partly a reason why FIEs/DEs indexes are (much) higher for indicators which have number of employees in the denominator than for indicators which have assets or equity in the denominator. On the other hand, value added – whose major component is labour costs – as a share of gross revenue/output/sales is in FIEs lower than in DEs.

The fact that value added as a share of gross revenue/output/sales in FIEs is much lower that in DEs deserves some additional attention. This might not only be the consequence of FIEs' superior capital intensity and consequent relatively lower importance of labour costs as the major component of value added. Compared to DEs, one of FIEs' basic characteristics is their more or less intensive vertical integration into their foreign parent companies' networks. The more a FIE is vertically integrated into its foreign parent company the less stages of manufacture is performed by a FIE itself, the higher share of its output is accounted by inputs imported from other parts of the foreign parent company and the lower is value added.[8] The available data does not permit us to verify this assumption. Only for illustration, the data for Slovenia partly support this view. In the Slovenian manufacturing sector, the level of inputs bought from outside the company (commercial goods, materials and services) as a share of gross revenue is by 15 per cent higher in FIEs than in DEs (1996 data). Lower value added as a share of gross revenue/ output/sales in FIEs, thus, might not be influenced only by FIEs' superior capital intensity, but also by the fact that a higher share of their output is accounted for by intermediate goods.

From the point of view of restructuring and further development, investment activity represents a crucial aspect of FIEs' operations. FIEs in general exhibit an investment activity which is to a major extent more intensive than that of DEs. Measured by investment outlays to assets ratio, FIEs' investment activity in the Czech manufacturing sector is 2.09 times higher than that of DEs; in Hungary 2.3 times higher; in Slovakia 1.52 times higher; and in Slovenia 1.46 times higher. No doubt, the pace of modernization and restructuring in FIEs is much higher than in DEs.[9] FIEs' investment activity is much more intensive in terms of the investment outlays to sales ratio, too. This is a proxy of how much of their income companies devote to investment purposes. In the case of the Czech Republic, this ratio is 1.73 times higher in FIEs than in DEs; in Hungary it is 2.97 times higher; in Slovakia 1.20 times higher; and in Slovenia 1.04 times (1996 data). In short, investment activity and future development seem to be much more in focus in FIEs than in DEs.

Finally, FIEs also exhibit superior export orientation. Superior export orientation of FIEs could really be attributed to the 'foreign ownership' factor itself, that is to the fact that a FIE is an integral part of its parent MNE network. In the words of Willmore (1993, p. 263), FIEs superior export intensity 'is to be expected on a priori grounds, for the costs of exporting are much lower for foreign firms which have access to market information and sales organizations through their parent companies overseas'.

4 CONCLUSIONS

Theory suggests that in an outward-looking, export-oriented host economy, inward FDIs are to a greater extent of Ozawa's comparative-advantage-augmenting type, which fosters existing or potential comparative advantages of a host economy. FDI upgrades host economy's comparative advantages through its allocative efficiency impact, by altering the distribution of industrial investment (macroeconomic restructuring), and through its industry (technical) efficiency impact, by increasing productivity through FIEs' (microeconomic restructuring) own activities and through their spillover effects on DEs. This chapter, based on the analysis of 1994–96 income statements and balance sheets of manufacturing FIEs and DEs in four transition economies – the Czech

Republic, Hungary, Slovakia and Slovenia – puts forward four major conclusions on allocative and industry efficiency impact of FDI in the analysed countries' manufacturing sectors.

1. *FIEs demonstrate much better performance indicators than DEs.* FIEs on average perform much better as far as return on equity, profit margin, total assets turnover and value added per employee, is concerned. It is difficult to say to what extent FIEs' superior performance is due to their higher allocative efficiency and to what extent is due to their industry efficiency. AD ratios for operating profit per equity and value added per employee indicate that quite a considerable portion of FIEs' superior performance is due to their higher allocative efficiency. However, the industry efficiency component is probably even more important as FIEs have higher profitability (net profit per equity/nominal capital) not only in manufacturing total, but also in the vast majority of individual manufacturing industries in which they are involved.

2. *FIEs' industrial distribution in the framework of manufacturing sector, is radically different than that of DEs indicating that a macroeconomic restructuring is going on through FDI.* By allocation of investment, which is different from the existing distribution of assets in host countries' manufacturing sectors, FDI fosters macroeconomic restructuring of the analysed host countries' manufacturing sectors. By tending to be located in manufacturing industries with above-average profitability, the value added per employee, export orientation, assets per employee (as a proxy for technical sophistication), FDI seems to foster the restructuring in an allocative efficient way.

3. *FDI fosters restructuring of the manufacturing sector in accordance with the analysed host countries' comparative advantages as indicated by RCA analysis.* FDI fosters shifts from those manufacturing industries where the analysed countries' manufacturing sectors have no or little comparative advantages *vis-à-vis* the EU towards industries where they have some or big comparative advantages. In other countries, with the exception of Slovenia, distribution of FIEs' manufacturing assets is very much in line with the pattern of comparative advantages *vis-à-vis* the EU. However, DEs in Hungary, Slovakia and Slovenia exhibit even superior industrial distribution than FIEs as far as comparative advantages *vis-à-vis* the EU is concerned. This suggests that (i) because of its allocative efficiency, FDI is a powerful vehicle of manufacturing restructuring in host CEE economies, but also that (ii) manufacturing DEs have already undergone a process of

restructuring which increased allocative efficiency of manufacturing DEs' assets by putting forward industries with comparative advantages *vis-à-vis* the EU.

4. *Analysis suggests four major areas in which FIEs show distinctively different operating indicators, which might explain their superior performance. Compared to DEs, FIEs are much larger in size, more capital-intensive, have much more intensive investment activity and are more export-oriented.* Of these four areas, one – distinctive differences in export orientation – can by definition be attributed to 'foreign ownership', that is, to the fact that FIEs are a part of larger MNEs' systems. This fact ensures them better access to foreign markets, including exports to other parts of a parent company. The other three distinctive features – larger company size, higher level of capital intensity and more intensive investment activity – are not necessarily correlated to 'foreign ownership', but statistically are characteristic for the world of MNEs.

NOTES

1. Koo uses the term 'sectoral efficiency'.
2. Notion introduced by Kojima in 1995 and further developed in his and Ozawa's macroeconomic theory of FDI (Ozawa, 1992a, p. 41).
3. Foreign privatization is (direct or indirect) foreign acquisition of a non-privatized host country enterprise (Rojec *et al.*, 1995).
4. In the RCA analysis for Slovenia based on 1995–96 data for total foreign trade of the manufacturing sector, the SRCA ratio for FIEs is 101 per cent and for DEs 118 per cent (Rojec, 1998).
5. More information can be obtained in Rojec, 1998.
6. Slovenian data gives an insight into two other operating aspects in which FIEs differ considerably from DEs. The first is reflected in much higher machinery and equipment to fixed assets ratio in FIEs than in DEs. In Slovenia, FIEs in manufacturing engage 51 per cent more of their fixed assets in the form of machinery and equipment than DEs (1996 data), meaning that FIEs engage a much smaller part of their assets in 'non-productive' land and buildings, which increases productivity of assets. The second aspect are better solvency indicators of FIEs than DEs. FIEs have a superior liquidity ratio (ratio between current receivables and cash and current liabilities) and also a better receivables turnover ratio (ratio between net sales and long-term and current operating receivables). The latter may be due to the fact that FIEs are an integral part of foreign parent MNEs' networks, which brings better and more reliable customers (Rojec, 1998).
7. In the Czech Republic, FIEs have higher assets per employee than DEs in 14 out of 21 manufacturing industries; in Hungary in 21 out of 23; in Slovakia in 12 out of 16; and in Slovenia in 15 out of 18 (1996 data).
8. This is a different outcome and explanation than in the case of Willmore's comparison of performance of FIEs and DEs in Brazil. He found that value added per output ratio is higher in the case of foreign firms and attributed this partially to the fact that FIEs are more vertically integrated, meaning that 'they process more stages of manufacture within the firm, relying less on outside producers or imports for a supply of intermediate inputs' (Willmore, 1993, p. 262).

9   Higher investment outlays to assets ratio in FIEs than in DEs may also be partly a result of worse assets structure in DEs. The Slovenian case, for example, shows that the share of machinery and equipment in fixed assets is much higher in FIEs than in DEs. This gives DEs a more unfavourable position for a comparison.

BIBLIOGRAPHY

Artisien, P., M. Rojec and M. Svetličić (eds) (1993), *Foreign Investment in Central and Eastern Europe*, Basingstoke and London: Macmillan Press.

Blomström, M. (1993), 'Foreign investment and productive efficiency: the case of Mexico, in S. Lall (ed.), *Transnational Corporations and Economic Development* (The United Nations Library on Transnational Corporations), London and New York: Routledge, pp. 273–87.

Buckley, P.J. and M. Casson (1985), *The Economic Theory of the Multinational Enterprise*, New York: St. Martin's Press.

Business International and Creditanstalt (1993), 1992 East European Investment Survey, Vienna: Business International.

Charap, J. and A. Zemplínerová (1994), 'Foreign direct investment in the privatization and restructuring of the Czech economy', *Development and International Cooperation*, **10** (18), 27–44.

Dunning, J.H. (1993a), *Multinational Enterprises and the Global Economy*, Wokingham, UK: Addison Wesley Publishing Company.

Dunning, J.H. (1993b), 'The prospects of foreign direct investment in eastern Europe', in P. Artisien, M. Rojec and M. Svetličić (eds), *Foreign Investment in Central and Eastern Europe*, Basingstoke and London: Macmillan Press, pp. 16–33.

EBRD (1994), *Transition Report 1994*, London: EBRD.

EBED (1995), *Transition Report 1995*, London: EBRD.

Hunya, G. (1996), 'Foreign direct investment in Hungary: a key element of economic modernisation', *Research Reports*, no. 226, The Vienna Institute for International Economic Studies (WIIW), February.

Jermakowicz, W.W. *et al.* (1994), 'Foreign privatisation in Poland: Studies and Analyses', no. 30, *Centre for Social and Economic Research*, Warsaw, October.

Koo, B.-Y. (1993), 'Foreign investment and economic performance in Korea', in S. Lall (ed.), *Transnational Corporations and Economic Development* (The United Nations Library on Transnational Corporations), London and New York: Routledge, pp. 288–313.

Korze, U. and M. Simoneti (1992), 'Privatisation of the tobacco company Ljubljana', *Central Europe Working Paper Series*, no. 1. Chapel Hill: International Private Enterprise Development Research Center, Kenan Institute of Private Enterprise, University of North Carolina.

McMillan, C.H. (1993), 'The role of foreign direct investment in the transition from planned to market economies', *Transnational Corporations*, **2** (3), 97–119.

Meyer, K.E. (1995), 'Direct foreign investment, structural change and development: can the east Asian experience be replicated in east central Europe', *Discussion Paper Series*, no. 16, London Business School, CIS-Middle Europe Centre, January.

Ozawa, T. (1992a), 'Foreign direct investment and economic development', *Transnational Corporations*, **1** (l), 27–54.

Ozawa, T. (1992b), 'Japanese MNCs as potential partners in eastern Europe's economic reconstruction', *Working Paper*, 2–92, Institute of International Economics and Management, Copenhagen.

Rojec, M. *et al.* (1995), 'Foreign direct investment and privatisation in central and eastern Europe: a comparative analysis of concepts, experiences and policy issues in the Czech Republic, Hungary, Poland and Slovenia', *ACE Research Project*, Centre for International Cooperation and Development, Ljubljana, mimeo.

Rojec, M. (1998), 'Impact of foreign direct investment on efficiency and restructuring of Slovenia's enterprise (manufacturing) sector', mimeo, Faculty of Social Sciences, Ljubljana.

Shimada, H. (1996), 'Impact of DFI on the supply side of the Singapore economy: focusing on total factor productivity', *ASEAN Economic Bulletin*, **12** (3), 369–79.

Stankovsky, J. (1996), 'The role of foreign direct investment in eastern Europe', *Austrian Economic Quarterly*, **1** (2), 109–20.

Svetličić, M. and M. Rojec (1994), 'Foreign direct investment and the transformation of central European economies', *Management International Review*, **34** (4), 293–312.

Szabó, K. (1992), 'Direct sale and joint ventures as a technique of privatisation', summary paper of the workshop organized by Central and Eastern European Privatisation Network (Ljubljana) on 'Direct Sales and Joint Ventures as a Technique of Privatisation', Budapest, 19–20 March, mimeo.

Szanyi, M. (1997), 'The role of foreign direct investments in restructuring and modernization of transition economies', mimeo, Institute for World Economics of the Hungarian Academy of Sciences, Budapest.

UNCTAD (1995a), *Foreign Direct Investment in Central and Eastern Europe*, TD/B/ITNC/Misc.2, UNCTAD secretariat, Geneva, 19 April.

UNCTAD (1995b), *World Investment Report 1995*, New York and Geneva: United Nations.

Willmore, L.N. (1993), 'The comparative performance of foreign and domestic firms in Brazil', in S. Lall (ed.), *Transnational Corporations and Economic Development* (The United Nations Library on Transnational Corporations), London and New York: Routledge, pp. 251–72.

UNECE (1995), 'Statistical survey of recent trends in foreign investment in east European countries', TRADE/R-636, Geneva, 23 November.

8. Production specialization in central European manufacturing

Waltraut Urban

1 INTRODUCTION

This chapter deals with changes in the production structure in the manufacturing industry that took place in the CECs after 1989. Section 2 gives a general outline of the problem of industrial restructuring in the CECs. In Section 3 the industrial profile of the different CECs is compared to each other. Section 4 examines the speed of structural change in individual CECs between 1989 and 1996. Section 5 focuses on the patterns of change and identifies the industries which became 'winners' and 'losers' of transition. Finally, in Sections 6 and 7, the impact of the foreign sector, that is foreign trade and direct investment, on the process of structural change is analysed. Our analysis is at the level of the 2-digit NACE – revision 1 classification (14 industries) for which comparable data were available for all countries.[1]

2 GENERAL OUTLINE OF THE PROBLEM OF INDUSTRIAL RESTRUCTURING IN THE CECS

Under socialist rule, manufacturing was the most favoured sector of the economy in the CECs. The shares of manufacturing in GDP were much higher than in comparable Western economies, and its structure differed considerably from that in comparable market economies as production patterns were decided by planning authorities instead of the market. Also, foreign trade with market economies was relatively small and trade with other socialist countries was determined by the peculiar rules of intra-CMEA division of labour. Furthermore, the lack of internationalization led to a decoupling from technical progress and associated structural changes in the West. Compared to the more advanced Western economies, the relatively lower level of GDP per capita in the CECs, implying different structures in industry, is important as well.[2] Accordingly, the transition to a market economy called for special adjustments in this sector beyond what was required elsewhere. However, the conditions for restructuring changed in the course of the transformation process.

The collapse of the socialist regimes in central and eastern Europe and the beginning of the transition from socialist to market economies in 1989/90 led to a temporary downturn of economic activity in general and industrial production in particular. GDP decreased considerably, but to a lesser extent than industrial production, which over the period of 1990–92 suffered from double-digit negative annual growth rates in all CECs investigated (Table 8.1). A process of *de-industrialization* was taking place, implying a passive (defensive) rather than active (strategic) process of restructuring in manufacturing.[3] Rates of decline in industrial production ranged between –12.3 per cent and –16.4 per cent over the 1990–92 period. After 1992, however, growth gained momentum in all CECs and in several cases industrial production increased even faster than GDP. We can, therefore, expect the process of structural change after 1992 to differ significantly from the previous period, which has been proved by all our results.

The industrial profile of the CECs deviated substantially from comparable economies in the West in 1989. Moreover, interesting differences were found if two distinct groups of west European countries were used as yardsticks. The first group consists of fairly advanced EU countries, termed 'EU-North' and the other of industrially less advanced EU countries, termed 'EU-South'.[4] Apart from a general excess of heavy industry, in particular the metal industry, and a structural deficit[5] in the paper and printing industry in the CECs compared to both groups of countries, the following important differences were found. A structural deficit of the CECs in the *sophisticated engineering branches* (electrical and mechanical engineering, transport equipment) compared to EU-North, but a surplus in these branches compared to EU-South. On the other hand, there existed major surpluses of the CECs in the food industry and in *labour-intensive* industries such as textiles, clothing and leather compared to EU-North, but structural deficits towards EU-South. Thus, the level of industrial development of the CECs at the beginning of the transition can be located somewhere between the more advanced and the less advanced west European countries. In *Slovenia*, the surplus in labour-intensive industries towards EU-North, in particular for textiles and clothing, was much more pronounced and the deficit in sophisticated engineering considerably smaller than in the other CECs. This indicates a comparatively greater specialization in labour-intensive products, on the one hand, and a relatively more advanced level of industrial development of this country, on the other (Figure 8.1).[6]

Table 8.1 Industrial production and GDP in the CECs, growth rates in per cent, 1990–96

	1990	1991	1992	1990–92	1993	1994	1995	1996	1993–96
Hungary									
GDP, real growth	−3.5	−11.9	−3.1	−6.3	−0.6	2.9	1.5	1.0	1.2
Industrial production, real growth	−10.7	−16.7	−17.4	−15.0	3.4	9.6	7.1	3.7	5.9
Czech Republic									
GDP, real growth	−1.2	−11.5	−3.3	−5.4	0.6	3.2	6.4	3.9	3.5
Industrial production, real growth	−5.1	−26.3	n.a.	−16.4[a]	−8.2	−0.2	8.2	4.6	0.9
Slovak Republic									
GDP, real growth	−2.5	−14.6	−6.5	−8.0	−3.7	4.9	6.9	6.6	3.6
Industrial production, real growth	−4.2	−25.9	−15.6	−15.7	−18.6	1.9	9.0	2.5	−1.9
Slovenia									
GDP, real growth	−4.7	−8.9	−5.5	−6.4	2.8	5.3	4.1	3.3	3.9
Industrial production, real growth	−9.0	−13.1	−14.7	−12.3	−4.1	6.2	2.0	−0.2	0.9

Note: [a] 1990–91.

Sources: WIIW Annual Database Eastern Europe, WIIW Industrial Database.

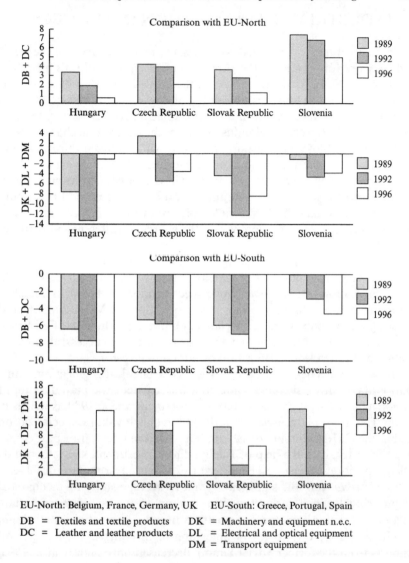

EU-North: Belgium, France, Germany, UK   EU-South: Greece, Portugal, Spain

DB = Textiles and textile products   DK = Machinery and equipment n.e.c.
DC = Leather and leather products   DL = Electrical and optical equipment
                                       DM = Transport equipment

Source: WIIW Industrial Database.

*Figure 8.1 Output share differences of selected labour-intensive and
            sophisticated engineering branches in CECs compared to
            the West*

3 INDUSTRIAL SPECIALIZATION IN THE CECS

As in many other industrialized countries, the food industry and the metal industry are found among the three top industries in all CECs both in 1989 and 1996. Beyond that, however, the individual CECs have concentrated on different industries to a different degree and have also changed their pattern of specialization during transition to a certain extent. In Hungary it was the chemical industry, in Czechoslovakia mechanical engineering and in Slovenia transport equipment which ranked third in size in 1989. By 1996, the picture looked somewhat different, with electrical equipment among the three top industries in Hungary and Slovenia, transport equipment in the Czech Republic and coke and refined petroleum products in Slovakia. A more detailed picture of intra-regional specialization is given in Figure 8.2 comparing the shares of different industries in individual countries to the respective CECs averages.[7]

Hungary showed in 1989 a higher than average share than the other CECs in the production of chemicals, mainly pharmaceuticals and in electrical equipment. However, while specialization in chemicals vanished during transition, due to the loss of the traditional CMEA markets and pressing import substitution, specialization in the production of electrical equipment declined first, but increased again after the successful modernization of branch leader Tungsram by a foreign investor.

In the *Czech Republic,* industries such as mechanical engineering, transport equipment, basic metals and to a lesser extent the manufacture of non-metallic mineral products played a prominent role in 1989 as well as in 1996. The 1989 picture clearly reflects Czechoslovakia's specialization within the CMEA division of labour, but while the Czech transport equipment industry, with the help of foreign direct investment, strengthened its relative position, mechanical engineering experienced a dramatic decline.

In *Slovakia,* too, the significantly above-average share of mechanical engineering declined during transition ending up at a nearly average share in 1996. Slovakia's prominent position in coke and refined petroleum products, partly due to favourable long-term contracts for crude oil imports from the former Soviet Union, decreased only slightly after 1993. Most remarkable is the 'new specialization' of Slovakia in the production of metals, following the extension of the aluminium production in the new Zavod SNP plant in Zdiar nad Hronom.

Slovenia is the only CEC to show a certain kind of specialization in labour-intensive industries such as textiles and clothing and leather and leather products. The above-average shares in wood and wood products and manufacturing n.e.c. comprising toys, sports articles, musical instruments and furniture as major product categories point in the same direction. The above-average production share of the paper and printing

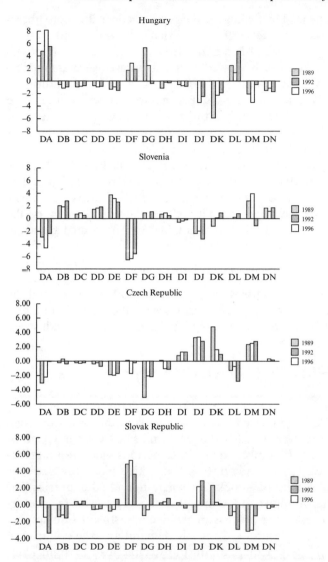

Notes: DA = Food products, beverages, tobacco; DB = Textiles, textile products; DC = Leather, leather products; DD = Wood, wood products; DE = Pulp, paper, paper products; DF = Coke, refined petroleum products; DG = Chemicals, chemical products; DH = Rubber, plastic products; DI = Other non-metallic products; DJ = Basic metals, fabricated metal products; DK = Machinery and equipment n.e.c.*; DL = Electrical and optical equipment; DM = Transport equipment; DN = Manufacturing n.e.c.*
* Not elsewhere classified.

Source: WIIW Industrial Database.

Figure 8.2 Shares of industries in total production relative to CEC averages

industry can be explained by the higher per capita income, the more liberal market for print media before 1989 and the rich endowment with natural resources (wood!) in Slovenia. Mostly affected by transition was the transport equipment industry which showed a high above average share in 1989 but a smaller than average share in 1996, due to the loss of traditional markets in Yugoslavia and former CMEA markets, which could not be compensated for. Also interesting is the emerging new specialization in mechanical and electrical engineering which is a change in line with the country's relatively advanced level of economic development.

Although the pattern of specialization depicted in Figure 8.2 shows many similarities in 1989 and 1996, a closer look reveals that it has changed, in many cases to a quite large extent, and in a few cases even new specialization patterns have emerged. This reflects the situation that, on the one hand, the old division of labour under CMEA is substituted gradually by a wider international division of labour, implying new patterns of specialization in the regional context as well. However, on the other hand, as noted above, due to the deep transformational recession, active restructuring of the manufacturing sector started only from 1992 onwards and the resources available for new investment being scarce, the expansion of production relied to a large extent on existing capacities of inherited industries.

4   SPEED OF STRUCTURAL CHANGE

In the first years of transition, industrial structures changed very rapidly in most CECs compared to developments in the west European countries in the same period. Moreover, in most CECs, the speed of change was also fast, if compared to those periods when rapid structural change in west European countries was taking place, for example, after the first and second oil shocks, or when individual countries had to prepare for and/or adjust to EU membership.[8] However, restructuring until 1992 was mainly a process of passive adjustment to changing relative prices, rapidly declining domestic demand and the collapse of CMEA markets. Different rates of output decline lead to significant shifts in the relative importance (production shares) of individual industries. To compare the industrial structure of one country at the aggregate level over time, a 'structural change indicator', S^* is applied. This summary measure reflects the weighted average difference in the share representation of different industries in total manufacturing in two different points in time. If S^* is close to 0, structural change over time in the country concerned is very small; the bigger this indicator, the faster the structural change (Table 8.2).

Table 8.2 *Structural change indicators* $(S^*)^a$

	1990	1991	1992	1993	1994	1995	1996	1990/92	1993/96
Hungary	1.04[b]	2.07[b]	1.21[b]	1.25	0.85	0.87	1.42	3.97	3.70
Czech part of Czechoslovakia	0.50	2.31	2.06	0.51	0.61	0.63	0.90	3.21	1.10
Slovak part of Czechoslovakia	0.77	1.59	1.29	1.94	1.05	0.88	1.05	2.43	2.56
Slovenia	0.89	0.70	0.59	0.55	0.57	0.39	0.64	1.31	1.42

Notes:
[a] Based on 2-digit NACE rev. 1 data for industrial production at constant prices. For definition see following equation:

$$S^* = \sqrt{\sum_k {}^{t_1}{}^{t_2}(sh_k^{t_1 t_2} - sh_k^{t_2})^2 \cdot {}^{t_3}(sh_k^{t_3}{}^1/100)}$$

k = individual industry
sh_k = share of industry k in total output at constant prices/employment (in %)
t_i = time index, where $i = 1, 2, 1$ denoting the earlier year.

[b] Comparable 2-digit NACE data were available from 1992 onwards only; the figures given have been aggregated from ISIC statistics by WIIW.

Source: Compiled from WIIW Industrial Database.

If ranked by the size of the summary measure S*, the change of the industrial structure between 1990 and 1992 was fastest in Hungary, followed by the Czech part of Czechoslovakia. Less significant change can be observed in the Slovak part of Czechoslovakia and the least in Slovenia. The sequence as well as the timely pattern of change correspond to the relative speed of transformation in these countries. Typically, the speed of change was highest in 1991, when the transformational recession was at its peak in most CECs. However, in Slovakia, it was highest in 1993, the first year of political independence and in Slovenia in 1990 already, due to the disintegration of the Yugoslav market preceding political secession.

Fast structural change comes about when a great number of industries change production shares to a significant degree and/or if some important industries with big weights in manufacturing change their shares considerably. Basically, structural change in 1990–92 was more equally distributed over the individual industries in Hungary and Slovenia and concentrated on a few important industries in the Czech and Slovak parts of Czechoslovakia. Most severely hit by output decline were industries which depended on CMEA markets to a large extent, such as mechanical engineering, transport equipment and electrical and optical equipment. In all CECs, the size of the summary indicator S* is greatly influenced by the development of the food industry – a large industry increasing its share in all countries due to the 'ratchet effect', which prevents demand for basic consumer goods from falling to the same extent as incomes.[9]

In the years after 1992, when growth gained momentum, the speed of structural change slackened in all CECs, indicating that the forced adjustment of production to the huge drop of demand had come to end and a new, but slower phase of active restructuring, with production expanding in most industries, had begun. However, different economic policies in individual CECs seem to have played a certain role as well. This is demonstrated by the very accentuated slow-down of structural change in the Czech Republic, reflecting the special kind of voucher privatization which is particularly non-conducive to restructuring at the level of individual companies. On the other hand, the speeding up of structural change in Hungary in 1996 anew, due to an increase of the share of the electrical and optical equipment industry mainly, is at least partly a consequence of this country's policy of promoting FDI.[10] Again, in all CECs, the size of S* was largely determined by the food industry, but contrary to the period before 1993, production shares of the food industry now declined in all CECs, except in Slovenia where it remained fairly constant. A more detailed analysis of the pattern of change at the level of individual industries is given below.

5 WINNING AND LOSING INDUSTRIES

Industries which during the transition performed better than the total manufacturing industry may be called 'winners' of transition, those which performed worse, 'losers' of transition. In terms of our structural change indicator S^*, winners are characterized by increasing shares and losers by decreasing shares in total manufacturing output. However, as a share reduction of a certain industry implies less than average growth, while a share increase refers to a better than average growth performance of this industry, winners and losers can be defined more directly in terms of growth rates of the individual industries relative to the growth of total manufacturing. We have to be aware, however, that according to this definition, if total manufacturing output is falling, any industry whose output is falling less than total, is termed a 'winner'. Therefore, in a period of recession, as in the CECs before 1993, a winner means 'less of a loser' rather.

5.1 Winners and losers 1990–92

As stated above, structural change of the manufacturing industry in this period took place when aggregate demand was decreasing in absolute terms: the sudden decline of demand from CMEA markets could be compensated only partly by the redirection of trade flows towards the West, and shrinking domestic demand was aggravated by rising import competition. As a result, we expect those industries to be losers which before 1990 had exported their products to CMEA markets mainly, and the quality of whose products was not sufficiently competitive on Western markets to allow for substantial redirection of trade. This is probably true for most investment goods, such as mechanical and electrical machinery and transport equipment. Another group of suspected losers are industries producing consumer goods, the purchase of which can be deferred and/or which are heavily exposed to Western import competition because of quality differences and/or consumer tastes, such as household appliances and consumer electronics as well as clothing and leather products.

On the other hand, due to the so called 'ratchet effect' that prevents demand from falling to the same extent as incomes, producers of basic consumer goods such as food and beverages are expected to increase their shares in total manufacturing output in the first phase of transition characterized by a 'transformational recession' (Kornai, 1993). Other types of industry with a good potential to be winners are those which were significantly under-represented under socialism, such as paper and paper products and publishing and printing. Finally, we suspected that industries producing raw materials and semi-finished products, which at least in the low-quality segment could compete well in Western markets, such as basic metals, non-metallic mineral products, (basic) chemicals, rubber and plastic products and so on, would perform better than the total manufacturing industry.[11] However, at the same time both the metal and the chemical industries used raw materials imported mainly from the Soviet Union and with the collapse of the CMEA they suffered a supply-side shock. As a result of this, a losing position could also be justified.

The actual performance of individual industries in the different CECs coincides largely with our expectations based on the assumption of a passive (defensive) rather than active (strategic) restructuring process in the first phase of transition (Table 8.3): The chemical and the metal industries being losers in several CECs confirms our 'supply shock' hypothesis.[12] Beyond that, in case of the latter, import restrictions for steel and general overcapacities in the European metal industry as well as high transport costs impeded the redirection of exports from CMEA to EU markets. In the Hungarian chemical industry, pharmaceuticals – playing the dominant role – did not fulfil Western quality standards and/or certain institutional requirements to be competitive on west European markets. Moreover, import substitution became particularly fierce in this field.

Although at the given level of aggregation it is difficult to explain each of the deviations from the expected scheme, a few suppositions will be given. The better than average performance of the Hungarian machinery industry, for instance, could be a consequence of the relatively early inflow of foreign direct investment, dampening to some extent the decline of production in this branch. The relatively better performance of the leather industry in the Czech part of Czechoslovakia and in Slovenia than expected indicate that perhaps because of higher quality, and in case of Slovenia better market experience as well, leather products from these two countries were more competitive compared to Western products than those from other CECs.

5.2   Winners and Losers 1993–96

During the period 1993–96, the average annual growth of GDP was positive in all CECs. Industrial production, with some delay, began to expand as well. In Hungary, the manufacturing sector grew even faster than GDP during the whole period, while in the other CECs growth of the industrial sector was only in some years higher than that of GDP Obviously CEC producers were at least partly successful in adjusting their production to market demand, supported by appropriate macroeconomic measures and

Table 8.3 *Winners and losers of transition, 1990–92ᵃ growth rates relative to national average in percentage points*

		Hungary	Czech Republicᵇ	Slovak Republic	Slovenia
DA	Food products, beverages, tobacco	8.6	**15.6**	3.3	**5.4**
DB	Textiles, textile products	−5.0	−1.9	−1.6	−2.0
DC	Leather, leather products	−3.2	0.5	−5.9	0.1
DD	Wood, wood products	**9.9**	1.3	−1.6	0.1
DE	Pulp, paper, paper products	5.9	**6.9**	10.5	3.0
DF	Coke, refined petroleum products	**9.7**	**−8.2**	1.8	**19.0**
DG	Chemicals, chemical products	−5.5	−1.9	1.0	**−4.5**
DH	Rubber, plastic products	**11.2**	−7.2	**4.9**	**4.9**
DI	Other non-metallic mineral products	1.3	1.4	0.3	2.7
DJ	Basic metals, fabricated metal products	**−7.7**	−2.9	**6.8**	1.5
DK	Machinery and equipment n.e.c.	0.7	−3.1	**−11.1**	**−4.1**
DL	Electrical and optical equipment	**−7.1**	**−9.9**	**−6.6**	**−6.7**
DM	Transport equipment	**−15.5**	**−8.6**	**−8.6**	−1.7
DN	Manufacturing n.e.c.	−6.3	**3.4**	2.2	0.8

Notes:
ᵃ The top three winners and losers are indicated by bold figures.
ᵇ 1990–91; because data are not strictly comparable between 1991 and 1992, no growth rates were calculated.

Source: Compiled from WIIW Industrial Database.

institutional changes. We must not forget, however, that in 1996 the levels of total industrial production (at constant prices) were still considerably below that of 1989 in all CECs. In all countries, internal financial resources for investment were still very limited after several years of recession. Although fixed asset investment in the manufacturing industry increased sharply in all CECs after 1992, the absolute levels were still low (probably with the exception of Hungary, due to the large inflow of FDI). This indicates that some adjustment of existing capacities to the new relative prices and demand patterns had to take place via company level restructuring and using relatively low amounts of investments.

Because of differences in the process of transition and (the evolution) of different patterns of comparative advantage in the individual CECs, we can assume the pattern of industrial restructuring after 1992 to differ substantially from the period before and also to vary more widely among the different countries. There were, however, some common features which could be explained on more general grounds.

To a great extent, the pattern of development in the period 1993–96 'mirrors' that of the previous period, at the aggregate level as well as with regard to individual industries. Many industries which had been major losers of transition before 1993 turned into winners, and vice versa. The food industry, a major winner in all CECs in the period before 1993, became a loser in Hungary, the Czech Republic and Slovakia; in Slovenia above-average growth slowed down to about average (Tables 8.3 and 8.4). This can be explained, on the one hand, by limited access to foreign markets and, on the other hand, by the income inelasticity of basic consumer goods. Thus, when incomes rise, their share in private consumption declines and industries supplying these goods can be expected to grow less fast than total manufacturing. Probably, for a similar reason, textiles and clothing and the leather industries have remained or become (major) losers in the CECs after 1992. This suggests that the industries are concentrated on low quality products mainly, characterized by low-income elasticities, and/or that in the field of more luxurious items with higher elasticities, imports took the lion's share of increased domestic demand.[13]

On the other hand, two of the more sophisticated engineering branches, electrical and optical equipment and transport equipment, which were major losers before 1993, turned into major winners thereafter. This must be seen in the light of growing domestic demand for consumer as well as investment goods, but also reflects improving international competitiveness of the CECs in this field, as is elaborated below, when dealing with exports of and FDI in individual industries. An important exception is Slovenia, where the transport equipment industry remained a loser. In 1989 this country had the highest share of the transport equipment sector of all CECs, but afterwards this industry suffered particularly hard from the disintegration of its major market in Yugoslavia.

Most interestingly, the mechanical engineering industry (DK), which can be classified as a sophisticated engineering branch as well, did not recover and remained a loser in all CECs. This industry largely depends on the demand for investment goods, which in absolute terms was still weak in its traditional markets. Moreover, the investment needed to modernize and to overcome existing quality gaps in this industry is relatively

Table 8.4 Winners and losers of transition, 1993–96[a], growth rates relative to national average in percentage points

		Hungary	Czech Republic	Slovak Republic	Slovenia
DA	Food products, beverages, tobacco	–5.1	–0.6	**–6.1**	0.1
DB	Textiles, textile products	–5.3	**–6.5**	**–7.1**	–1.1
DC	Leather, leather products	**–9.3**	**–6.5**	–4.1	**–11.2**
DD	Wood, wood products	–1.7	**–5.2**	0.0	0.3
DE	Pulp, paper, paper products	–4.7	0.6	4.7	–2.3
DF	Coke, refined petroleum products	–6.2	2.2	**–6.1**	**–9.5**
DG	Chemicals, chemical products	–7.2	0.3	**5.3**	**3.8**
DH	Rubber, plastic products	**5.7**	**6.4**	**6.6**	1.8
DI	Other non-metallic mineral products	–0.6	–0.3	–1.9	2.5
DJ	Basic metals, fabricated metal products	3.9	0.1	2.0	–1.0
DK	Machinery and equipment n.e.c.	–1.9	–4.3	–3.2	–0.9
DL	Electrical and optical equipment	**19.5**	**5.6**	5.0	**13.1**
DM	Transport equipment	**23.9**	**5.7**	**16.5**	**–6.8**
DN	Manufacturing n.e.c.	**–7.0**	–1.6	2.1	**3.0**

Note: [a] The top three winners and losers are indicated by bold figures.

Source: Compiled from WIIW Industrial Database.

high. For reasons that have to be analysed in more detail, there has been little willingness on the side of domestic as well as foreign investors so far to put money into this industry.

Another common feature of the development after 1992 is the significantly better than average performance of the rubber and plastic industry (DH). This industry has remained a winner in Hungary, Slovakia and Slovenia and has turned from a major loser into a major winner in the Czech Republic. Obviously, as in some sophisticated engineering branches, the CECs have built up a comparative advantage in this field.

However, to a considerable extent, output was supported by the demand for components, in particular tyres, from the rapidly expanding transport equipment industry in central Europe. This is reflected in the less impressive growth of the production of rubber and plastic products in Slovenia, where the transport equipment industry performed below average only.

Also common to the CECs is the deteriorating performance of coke and refined petroleum products (DF), which can be explained by lower energy consumption, the phasing-out of preferential contracts for crude oil with the former Soviet Union and existing overcapacities in this field. The paper and printing industry (DE), relatively underdeveloped under socialism and thus a major winner of transition in the period 1990–92, has reached a certain level of saturation in some CECs and is at the point of becoming an industry with below-average growth.

6 FOREIGN TRADE AND PATTERNS OF CHANGE IN PRODUCTION

The process of internationalization, through foreign trade and investment, has affected the ongoing process of industrial restructuring in the CECs. The opening-up of the national economy to foreign goods and FDIs was a very important element of the process of transition from socialist to market economies in all CECs. We, therefore, expect an increasing impact of foreign trade and investment on the allocation of resources and thus on structural change. At the beginning of the transition, however, CEC foreign trade and its impact on production was dominated by the collapse of the CMEA markets, as mentioned above. We can, therefore, expect the effects of increasing trade on production with the West to become visible only later on. Our analysis of the growth rates of production and those of exports in individual industries confirms this notion. The correlation between production growth and export growth of individual industries was very weak for the period 1990–92 in all CECs, but, except for Slovenia, a significant relation was found for the period 1993–96. However, for the sake of comparability of trade and production data at the level of individual industries, we had to confine our analysis to CEC trade with EU countries.[14] As the EU is the greatest single market for all CECs analysed, and in the light of the even closer trade relations expected for the future, this procedure seems justified on empirical grounds as well.[15] Nevertheless, it has to be borne in mind that our results may differ from those based on national (total) trade data presented for selected central and east European countries by other researchers in this field.[16]

The regression line used in our empirical analysis is the following:

$$y = a + \beta x + u$$

where y = growth rate of production (in national currency, at constant prices)

x = growth rate of exports (in US dollars)
a = constant term
u = error term.

For the period 1993(4)–96,[17] our analysis showed a significant correlation of production and export growth for Hungary, the Czech Republic and Slovakia, but not for Slovenia (Appendix, Figures 8.A.1–8.A.4). The low correlation between production growth and growth of exports to the EU in Slovenia can be explained by the fact that before transition industrial production in Slovenia was much more oriented towards EU markets than in the other CECs and thus trade regime changes thereafter played a minor role.

The regression coefficient, b, was by far the highest for Hungary, indicating that on average an increase of exports of one percentage point in a certain branch was related to an increase of production in the same branch of 0.4 percentage points while in the Czech Republic and Slovakia the respective increment was between 0.2 and 0.3 percentage points only (Figures 8.A.1–8.A.3). The constant term, a, indicating production growth independent of export growth, was statistically insignificant for all CECs, which suits well for small open economies.[18]

6.1 Foreign Trade as an Engine of Growth in Manufacturing

During the period 1993–96, total manufacturing exports, in particular to the EU, were growing much faster than production in the CECs. (Real export growth is approximated by denomination of exports in US dollars.) Our findings of a significant correlation between growth of exports and production of individual industries indicate that not only at the aggregate level, but at the level of individual industries as well, foreign trade was an engine of growth during this period.

Applying our framework of 'winners' and 'losers' of transition, outlined above, to the Figures 8.A.1–8.A.3, we would expect the major winners to be found in the upper right-hand corner of the figures, representing high growth rates of production as well as exports. This is perfectly true in all three countries for the transport equipment industry and/or electrical engineering, to mention two prominent cases of industries marked out as major winners in Table 8.4 above. The major losers, on the other hand, should show up in the lower left-hand corner of Figures 8.A.1–8.A.3, character-ized by low growth rates of production and exports, which is the case for the relatively labour intensive leather industry and textiles and clothing industry, as well as the food industry in all CECs. In Slovenia, although in general no significant correlation between production growth and export growth of individual industries was found, electrical engineering also shows up in the upper right-hand corner and the leather industry in the lower left-hand corner of Figure 8.A.4.

However, in each country, we find industries which – apart from devia-tions immanent to every econometric analysis – seem not to conform to the general pattern of production and export growth as indicated by the regression line. The reasons for these deviations may be country-specific but industry-specific as well.

6.2 Deviations from the Observed General Pattern ('Outliers')

Considerable deviations of individual industries from the regression line give an indication whether an industry in a specific country is perhaps more than averagely dependent on the growth of exports to the EU, or less.

Outliers *above* the regression line are characterized by a higher than expected growth of production at a given level of export growth to the EU or, putting it the other way round, the growth of exports to the EU is lower than expected at a given level of production growth. These industries, therefore, seem to depend less than the average on the growth of EU markets and more on domestic market and/or non-EU markets instead.

Outliers *below* the regression line are characterized by a lower than expected growth of production at a given level of export growth or, alternatively formulated, the growth of exports to the EU is higher than expected at a given level of production growth. These indus-tries, therefore, seem to depend more on the growth of EU markets than average.

However, apart from the paper and printing industry situated above the regression line in all three CECs, which can be explained by the above-mentioned catch-up demand of transition countries in advertis-ing, packaging, print media and so on, many differences between the individual CECs were found. In *Hungary*, for instance, growth of the electrical and optical equipment and the rubber and plastic industries appears to be rather related to the domestic and/or non-EU markets, while the transport equipment industry seems more dependent on EU markets than average. An explanation may be that the former were major suppliers of the latter. Furthermore, the production of consumer electronics for the domestic market has become an important segment of the electrical and optical equipment industry in Hungary and plastic products are used to a large extent in packaging. In the *Czech Republic*, electrical engineering is also more domestic/non-EU market-oriented than average, but contrary to Hungary and similar to *Slovakia*, the transport equipment industry, too, shows up above the regression line indicating above average dependence on domestic/non-EU markets. This points to different marketing strategies of major (foreign) producers in this field.[19]

Moreover, in all three CECs, the textile and clothing and the leather industries can be found considerably below the regression line, pointing to above-average orientation towards EU markets of these industries. Although, to a somewhat lesser extent, this is true for the mechanical engineering sector (DK) as well. This may be explained by the relatively sluggish domestic demand in these fields, already noted above.

Finally, before turning to the role of FDI in industrial restructuring, a few words on the *question of causality* with regard to production and export should be mentioned:

Correlation by itself does not imply any direction of causality. This can be derived from a certain hypothesis only. For instance, if we assume a demand-orientated model, then our results may be interpreted as foreign demand (that is, exports) inducing further production and thus shaping the production structure. However if we suppose a supply-oriented model, where domestic supply pushes exports, production determines the structure of exports and is to be explained first. For instance, as elaborated by Rothschild (1966),[20] excess capacities during recession will induce entrepreneurs to push exports more strongly to compensate for the lack of domestic demand. Another example are multinational companies which, as part of their corporate strategy, push exports and thanks to their corporate linkages and better knowledge of international markets are able to do so. In the case of the CECs the excess supply hypothesis in a modified form could be applied to the excess capacities inherited from the socialist era in many industries and in certain industries, the high export growth could at least partly be explained by the relatively high degree of foreign penetration. Thus, the results of the correlation analysis above should be interpreted as a mixture of both export-push and export-pull factors.

7   THE ROLE OF FDI IN INDUSTRIAL RESTRUCTURING

In all CECs, enterprises where FDI is involved (foreign investment enterprises, FIEs) show on average a higher share in exports and in investment than in production and sales, respectively (Chapters 6 and 7). This means that they have a higher propensity to export and invest than purely domestic enterprises. We, therefore, expect them to contribute significantly to the restructuring process in manufacturing.

In Hungary, for instance, in 1996, the share of FIEs in total sales of manufacturing companies was 61.4 per cent, but reached 73.9 per cent in sales for exports and 79.9 per cent in investment outlays. (In Slovenia the difference between the respective figures was less dramatic: 19.6 per cent, 25.8 per cent and 20.3 per cent.)[21] This is generally the case, not because foreign investors put their capital mainly in very export-oriented branches, but because they realize higher than average export quotas in nearly every industry they invest. We find (major) winners, (major) losers and industries performing around average among those industries which have attracted the highest shares of foreign capital in each country. From an overall point of view, FDI in the four CECs analysed is concentrated in the food industry, transport equipment, chemicals and electrical and optical equipment. Out of these, the food industry is largely domestic-market oriented while electrical engineering in all CECs shows an above average propensity to export. With regard to the two other industries the picture is mixed.

The higher export propensity of FIEs can be attributed to the higher efficiency and quality of output and to their advantage of international corporate linkages which gives them better access to foreign markets than domestic firms. This applies not only to greenfield investments but acquisitions as well, which comprise a large part of FDI due to privatization, and which do not add to the production capacity in the short run. However, quality upgrading and productivity increase due to FDI helped acquired enterprises to become internationally more competitive and increase production and exports in the longer term. We might thus speak of an 'export push' resulting from FDI, as stated above, meaning that *ceteris paribus* industries with a higher foreign penetration will perform better in exports. (Notably, there is also evidence of an import pull by FIEs.)

From the above-average performance of FIEs in exports and the quite significant correlation found between the growth of exports and production in individual industries (Figures 8.A.1–8.A.3), we can expect a certain impact of the rate of foreign penetration in individual industries on production growth and thus on the pattern of structural change in manufacturing. This hypothesis was tested by running (linear) regressions between production growth and rates of foreign penetration of individual CEC industries.

As FDI was negligible in the CECs before 1993 (probably with the exception of Hungary), our analysis is focused at production growth for the period 1993–96. For measuring the rate of foreign penetration, depending on the availability of data at the level of individual industries, the following indicators were used: the shares of FIEs in *nominal capital* for Hungary and Slovenia, the shares of FIEs in *equity capital* for the Czech Republic and FIE shares in *output* for Slovakia.[22] Given the fact that investment usually takes some time to affect production, a certain 'time-lag' between FDI and growth of production could be expected, yet our data set was too small to test sophisticated lag structures. However, a simple cross-section analysis over all countries and industries gave us some indication that in general the rate of foreign penetration prevailing in 1994 was most important for explaining production growth 1993–96. (The rates of foreign penetration in 1995 provided a good explanation as well, but FIE rates in 1996 turned out to be insignificant.)

With regard to the individual countries, a significant correlation between foreign penetration and production growth in individual industries was found for *Hungary,* the *Czech Republic* and *Slovakia*; but not for *Slovenia* (Figures 8.A.5–8.A.8). However, with the exception of the Czech Republic, this correlation became insignificant when the transport equipment industry, which shows an extremely high rate of both foreign penetration and production growth in all three countries, was excluded from the sample. On the other hand, in all three CECs correlation coefficients increased considerably and the size of regression coefficients changed if only one important outlier was eliminated, for instance, the food industry in Hungary, electrical engineering in the Czech Republic and the rubber and plastic industry in Slovakia.[23]

In Slovenia, the transport equipment industry is also characterized by a high rate of foreign penetration, but contrary to the other CECs, production growth was negative in the period 1993–96. As already noted in Section 5.2, this was due to the loss not only of the CMEA markets but of the major markets in former Yugoslavia as well. Given the important role this industry played in other CECs for the significance of the overall relation between FIE penetration and production growth, the 'inverse' performance of this industry in Slovenia provides a major explanation why no significant correlation between production growth and foreign penetration was found in this country. Other reasons could be the overall low level of FDI and various obstacles to FDI in particular industries in Slovenia.

Taken together, our findings suggest that there is a certain impact of FIE on production growth and thus the production structure in manufacturing, but the impact might be quite different in different industries of a country. In Hungary, for instance, the rate of foreign penetration in 1994 was nearly the same in the transport equipment and in the non-metal mineral industries, but in the former production growth for the period 1993–96 was 30 per cent while in the latter it was 5 per cent only. Or seen from the other side, production growth in the transport equipment and in the electrical engineering industries were nearly the same in the Czech Republic, but the rate of foreign penetration was beyond 35 per cent in the former and only about 10 per cent in the latter industry. This is no great surprise, as FDI is just one out of many factors to determine production growth of individual industries. Moreover, it has to be taken into account that, by definition, FIEs include all enterprises where foreign investment is involved, no matter to what extent. Therefore, the share of FIEs in (nominal/equity) capital of an industry does not always truly reflect the share of foreign capital invested in this industry.[24] Another problem is the relatively high level of aggregation in our analysis which may conceal relations that would become visible only at a more disaggregated level of industries.[25]

A further interesting result of our analysis refers to the 'outliers' discussed in Section 6.2. Industries which seem to depend more than average on the growth of EU markets are often characterized by higher rates of foreign penetration as would be expected from the regression lines in Figures 8.A.5–8.A.7.[26] Good examples are the leather industry, textiles and clothing and, in the case of the Czech Republic and Slovakia, mechanical engineering as well. As a result of this we may conclude that the relatively high export growth in these industries can at least partly be attributed to the FIEs engaged in this field. However, for domestic/non-EU market-oriented industries no such straightforward explanation was found.

In general, our results indicate that there is a definite impact of FDI on structural shifts in manufacturing, although it does not hold true for every industry to an equal extent. However, given a certain overall relationship, political measures influencing the pattern of FDI, for instance, different privatization measures, have an effect on industrial restructuring as well.

NOTES

1. This classification is more aggregated than that used in the FIE database (2-digit ISIC; 23 industries), but data for industrial production in the Czech and the Slovak Republic were available at the 2-digit NACE level only. In the Appendix, a list of NACE industries and the corresponding ISIC codes are given.
2. The hypothesis of the occurrence of uniform development patterns in industry has been frequently examined – see, for example, Chenery and Taylor (1968) and Syrquin (1988).

3. Compare Grosfeld and Roland (1995).
4. EU-North comprises Belgium, France, the United Kingdom and (West-) Germany; the choice of these countries as representative of the industrially more advanced EU countries was guided by the availability of comparable industrial data. EU-South includes Greece, Portugal and Spain. The terms 'North' and 'South' are meant to indicate differences in industrial development rather than the geographical location of the countries within the EU.
5. We compared the share of each single industry in total manufacturing output of a CEC to the share of the same industry in EU-North and EU-South. The resulting positive or negative deviations were interpreted as 'structural surpluses' or 'structural deficits' of the CEC as compared to the group of Western countries under consideration.
6. Also, there existed a structural deficit in the metal industry compared to EU-North and in coke and refineries compared to both, EU-North and EU-South. Furthermore, there was a structural surplus in the paper and printing industry and a deficit in the food industry with regard to both country groups.
7. Unweighted average of production shares in Hungary, the Czech and Slovak Republics and Slovenia. It is largely shaped by the very high share of Hungary in the food industry (DA) and the very low share of Slovenia in coke and refineries (DF). Thus, the other CECs all show below-average shares in the first case and above-average shares in the latter.
8. See Urban (1995), p. 20.
9. See Urban (1997), p. 15.
10. In Slovenia, the increase in structural change was largely due to an increase in the share of electrical and optical equipment, but a significant further reduction in the share of basic metals and mechanical engineering as well.
11. Because it is a very mixed category, we did not attempt any predictions for manufacturing n.e.c. (DN).
12. In Slovakia, the production of basic metals was less over-represented than in the other CECs in 1989 but expanded significantly when the new aluminium plant, Zavod SNP, in Ziar nad Hronom was completed.
13. Even in the low-quality range of leather and textile products, import competition from low-wage Asian countries, especially China, became very fierce.
14. For CEC exports to the EU, we have used EU imports from the individual CECs and have made them comparable to the production statistics at the 2-digit NACE level, using the proper Eurostat keys from EUROSTAT (1996).
15. As we are comparing growth rates of exports and production for the period 1993–96 our analysis is in terms of CEC exports to EU (12).
16. See, for example, Lemoine (1997), pp. 14–19, dealing with Hungary, the Czech Republic and Poland.
17. For the Czech and the Slovak Republic, proper data for exports to the EU are available from 1993 onwards, after the two countries had become independent states. Therefore, growth rates could be calculated for the years 1994–96 only.
18. In another study dealing with a wider range of countries, using a similar regression equation, a statistically significant constant term was found for Poland, in line with its large domestic market and its self-supporting growth process (Urban, 1997).
19. For example, Magyar Suzuki in 1996 exported 70 per cent of all 'Swifts' and 'Subarus', while Škoda–VW gained half of its revenues in 1995 from domestic sales. In 1996 the company's share in the new car market was 55 per cent. In Slovakia, the relatively large components industry is mostly supplying to Czech producers, including Škoda–VW, Tatra, Liaz and Avia. Again, the best selling car brand in Slovakia is Škoda with a market share of roughly 30 per cent in 1996; see WIIW (1998), Annex B.
20. 'In actual economic reports, however, it is often pointed out that exports are either increased or decreased according to the fluctuations of domestic sales. Consequently, the volume of exports should not merely be considered as a quantity of passive

21. adjustment, for it is manipulated in an active manner, at least by enterprises of certain economic branches' (Rothschild, 1966, p. 270).
21. WIIW, Database on Foreign Investment Enterprises. In the Czech and the Slovak Republic, the latest available data for FIE export sales are for 1994 only. In this year, the shares of FIEs came up to about 12 per cent in total sales, 16 per cent in export sales and 24 per cent in investment outlays for both countries.
22. For Slovakia, FIE shares in equity capital at the level of individual industries were available from 1995 onwards only.
23. By this measure, r square increased from 0.34 to 0.41 in Hungary, from 0.53 to 0.68 in the Czech Republic and from 0.33 to 0.60 in the Slovak Republic.
24. An extreme example is the petroleum industry in Hungary which, measured by the share of FIE in nominal capital, in 1996, showed a foreign penetration rate of 100 per cent albeit the share of foreign capital invested in this industry, which is a state-owned monopoly, is only very small. However, because of certain special features of this industry in the other CECs as well, the coke and refined petroleum industry (DF) was completely excluded from our regression analysis.
25. In Hungary, for instance, the different statistical basis for production data from national industrial statistics, including enterprises with more than 20 employees (1994) only, and our FIE data, including all enterprises, could, to a certain extent, give misleading results.
26. These industries show up *below* the regression line; for industries *above* the regression line foreign penetration is lower than expected. It has to be borne in mind, however, that above and below the regression line is not identical with above and below the average rate of foreign penetration in a CEC.

REFERENCES

Chenery, H.B. and L. Taylor (1968), 'Development patterns: among countries and over time', *Review of Economics and Statistics*, **50** (4), pp. 391–416.
Eurostat (1996), 'NACE Rev. 1. Statistical classification of economic activities in the European Community, Statistical Document', no. 2E.
Grosfeld, I. and G. Roland (1995), 'Defensive and strategic restructuring in central European enterprises', Centre for Economic Policy Research, *Discussion Paper*, no. 1135, March.
Kornai, J. (1993), 'Transformational recession. A general phenomenon examined through the example of Hungary's development', *Economie Appliqué*, **XLVI** (2), pp. 181–227.
Lemoine, F. (1997), 'Industrial recovery in central European countries: sectoral trends, foreign trade and direct investments', paper for the ACE workshop on 'Emerging Market Organisation and Corporate Restructuring in Central and Eastern Europe', May, mimeo.
Rothschild, K.W. (1966), '"Pull" und "push" im export', *Weltwirtschaftliches Archiv*, **97** (2), pp. 250–72.
Syrquin, M. (1988), 'Patterns of structural change', in H.B. Chenery and T.N. Srinivasan (eds), *Handbook of Development Economics*, vol. 1, Amsterdam, Elsevier Science Publishers B.V. pp. 203–73.
Urban, W. (1995), 'The industrial structure of central and east European countries as compared with Austria and some other west European countries', mimeo, The Vienna Institute for International Economic Studies (WIIW), Vienna.

Urban, W. (1997), 'Patterns of structural change in manufacturing in transition countries', in M. Landesmann *et al.* (eds), *WIIW Structural Report 1997*, The Vienna Institute for International Economic Studies (WIIW), Vienna.

WIIW (1998), 'Development prospects of the transport equipment sector in the central and eastern European countries', mimeo, The Vienna Institute for International Economic Studies (WIIW), Vienna.

APPENDIX 8.A

Table 8.A.1 NACE rev. 1 – classification[a]

D	Total manufacturing
DA	Food products, beverages and tobacco (15, 16)
DB	Textiles and textile products (17, 18)
DC	Leather and leather products (19)
DD	Wood and wood products (20)
DE	Pulp, paper and paper products, publishing and printing (21, 22)
DF	Coke, refined petroleum products and nuclear fuel (23)
DG	Chemicals, chemical products and man-made fibres (24)
DH	Rubber and plastic products (25)
D1	Other non-metallic mineral products (26)
DJ	Basic metals and fabricated metal products (27, 28)
DK	Machinery and equipment n.e.c. (29)
DL	Electrical and optical equipment (30, 31, 32, 33)
DM	Transport equipment (34, 35)
DN	Manufacturing n.e.c. (36, 37)

Note: [a] The figures in brackets refer to the respective ISIC codes.

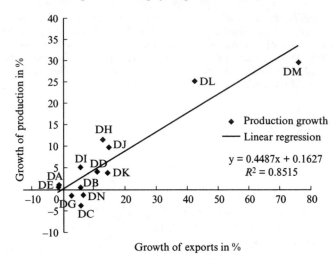

Notes: see Table 8.A.1.

Source: WIIW Industrial Database.

Figure 8.A.1 Hungary 1993–96

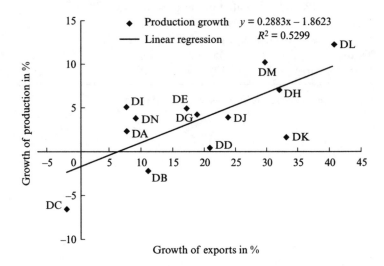

Notes: see Table 8.A.1.

Source: WIIW Industrial Database.

Figure 8.A.2 Czech Republic 1994–96

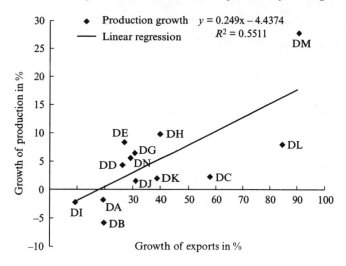

Notes: see Table 8.A.1.

Source: WIIW Industrial Database.

Figure 8.A.3 Slovakia 1994–96

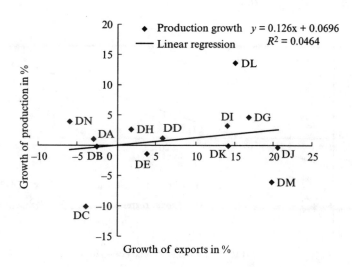

Notes: see Table 8.A.1.

Source: WIIW Industrial Database.

Figure 8.A.4 Slovenia 1993–96

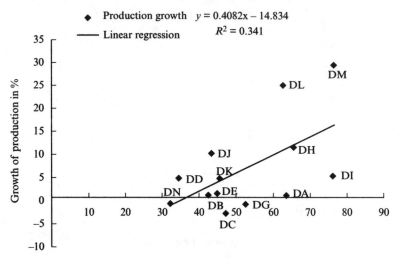

Notes: see Table 8.A.1.

Source: WIIW Industrial Database and WIIW FIE Database.

Figure 8.A.5 Hungary 1993–96

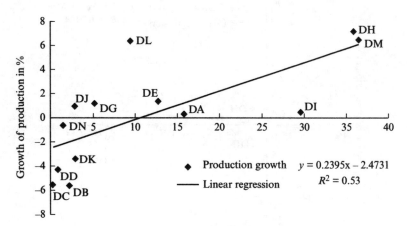

Notes: see Table 8.A.1.

Source: WIIW Industrial Database and WIIW FIE Database.

Figure 8.A.6 Czech Republic 1993–96

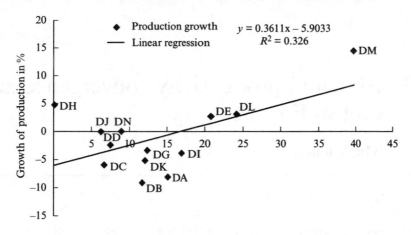

FIE shares in output (1994) in %

Notes: see Table 8.A.1.

Source: WIIW Industrial Database and WIIW FIE Database

Figure 8.A.7 Slovak Republic 1993–96

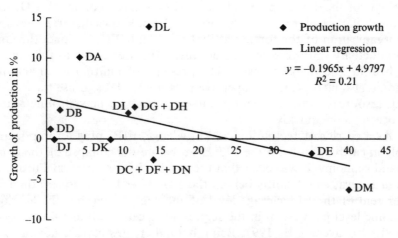

FIE shares in nominal capital (1994) in %

Notes: see Table 8.A.1.

Source: WIIW Industrial Database and WIIW FIE Database.

Figure 8.A.8 Slovenia 1993–96

9. FIEs and productivity convergence in central Europe

Mark Knell

1 INTRODUCTION

FDI can play an important role in facilitating technical change and technological learning in the countries undergoing economic transformation in central Europe. The growth of inward FDI has been phenomenal, with more than US\$ 27 billion coming into the region from 1990 to 1996. The main reason why these countries try to attract foreign investment is the prospect of acquiring the necessary technology and skills needed to close the 'productivity gap' with the EU. FIEs can be important carriers of technical knowledge and a source of new technology for the domestic-owned enterprises in host economies. FDI has a direct impact on productivity through direct knowledge transfers and reorganization of the foreign affiliate and an indirect impact through 'productivity spillovers' to DEs because FIEs are unable to fully internalize the knowledge transfer. The presence of multinational activity should also increase the competitive pressure for DEs to use their existing resources more efficiently and to introduce new products and processes more quickly.

As a carrier of technological knowledge, FIEs play an important role in catching up with the EU. Even before the collapse of the command economy, it was clear that the productivity of central European industry was significantly behind the EU. After falling to less than 34 per cent of the EU average level of income per person, the average income level per person in the region advanced to almost 40 per cent of the EU average by 1997. Being behind creates certain advantages for catching-up if the region can create the absorptive capacity (or technical competence) to take advantage of the productivity spillovers. This 'social capability', as Abramovitz (1989) describes it, depends not only on the level of education and R&D activity, but also on the institutional setting including finance, infrastructure, corporate governance and industrial networks. The long-term potential for economic growth in central Europe depends, therefore, on both the opportunity and social capability for domestic firms to access technology in the global economy.

This chapter examines the impact of MNCs activity on the productivity growth of manufacturing industries in four CECs: the Czech Republic, Hungary, Slovakia and Slovenia. It covers the period from 1993 to 1996 when both FIEs and DEs in the region began shifting away from a defensive restructuring strategy towards a more strategic one (Grosfeld and Roland, 1995). As FIEs enter the region, foreign affiliates are assimilated into the global strategy of the parent firm, facilitating the shift toward a more strategic behaviour. Competitive pressure and knowledge spillovers create the potential for DEs to follow a more strategic restructuring strategy. Evidence of this should appear initially as relatively higher productivity in the FIEs and as a closing productivity gap between the FIEs and the domestic enterprises. If the productivity of FIEs is similar to the productivity levels in the EU, then the evidence will indicate a convergence of labour productivity.

This study uses Austria as an approximation of EU productivity levels since the variances in productivity are low at the 2-digit industry level and Austria is the only member State to have a common border with all four countries. Evidence of productivity spillovers between foreign-owned affiliates and domestically owned enterprises in central Europe and similar productivity levels between FIEs and Austrian industry should, therefore, show that there is a closing productivity gap.

The data used in this chapter measure the share of foreign ownership at the 2-digit International Standard Industrial Classification (ISIC) industry from 1993 to 1996. FIEs include all enterprises with some foreign share in their equity capital. (Chapters 2 and 3 describe these data more fully.) The following section explores the relationship between FIEs and productivity gaps further. Section 3 describes the patterns of multinational activity in central Europe and Section 4 draws some conclusions on productivity of FIEs and spillovers to domestic-owned firms. The region is then compared with Austria in Section 5 to show whether the multinational firms in central Europe have similar productivity levels. Section 6 examines the relationship between innovation, R&D and multinational activity in central Europe. The final section explores certain issues related to multinational activity and productivity convergence.

2　CAN FDI CLOSE THE PRODUCTIVITY GAP?

The appearance of endogenous growth theory has encouraged research in the relationship between multinational activity and long-run growth (de Mello, 1997). Foreign investment only affects growth in the short run in the growth model of Solow (1956) since the assumption of diminishing returns to capital inputs has no permanent impact on output growth and that the host country would converge to the same productivity level as if the inward FDI never occurred. FDI can have a permanent effect on the host country by offsetting the diminishing returns through exogenous technological shocks. Productivity convergence occurs automatically because technology is public knowledge that can spillover without difficulty.

In the endogenous growth models of Romer (1986, 1990) and Grossman and Helpman (1991), technical knowledge can also be firm-specific (or tacit) and excludable in that it requires certain rights. Productivity gaps persist because of positive feedback, generated by technological learning external to the firm, exceeds the negative feedback engendered by diminishing marginal returns internal to the firm. In this context, FDI becomes an important channel for domestic firms to gain access to rights and technical knowledge of foreign firms. FDI can help close the productivity gap through increased competitive pressure, access to new markets, acquisition of new skills, improved corporate governance and additional collaborative arrangements. By providing the affiliate with access to finance and a wider range of intermediate products, FDI can increase productivity directly in the affiliate and indirectly in local domestic-owned enterprises through knowledge spillovers. The mobility of skilled labour, leasing and licensing of technology, outsourcing of production activities, and other JVs can facilitate spillovers from affiliates to local firms. In these models the existence of technology transfer and local spillovers prevent the unbounded decline of the marginal productivity of capital and makes long-term growth possible.

A basic shortcoming of the endogenous growth models is that they do not consider the strategic behaviour of the firm. While these models recognize that tacit knowledge can be costly to transfer even within the multinational corporation, they neglect the role that strategic behaviour plays in generating productivity spillovers. Dunning (1994) argues that MNCs can limit access of affiliates to certain markets, the range of products they produce, the kinds of technology they adopt, R&D activity they undertake, and their pattern of networking with domestically owned firms. MNCs can also reduce competition and taxes paid in the host country through market domination and transfer pricing. Limiting competition and access to certain technologies will result in fewer productivity spillovers and restrict domestic production to simple technologies and low value-added activities. Bardham (1998) also shows that MNCs can restrict domestic production when they set up affiliates with the main purpose of protecting existing property rights and taking out patents in the host country. While Dunning (1994) sees FDI as a potentially important channel for transferring technology, the global strategy of a multinational can also reduce the opportunities for technology spillovers and hence, long-term growth in the host country.

Productivity spillovers tend to occur more frequently in countries with relatively high absorptive capacities. While countries with relatively low technological levels carry a certain advantage in catching-up, the ability to absorb technical knowledge will depend on technological capabilities of the affiliate and the local producers. The strategic behaviour of a MNC in a particular country will depend on the technological capabilities of that country and the relative price levels between the two countries. Countries (and firms) without the capability to assimilate new technology tend to attract mainly market- or resource-seeking foreign investment, and countries with this capability tend to attract more efficiency- and asset-seeking foreign investment (Dunning, 1994). There would be few, if any, productivity spillovers in countries (or firms) without the relevant technological capabilities. The model of Verspagen (1991) shows why countries with a high learning capacity and/or small productivity gap are likely to catch up, while other countries will tend to fall further behind (Kokko, 1992).

There are numerous case studies of technology transfer and productivity spillovers induced by multinational activity in central Europe but no comprehensive analysis of the effects of this investment on the industrial structure. Difficulties in obtaining appropriate data limit the ability to undertake such a study, but there are also few studies of other countries where detailed manufacturing data are available. Blomström and Kokko (1998) provide a review of the literature on the spillover effects from multinational activity. Empirical analysis of intra-industry spillovers by Caves (1974) on Australia, Globerman (1979) on Canada, and by Blomström and Persson (1983) on Mexico all point to the existence of significant spillovers. Nadiri (1991) reaches similar conclusions in a study of US investment in France, Germany, Japan and the UK from 1968 to 1988. Blomström and Wolff (1994) confirm these findings using the case of Mexico from 1970 and 1975 and ask whether there is a relationship between these spillovers and technological change. By contrast, studies of manufacturing industries in Morocco by Haddad and Harrison (1993) and Venezuela by Aitken and Harrison (1991) show that impact of multinational activity varies considerably across industries and that spillovers may be limited to industries that are less knowledge-intensive. All these studies suggest that the ability of domestic-owned firms to access the potential productivity spillovers maybe created by FIEs depends crucially on the social and technological capabilities possessed by firms in the country.

This chapter adopts the intra-industry approach developed by Blomström and Wolff (1994). Being one of the few studies that uses industry-based data to analyse the relationship between technology and productivity spillovers also provides an opportunity to compare Mexico with central Europe. In their study, Blomström and Wolff construct a simple model of productivity convergence between local and foreign firms that depends on the labour productivity gap between local and foreign-owned firms and the degree of foreign ownership of an industry. Their main conclusion was that multinational activity has a significant impact on the convergence of productivity between foreign and domestic firms and between Mexican industries and manufacturing firms in the USA. This study will develop a similar inter-industry approach to show whether spillovers do occur in central Europe from 1993 to 1996.

3   MULTINATIONAL ACTIVITY GROWTH IN CENTRAL EUROPE

Previous studies on productivity spillovers through multinational activity focused on countries with relatively little structural change. Although firms in the CECs have started to follow longer-term strategies after 1993, there has still been considerable structural and institutional changes through the 1990s. Table 9.1 shows the extent of these changes through the growth of employment between FIEs and DEs. Industries with high employment growth in the FIEs indicate that firms received investment for the first time from 1993 to 1996 (except Slovenia). The most prominent example is the coke and petroleum industry in Hungary which shifted almost in entirety to become an FIE in 1996. Data on the number of firms in the CECs indicate that most industries experienced a growth in both FIEs and domestic-owned firms indicating that many of the FIEs are affiliates created by the parent firm and not through privatization to a foreign firm. Where there are high growth rates in FIE employment and negative growth rates in domestic-owned firms, it is very likely that nominal ownership changed during the period covered in the study.

Table 9.1 Average annual employment growth of the CECs by type of ownership, 1993–96

ISIC Code	Industry	Czech Republic		Hungary		Slovakia		Slovenia	
		FIE	DE	FIE	DE	FIE	DE	FIE	DE
15 + 16	Food, beverages and tobacco	9.4	-1.9	-2.7	-2.1	-2.5	-1.8	12.4	-0.5
17	Textiles	518.7	-8.5	6.4	5.9	7.7	-10.6	-1.9	-4.9
18	Wearing apparel and fur	76.0	-2.5	4.0	5.8	23.1	-4.5	-4.1	-2.7
19	Leather products	-7.1	-11.4	19.8	-7.2	155.9	-16.0	–	–
20	Wood products	43.9	-8.7	14.5	2.0	31.9	-3.3	-16.8	0.8
21	Pulp and paper products	34.1	-1.2	-7.1	4.6	in 22	in 22	18.4	-1.2
22	Printing and publishing	167.0	-1.4	3.2	1.3	2.8	-2.1	2.1	-2.5
23	Petroleum and coke	–	-21.4	451.5	-33.3	in 24	in 24	–	–
24	Chemicals and chemical products	22.7	4.0	18.9	-15.4	-3.3	-9.2	9.2	-0.6
25	Rubber and plastics	62.5	-2.6	10.5	7.0	–	-7.3	4.1	-3.7
26	Non-metallic mineral products	21.0	-9.1	4.1	2.3	14.6	-9.8	13.6	-1.4
27	Basic metals	20.9	-1.9	53.7	7.9	in 28	in 28	7.5	-1.7
28	Fabricated metals	48.2	-2.6	-0.3	0.5	16.5	-2.2	31.6	-3.5
29	Machinery and equipment	43.4	-8.7	14.2	25.0	in 30	in 30	0.5	-8.6
30	Office machinery and computers	–	-8.9	-3.7	32.5	6.7	-6.1	–	–
31	Electrical machinery	158.0	-4.1	11.6	0.2	85.6	-4.1	-6.9	-0.4
32	Radio and television	830.1	-6.0	24.8	-4.8	79.0	-10.7	7.1	-6.8
33	Precision instruments	29.0	-3.6	7.9	1.1	-18.6	-12.2	-2.0	0.0
34	Motor vehicles	9.0	-8.6	5.5	-4.5	in 35	in 35	0.8	-5.4
35	Other transport equipment	1.0	-3.9	-6.5	-14.5	12.7	-7.4	–	–
36	Manufacturing n.e.c.	238.0	-7.0	-0.2	1.0	68.8	-12.0	17.4	-1.0
37	Recycling	–	-11.2	36.5	57.4	–	-3.6	–	–
D	Total manufacturing	33.7	-5.6	8.6	1.1	7.8	-6.6	3.2	-2.9

Notes: Data for Slovenia is for 1995 instead of 1993 and does not include sectors with less than 3 multinational firms. Data for some industries in Slovakia aggregates the sector below. n.e.c. = not elsewhere classified.

Source: WIIW Database on Foreign Investment Enterprises.

183

The extent of structural and institutional changes will have an important influence on both the short- and long-term effects of productivity growth in the CECs. Since technology transfer within multinational firms involves a commitment of real resources, it may take time before the real effects can be felt (Teece, 1976). Spillover effects are likely to be sporadic during this stage of economic transformation, often being confined to industries that have developed a network of FIEs and domestic-owned firms. In some cases, such as the office machinery and computing equipment industry in Hungary, extensive outsourcing to domestic-owned enterprises have increased the productivity of these firms above the FIE. As a consequence, interpretation of the data should be taken with caution since it reflects the uneven pattern of technology accumulation characteristic of the economic transformation of the region.

4 PRODUCTIVITY GAPS BETWEEN FOREIGN AND DOMESTIC FIRMS IN CENTRAL EUROPE

FIEs had significantly higher labour productivity than domestic enterprises in central Europe. Labour productivity of DEs in the Czech Republic and Slovenia was, on average, less than half the productivity of FIEs, measured as net sales per employee. The difference was somewhat less in Hungary and Slovakia. With few exceptions, labour productivity was higher in every industry. The most notable exception was the Hungarian petroleum and coke industry, which received foreign investment for the first time in 1994. Other exceptions included the primary metal industry in Slovenia and Slovakia, printing and publishing in the Czech Republic, and office and computing equipment in Hungary.

Table 9.2 shows no clear trend in the convergence in labour productivity between MNs and DEs across industries when measured as gross output or sales per employee. The aggregate productivity gap appears to have closed slightly in Slovenia and the Czech Republic, but there are numerous examples where it has increased. In Hungary and Slovakia the gap appears to have widened significantly, but there are clear exceptions such as in the office and computing equipment sector in Hungary. Investment related to privatization and uncertainty about the future of institutional change explains some of the uneven patterns of relative productivity growth. Spillovers also tend to occur over time as competition increases, backward and forward linkages develop, and outsourcing becomes more prevalent.

Table 9.3 shows that the productivity gap between foreign firms and domestic firms appears smaller when measured as value added. Measured

Table 9.2 *Convergence of output/sales per employee between DEs and FIEs*

ISIC Code	Industry	Ratio of labour productivity levels between DEs and FIEs							
		Czech Republic		Hungary		Slovakia		Slovenia	
		1993	1996	1993	1996	1993	1996	1995	1996
15 + 16	Food, beverages and tobacco	0.95	0.64	0.58	0.54	0.84	0.64	0.78	0.77
17	Textiles	0.89	0.95	0.63	0.42	0.97	0.78	0.78	0.72
18	Wearing apparel and fur	1.09	1.09	0.64	0.73	1.29	0.99	0.58	0.78
19	Leather products	1.11	0.78	0.62	0.75	0.41	0.94	–	–
20	Wood products	0.62	0.74	0.46	0.39	0.90	0.64	0.67	0.88
21	Pulp and paper products	0.61	0.62	0.55	0.38	**in 22**	**in 22**	0.32	0.66
22	Printing and publishing	2.08	0.58	0.42	0.12	0.73	0.60	1.32	1.25
24	Chemicals and chemical products	0.68	0.74	0.86	0.61	1.67	1.47	0.67	0.69
25	Rubber and plastics	0.52	0.58	0.35	0.45	–	0.94	0.99	1.03
26	Non-metallic mineral products	0.44	0.36	0.59	0.41	0.36	0.67	0.52	0.47
27	Basic metals	0.70	0.51	0.75	0.51	**in 28**	**in 28**	1.78	1.06
28	Fabricated metals	1.24	0.37	0.42	0.63	1.46	0.70	0.70	0.68
29	Machinery and equipment	1.05	0.76	0.66	0.32	**in 30**	**in 30**	0.61	0.79
30	Office machinery and computers	–	2.41	1.13	2.30	0.36	0.32	0.43	–
31	Electrical machinery	0.67	0.68	0.76	0.54	0.29	0.43	0.74	0.63
32	Radio and television	0.31	0.45	0.34	0.21	0.19	0.18	0.44	0.65
33	Precision instruments	1.02	0.80	0.51	0.65	1.23	1.34	1.28	1.33
34	Motor vehicles	0.27	0.33	0.32	0.14	**in 35**	**in 35**	0.22	0.15
35	Other transport equipment	0.90	1.22	0.62	0.52	0.58	0.22	–	–
36	Manufacturing n.e.c.	0.63	0.27	0.75	0.61	0.37	0.56	0.72	0.57
D	Total manufacturing	0.48	0.52	0.66	0.35	0.69	0.48	0.44	0.46

Notes: Data for Slovenia is for 1995 instead of 1993 and does not include sectors with less than three multinational firms. Data for some industries in Slovakia aggregates the sector below. n.e.c. = not elsewhere classified.

Source: WIIW Database on Foreign Investment Enterprises.

Table 9.3 Convergence of value added per employee between DEs and FIEs

ISIC Code	Industry	Ratio of labour productivity levels between DEs and FIEs					
		Czech Republic		Slovakia		Slovenia	
		1993	1996	1993	1996	1995	1996
15 + 16	Food, beverages and tobacco	0.70	0.47	0.73	0.56	0.64	1.02
17	Textiles	1.33	0.93	1.11	0.73	0.86	1.10
18	Wearing apparel and fur	1.05	1.12	1.22	0.79	1.49	1.02
19	Leather products	1.05	0.69	0.31	0.63	–	–
20	Wood products	0.47	0.58	1.78	0.65	1.08	1.21
21	Pulp and paper products	0.50	0.55	**in 22**	**in 22**	0.48	0.96
22	Printing and publishing	1.87	0.72	0.91	0.55	1.53	1.39
24	Chemicals and chemical products	0.49	0.39	1.44	1.18	0.89	0.96
25	Rubber and plastics	0.59	0.56	–	1.05	0.96	1.04
26	Non-metallic mineral products	0.62	0.39	0.47	0.75	0.47	0.46
27	Basic metals	0.75	0.47	**in 28**	**in 28**	0.99	0.61
28	Fabricated metals	0.86	0.64	1.13	0.64	0.76	0.93
29	Machinery and equipment	1.40	0.79	**in 30**	**in 30**	0.57	0.72
30	Office machinery and computers	–	1.21	0.38	0.41	0.52	–
31	Electrical machinery	1.15	0.89	0.79	1.04	0.67	0.57
32	Radio and television	0.10	0.40	0.24	0.30	0.40	0.67
33	Precision instruments	0.85	1.00	1.22	1.36	2.32	1.63
34	Motor vehicles	0.81	0.53	**in 35**	**in 35**	0.57	0.45
35	Other transport equipment	2.93	1.45	1.36	0.48	–	–
36	Manufacturing n.e.c.	1.18	0.69	0.50	0.52	0.97	0.74
D	Total manufacturing	0.66	0.55	0.77	0.56	0.66	0.73

Notes: Data for Slovenia is for 1995 instead of 1993 and does not include sectors with less than three multinational firms. Data for some industries in Slovakia aggregates the sector below. n.e.c. = not elsewhere classified

Source: WIIW Database on Foreign Investment Enterprises.

on this basis, labour productivity of DEs in 1993 appeared about two-thirds of FIE in Slovenia and the Czech Republic and three-fourths in Slovakia. Moreover, the productivity gap appears to have widened significantly in the Czech Republic as a whole, a very different conclusion from what the gross output measure suggests. This may be due to different relative prices of intermediate goods or factor prices between the FIEs and domestic-owned enterprises. There is evidence across the CECs, and especially in the Czech Republic, that FIEs sometimes pay significantly higher wages and that depreciation in the domestic firms is much lower because the age of capital is much higher.

Table 9.4 shows that the gap between DEs and FIEs appears even wider in Hungary when measured as capital intensity. The capital intensity was about 1.75 times higher in foreign firms than in domestic-owned firms except in Slovenia where the difference was much smaller. Although the FIEs generally have a higher capital intensity than domestic firms, there are numerous examples where it is the other way around. There is no pattern that is consistent across central Europe, but there are notable examples especially in the electrical machinery and wood products industries in Slovenia and the apparel and leather industries in the Czech Republic. By contrast, the differential in capital intensity fell in the Czech Republic and Slovenia indicating that domestic firms have been increasing their investment in fixed capital faster than the FIEs from 1993–96.

Tables 9.2, 9.3 and 9.4 show an uneven pattern of multinational activity which reflects in some rather large productivity differences across central Europe. Figure 9.1 shows the ratio of labour productivity levels between domestic and foreign firms in aggregate manufacturing from 1993 to 1996. This figure suggests that there has been little productivity spillovers within the CECs with the possible exception of Slovenia. The rapidly widening productivity gap in Hungary and Slovakia illustrates this point. However, the elimination of the coke and petroleum sector from Hungary softens the decline significantly and shows how a sector with large changes in ownership can affect relative productivity data and any regression analysis.

5   TESTING FOR PRODUCTIVITY SPILLOVERS

Blomström and Wolff (1994) estimate productivity spillovers in two ways: (1) the rate of labour productivity growth of domestic-owned firms within an industry; and (2) the rate of convergence in labour productivity levels between local and foreign firms within a sector. Both regression forms yielded consistent results in their study of Mexico. Because of certain inconsistencies in the official employment data and the data on FDI, this

Table 9.4 Convergence of capital intensity between DEs and FIEs

ISIC Code	Industry	Ratio of capital intensity levels between DEs and FIEs							
		Czech Republic		Hungary		Slovakia		Slovenia	
		1993	1996	1993	1996	1993	1996	1995	1996
15 + 16	Food, beverages and tobacco	1.08	0.62	0.42	0.29	0.73	0.51	0.42	0.59
17	Textiles	0.19	1.35	0.72	0.36	1.11	0.81	2.48	2.52
18	Wearing apparel and fur	2.38	2.36	0.63	0.44	1.22	0.92	0.53	0.48
19	Leather products	6.23	2.12	0.51	0.17	0.31	1.84	–	–
20	Wood products	0.67	1.39	0.64	0.20	1.78	1.28	17.72	6.76
21	Pulp and paper products	0.62	1.38	0.91	0.92	in 22	in 22	0.18	0.39
22	Printing and publishing	0.14	0.83	0.55	0.39	0.91	0.96	1.39	1.52
24	Chemicals and chemical products	0.65	0.49	0.95	0.46	1.44	1.08	0.47	0.59
25	Rubber and plastics	0.42	0.64	0.31	0.24	–	1.44	1.76	2.13
26	Non-metallic mineral products	0.39	0.32	0.41	0.17	0.47	0.49	0.35	0.43
27	Basic metals	0.51	0.80	0.36	0.33	in 28	in 28	4.06	4.33
28	Fabricated metals	0.63	0.45	0.34	0.45	1.13	0.75	0.41	0.78
29	Machinery and equipment	0.67	0.99	0.56	0.20	in 30	in 30	0.78	0.93
30	Office machinery and computers	–	16.80	0.63	1.29	0.38	0.74	–	–
31	Electrical machinery	0.26	0.87	0.36	0.17	0.79	1.08	0.78	0.59
32	Radio and television	0.52	0.92	1.21	0.76	0.24	1.73	10.79	12.85
33	Precision instruments	0.92	0.78	1.27	0.69	1.22	1.66	0.53	0.52
34	Motor vehicles	0.52	0.55	0.54	0.24	in 35	in 35	0.55	0.63
35	Other transport equipment	0.82	0.83	0.71	0.90	1.36	0.99	–	–
36	Manufacturing n.e.c.	0.28	0.89	0.62	0.48	0.50	0.72	1.43	2.13
D	Total manufacturing	0.54	0.62	0.56	0.27	0.77	0.70	0.60	0.66

Notes: Data for Slovenia is for 1995 instead of 1993 and does not include sectors with less than three multinational firms. Data for some industries in Slovakia aggregates the sector below. n.e.c. = not elsewhere classified.

Source: WIIW Database on Foreign Investment Enterprises.

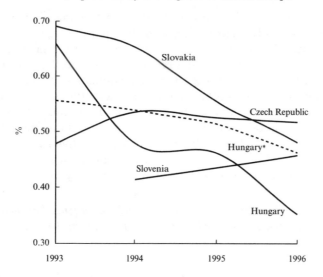

Notes: Hungary* (dotted line) excludes the coke and petroleum industry.

Source: WIIW Database on Foreign Investment Enterprises.

Figure 9.1 Ratio of labour productivity levels between DEs and FIEs in central Europe, 1993–96

analysis will only adopt the second convergence measure. As in Blomström and Wolff (1994), the independent variables include the degree of foreign ownership of the industry and the gap in labour productivity between domestic- and foreign-owned firms in 1993.

The equation for the convergence is written as:

$$CONVERGENCE = \alpha + \beta_1\, FIE + \beta_2\, GAP + \varepsilon$$

where *FIE* is the share of sales in foreign-owned firms in total sales and *GAP* is the ratio of gross output per employee in domestic-owned firms to the ratio of gross output per employee in foreign-owned firms in 1993. Evidence that multinational activity is generating enough spillovers for productivity convergence is present when $\beta_1 > 0$, and evidence that the relatively size of the productivity gap in 1993 leads to productivity convergence is present when $\beta_2 < 0$.

Table 9.5 summarizes the estimation results for the four countries. The negative sign for the coefficient on *FIE* suggests that there are not enough spillovers from multinational activity in central Europe to close the productivity gap. Productivity convergence between foreign and domestic firms appears faster in those industries with a lower share of sales accounted for by FIEs. However, the coefficient is not significant for either the Czech Republic or Slovenia and in both cases the sign turns positive when estimated without *GAP* and remains insignificant. The negative sign for the coefficient on *GAP* suggests that the initial size of the productivity gap does influence the probability of productivity convergence, as suggested by Abramovitz (1989). The one exception is Hungary, but the sign changes once you take out the office machinery and computing industry which already have relatively higher labour productivity in the domestic-owned firms. Also, the estimation for Slovenia should be treated with caution because it includes only the change over one year.

Table 9.5 Regression analysis of productivity convergence between FIEs and domestic-owned manufacturing firms in the CECs

Independent variables	Czech Republic	CONVERGENCE		
		Hungary	Slovakia	Slovenia
Constant	1.406	1.199	2.074	1.473
	(7.83)	(2.49)	(5.98)	(5.61)
FIE	−0.284	−1.081	−2.265	−0.241
	(0.64)	(1.91)	(2.23)	(0.48)
GAP	−0.564	0.409	−0.816	−0.469
	(3.54)	(0.87)	(3.06)	(1.86)
R^2	0.44	0.28	0.46	0.22
F-statistic	6.41	3.38	5.12	1.95
Sample size	19	20	15	17

Note: Absolute value of the *t*-statistic shown in parentheses. Hungary does not include the coke and petroleum industry because it appears as an outlier.

6   CATCHING-UP WITH THE EU

A related issue to whether there is productivity convergence between foreign firms and domestic firms is whether the productivity level of foreign firms is comparable to the EU. Austria provides a good approximation of EU productivity levels since the variances in productivity are low at the 2-digit industry level and Austria is the only member State to have a common border with all four countries. Table 9.6 shows considerable unevenness in the productivity levels between Austria and the different

Table 9.6 *Central European productivity level by type of ownership and industry as a proportion of Austrian productivity level measured in PPP, 1996.*

ISIC Code	Industry	Czech Republic		Hungary		Slovakia		Slovenia	
		FIE	DE	FIE	DE	FIE	DE	FIE	DE
15 + 16	Food, beverages and tobacco	1.17	0.75	0.88	0.48	0.97	0.63	0.99	0.76
17	Textiles	0.45	0.42	0.18	0.08	0.34	0.26	0.63	0.45
18	Wearing apparel and fur	0.55	0.60	0.16	0.12	0.50	0.49	0.85	0.66
19	Leather products	0.57	0.45	0.51	0.39	0.26	0.25	–	–
20	Wood products	0.67	0.50	0.87	0.34	0.53	0.34	0.62	0.54
21	Pulp and paper products	0.75	0.46	1.33	0.51	in 22	in 22	0.52	0.35
22	Printing and publishing	1.03	0.59	0.99	0.12	0.87	0.52	0.59	0.74
23	Petroleum and coke	–	1.71	2.42	8.40	in 24	in 24	–	–
24	Chemicals and chemical products	1.05	0.78	0.29	0.18	0.64	0.94	1.01	0.70
25	Rubber and plastics	0.98	0.57	0.63	0.28	0.91	0.86	0.77	0.80
26	Non-metallic mineral products	1.12	0.40	0.69	0.28	0.70	0.47	1.04	0.49
27	Basic metals	0.97	0.50	1.16	0.59	in 28	in 28	0.50	0.53
28	Fabricated metals	1.38	0.52	0.37	0.23	1.08	0.76	0.97	0.65
29	Machinery and equipment	0.55	0.42	0.70	0.22	in 30	in 30	0.76	0.59
30	Office machinery and computers	0.12	0.28	1.19	2.75	1.00	0.32	–	–
31	Electrical machinery	0.82	0.55	0.56	0.31	0.85	0.36	0.91	0.57
32	Radio and television	0.65	0.29	1.34	0.29	1.50	0.26	0.90	0.59
33	Precision instruments	0.56	0.45	0.51	0.33	0.49	0.66	0.56	0.75
34	Motor vehicles	1.03	0.34	3.40	0.47	in 35	in 35	2.04	0.31
35	Other transport equipment	0.24	0.29	0.36	0.19	1.25	0.27	–	–
36	Manufacturing n.e.c.	1.81	0.49	0.25	0.16	0.92	0.52	1.19	0.68
D	Total manufacturing	1.06	0.55	0.90	0.32	1.07	0.52	1.19	0.55

Notes: Data for Slovenia is for 1995 instead of 1993 and does not include sectors with less than three multinational firms. Data for some industries in Slovakia aggregates the sector below. n.e.c. = not elsewhere classified.

Source: WIIW Database on Foreign Investment Enterprises.

191

CECs. As an aggregate the labour productivity of FIEs in central Europe is comparable to the labour productivity of Austrian firms when measured in purchasing power parities. Labour productivity in the domestic-owned firms was roughly half of the foreign firms, which reflects the better technology of Austrian (and European) production.

There are numerous cases where productivity levels are higher in the CECs, but the automotive industry in Hungary and the Czech Republic and the office machinery and computer industry in Hungary have become interesting cases. In both cases domestic outsourcing has become an important potential source of productivity spillovers (Radošević and Hotopp, 1999). By contrast FIEs in the automotive industry had significantly higher labour productivity than domestic firms and in the case of Hungary it was also significantly higher than in Austria, when measured in PPP. Volkswagen becomes an important investor in Škoda, but often outsources production to Škoda General Manufacturing, a domestic-owned firm. The most obvious example of domestic outsourcing appears in office machinery and computer equipment in Hungary. A concentration of foreign investment by several well-known European and US firms appears in computing equipment with many of them outsourcing their production to domestic-owned firms, especially Videoton (Szalavetz, 1997). These cases suggest that there may be considerable scope for the transfer of technology to central Europe.

7   INNOVATIVE ACTIVITY AND PRODUCTIVITY CONVERGENCE IN CENTRAL EUROPE

An implication of the models of endogenous growth is that R&D activity is a key source of economic growth and productivity convergence. The importance of this activity is found in the way firms create an ability to absorb new technologies from abroad, or from FIEs operating in their home market. In central Europe there is no clear relationship between output growth and R&D expenditures and there is no clear relationship between the share of multinational activity in the economy and R&D expenditures. This suggests that FIEs are not attracted to R&D activity within central Europe. In Slovenia, where an extensive innovation survey was carried out in 1997, there is a clear relationship between the rate of innovation and R&D activity, but not between innovative activity and multinational activity. A simple linear regression model of a cross-section of 20 manufacturing industries shows this relationship (t-statistic in parentheses):

$$\text{INNOVATE} = 0.101 + 0.958\text{R\&D} + 0.002\text{FIE}$$
$$\quad\quad\quad (4.60)\quad (15.47)\quad\quad\quad (0.007)$$
$$R^2 = 0.94$$

The regression shows the relationship between the percentage of firms that induced new products or processes during 1996 (innovate) and the percentage of firms that engaged in *R&D* and the share of firms with some *FIE*. The results confirm that there is a very close and significant relationship between firms that engage in R&D activity and those that innovate but no relationship between firms with foreign investment and innovative activity. There are many exceptions to the rule, such as the Hungarian pharmaceutical industry which makes 40 per cent of total R&D activity and is predominantly owned by MNCs, but there is no clear relationship between R&D activity and sales by FIEs across central Europe.

A small innovation survey carried out during 1996 in Hungary that distinguishes between FIEs and DEs suggests that foreign affiliates tend to engage in more innovative activities, but they do not necessarily introduce more new products. Table 9.7 shows that foreign affiliates tend to carry out product development, license and know-how purchase more frequently than DEs. This tendency appears at all levels of

Table 9.7 R&D activity and technology transfer (percentage of total firms) in Hungary, 1996

Percentage	Metal-processing machinery		Vehicle industry		Telecommunications equipment	
	DE	FIE	DE	FIE	DE	FIE
Base research	1.4	7.0	0	0	2.9	0
Applied research	7.0	17.5	10.5	16.4	18.6	8.8
Experimental research	17.0	35.3	12.1	17.2	29.4	29.6
Product development	43.6	55.5	23.1	41.8	32.3	56.9
Licence purchase	6.0	11.6	7.2	8.2	8.6	31.3
Know-how purchase	3.7	9.4	5.3	8.2	2.9	14.4
R&D activity exists	45.6	62.0	27.7	58.2	47.4	63.9

Notes: Survey included 330 firms in metal processing; 147 firms in motor vehicle industry; and 79 firms in telecommunications equipment industry.

Source: Tamás (1997).

194   *Integration through foreign direct investment*

the innovation process. These results also appear somewhat surprising when compared with the survey results on innovative activity contained in Table 9.8. A much higher percentage of FIEs appears active in product development, but domestic firms were more likely to introduce new products. This was especially the case in telecommunications where the FIEs did not introduce any new products during 1996. The introduction of new technology processes was more uneven, with more domestic-owned enterprises introducing processes in the motor vehicle industry, but less in metal processing and telecommunications. This lack of innovation suggests, as Éltető (1998) points out, that the market share motivated foreign investors more than the science and technology system in Hungary. It may also explain why there is no correlation between FDI and innovative activity across industries in central Europe.

Table 9.8   Innovation activity in Hungary by type of ownership (percentage of total firms), 1996

Percentage	Metal-processing machinery		Vehicle industry		Telecommunications equipment	
	DE	FIE	DE	FIE	DE	FIE
New product introduced	73.7	70.5	71.9	71.8	80.2	0
New technology introduced	46.7	63.0	70.7	29.5	50.2	63.4
Introduction of ISO 9000	38.1	50.7	25.5	25.4	28.8	52.3

Notes: Survey included 166 firms in metal processing; 51 in the motor vehicle industry; and 40 in the telecommunications equipment industry. ISO 9000 is a standard of quality.

Source: Tamás (1997).

8   CONCLUSIONS

The data presented in this chapter show that both the productivity of labour and capital of FIEs is much higher than their domestic counterpart and, as a whole, comparable to labour productivity levels of Austria when measured in PPP. There is, however, no direct evidence of widespread productivity spillovers from FIEs to domestic-owned firms. This is found in the negative relationship between the share of sales of FIEs and the rate of convergence between foreign- and domestic-owned firms. Yet, these results support the advantage of backwardness suggested by

Abramovitz (1989) and they suggest that the domestic-owned firms have the opportunity for productivity convergence, but future prospects will depend on whether these firms have the technological capability to absorb the new technology.

There are certain problems with carrying out an analysis such as this one. Jenkins (1990) discusses some of the difficulties in completing an empirical analysis of FDI at the sectoral level and argues that conventional cross-section analysis of the behaviour of firms at the industry level does not provide adequate evidence of the relationship between FDI and growth. Instead, he suggests that longitudinal industry studies provide a better methodology. One particular problem is that there is a high correlation between FDI and the size of the firm. The data used in this analysis clearly shows that FIEs are generally larger than the domestic-owned firms. Larger firms tend to have certain economies of scale that bias productivity data upwards.

The results in this chapter do not imply that FDI plays no role in facilitating technical change and technological learning. Considering that it takes time to successfully transfer new technology, especially when central Europe is also undergoing an extensive institutional change, the results of the analysis may not seem that surprising. The uncertainty with respect to the data collection process can also create certain biases. Nevertheless, the analysis does suggest that FIEs may not be the panacea that central Europe is looking for. Perhaps more worrying for these countries is the technological infrastructure and absorptive capacities of domestic firms, for this will determine whether they can catch-up with the EU in the long term.

REFERENCES

Abramovitz, M. (1989), *Thinking About Growth*, Cambridge: Cambridge University Press.

Aitken, B. and A. Harrison (1991), 'Are there spillovers from foreign direct investment? Evidence from panel data for Venezuela', mimeo, World Bank.

Bardhan, P. (1998), 'The contributions of endogenous growth theory to the analysis of development problems: an assessment', in F. Coricelli, M. di Matteo and F. Hahn (eds), *New Theories in Growth and Development*, London: Macmillan, pp. 97–110.

Blomström, M. and A. Kokko (1998), 'Foreign investment enterprises and spillovers', *Journal of Economic Surveys*, **12**, pp. 247–77.

Blomström, M. and Persson (1983), 'Foreign investment and spillover efficiency in an underdeveloped economy: evidence from the Mexican manufacturing industry', *World Development*, **11**, pp. 493–501.

Blomström, M. and E. Wolff (1994), 'Foreign investment enterprises and productivity convergence in Mexico', in W. Baumol, R. Nelson and E. Wolff (eds),

Convergence of Productivity: Cross-national Studies and Historical Evidence, Oxford: Oxford University Press, pp. 263–84.

Caves, R.E. (1974), 'Multinational firms, competition and productivity in host-country markets', *Economica*, **38**, pp. 1–27

Dunning, J.H. (1994), 'Re-evaluating the benefits of foreign direct investment', *Transnational Corporations*, **3**, pp. 23–51.

Éltető, A. (1998), 'The economic performance of firms with foreign investment in Hungary', *Institute for World Economy Working Paper*, no. 94.

Grosfeld, I. and G. Roland (1995), 'Defensive and strategic restructuring in central European enterprises', *CEPR Discussion Paper*, no. 1135.

Grossman, G. and E. Helpman (1991), *Innovation and Growth in the Global Economy*, Cambridge: MIT Press.

Haddad, M. and A. Harrison (1991), 'Are there positive spillovers from direct foreign investment? Evidence from panel data for Morocco', *Journal of Development Economics*, **42**, pp. 51–74.

Jenkins, R. (1990), 'Comparing foreign subsidiaries and local firms in LDCs: theoretical issues and empirical evidence', *Journal of Development Studies*, **26**, pp. 205–28.

Kokko, A. (1992), 'Foreign direct investment, host country characteristics and spillovers', Ph.D. Thesis, Stockholm School of Economics.

de Mello, L.R. (1997), 'Foreign direct investment in developing countries and growth: a selective survey', *Journal of Development Studies*, **34**, pp. 1–34.

Nadiri, M.I. (1991), 'U. S. direct investment and the production structure of the manufacturing sector in France, Germany, Japan, and the U.K.', *NBER Working Paper*.

Radošević, S. (1997), 'Technology transfer in global competition: the case of economies in transition', in D.A. Dyker (ed.), *The Technology of Transition: Science and Technology Policies for Transition Countries*, Budapest: Central European University Press, pp. 126–58.

Radošević, S. and U. Hotopp (1999), 'The product structure of central and eastern European trade: the emerging patterns of change and learning', *MOCT–MOST*, **9**, pp. 171–99.

Romer, P.M. (1986), 'Increasing returns and long-run growth', *Journal of Political Economy*, **94**, pp. 1002–37.

Romer, P.M. (1990), 'Endogenous technological change', *Journal of Political Economy*, **98**, pp. S71–S102.

Solow, R. (1956), 'A contribution to the theory of economic growth', *Quarterly Journal of Economics*, **70**, pp. 65–94.

Szalavetz, A. (1997), 'Sailing before the wind of globalization: corporate restructuring in Hungary', Institute for World Economics, Hungarian Academy of Sciences, Working Paper, no. 78.

Tamás, P. (1997), *Egy távlatosabb nemzeti technologiapolitika alapvetései a piaci körülmények között müködö gazdasági szervezetek oldaláról (Basic Features of a Long-term National Technology Policy from the Side of the Economic Organizations Functioning in Market Circumstances)*, Budapest: OMFB.

Teece, D. (1976), 'Technology transfer by multinational firms: the resource costs of transferring technological know-how', *Economic Journal*, **87**, pp. 242–61.

Verspagen, B. (1991), 'A new empirical approach to catching up or falling behind', *Structural Change and Economic Dynamics*, **2**, pp. 359–80.

10. The impact of FDI on the foreign trade of CECs

Andrea Éltető

1 INTRODUCTION

Relations between FDI and foreign trade can be examined from several points of view. One approach is to consider FDI a substitute for trade (exports). In this case the foreign investor decides to invest in the host country instead of exporting to it. Another is to observe the effects of FDI on the host country's foreign trade. The first approach provides more of an *ex ante* analysis, while the second views an *ex post* situation. This chapter adopts the second approach. It observes the effects exerted by FDI and the resulting FIEs on the foreign trade of four CECs: the Czech Republic, Hungary, Slovakia and Slovenia.[1]

The presence and structure of FDI can significantly influence the structure of foreign trade in the recipient country and the effect of the activity of FIEs depends on the investment motives and the host country's structural characteristics. FDI can be *trade-substituting* if it goes to import-substituting activities that supply the domestic market, *trade-promoting*, if its aim is to supply other markets, *trade-complementing*, if it is directed towards rationalized production and backup facilities in export markets, or *trade-diverting*, if it aims to exploit unfilled quotas under preferential trade agreements (Narula, 1996).

These types cannot be clearly distinguished, because investment motivations are often complex, while an increasing proportion of trade is intra-firm within multinational corporations. However, there are two clearly discernible types of FDI that are especially relevant to the small countries examined in this chapter. The effect on the trade structure depends on whether the investment is oriented towards exports or towards the domestic market.[2]

Efficiency-seeking investment is induced by factor-cost differences, caused by different relative factor endowments. The investor is generally a large

197

company with standardized products. To benefit, the recipient country should have a liberalized trade system as well as cost advantages. The four countries analysed here are relatively well endowed with skilled and cheap labour. This is an investment-attracting factor for an investor from a developed country, and accounts for the majority of the greenfield investments. It is characteristic of this group of FIEs to produce mainly for foreign markets. They are mainly active in labour and skilled labour-intensive sectors and some subsectors of the engineering and electronics industries, for which labour-intensive production stages are transferred to the CECs.

Market-seeking investment is found in sectors where economies of scale are present or products are differentiated. Such investments are designed to supply a well-defined market segment in the host country (domestic) or neighbouring countries (regional). For the second to apply, the trade barriers and transport costs (in a wide sense) need to be negligible. In the case of market-seeking investments, the parent company treats its affiliate as an individual production unit, which it only integrates into its international network to a limited extent. The affiliate's products are sold in the local or regional market. The more protected the targeted market, the more attractive it is for market-seeking investors. That is why such firms are often in the food industry, where protection is higher because agriculture and food tend to be excluded from the preferential agreements covering most of the CECs' foreign trade.

These two types of investment have different effects on the host country's balance of trade. Export-seeking investments may improve the trade balance, even if case studies show that many firms tend to import most of their inputs initially. Market-seeking firms, on the other hand, may worsen the trade balance, if their exports are negligible and many of their inputs are imported. However, in the four countries examined, exports may be sizeable even for market-seekers, because the smallness of the domestic economy enhances the importance of the regional market. Smallness induces a relatively high degree of openness (ratio of trade to GDP), because compared to large countries, small countries produce a more limited range of goods and services and usually lack resources. In effect, what would be internal trade for a large country is international trade for a small one. This is especially pronounced where previously larger States have broken up, which is the case with the Czech Republic, Slovakia and Slovenia. The importance of the regional market was further enhanced as investment opportunities for Western firms in the four countries opened up almost concurrently.

2 EXPORT SIZE AND INTENSITY

Foreign investors 'discovered' the CEC region in the 1990s. Both efficiency-seekers and market-seekers have made significant investments here, through greenfield projects and privatization deals. There are two aspects in which FIEs have outstandingly high shares in each of the four countries: investment outlays and export sales.

A close relationship exists between the penetration of the FIEs in each sector and their export performance (Table 10.1). The export share of FIEs divided by their shares in the nominal/equity capital can be called 'exports-to-capital ratio'. Index values above one show that the export share of FIEs in an industry is generally higher than their shares in the nominal (or equity) capital of the same industry. This over-representation is marked in the wood, textile, publishing and printing, basic metals, radio and TV sets and furniture industries in Slovenia. There are also high exports-to-capital ratios in the Czech wood, furniture, leather, clothing and precision instrument industries and in Slovakia in the industries radio and TV sets, instruments and leather. Hungary differs somewhat in not showing any extremely high scores, because the FIEs in every sector have an important role in exports and there is a high penetration of FIEs in every sector. Values below one mean that the export share of the FIEs are low relative to their capital share. This is typical of certain industries oriented towards the domestic market, such as food, minerals and chemicals.

It is interesting to see the differences among countries for each manufacturing branch. The values are dispersed especially widely for wood, publishing and printing, textiles and basic metals. As to the Czech Republic, 1996 values (export data are no more collected) would presumably be lower than for 1994 because the FIEs' share in equity capital rose considerably in some branches (5 times in wood, 13 times in radio and TV sets, 4 times in clothing, and so on). With Slovenia, high exports-to-capital ratios occur even though the FIEs' share in exports is not high, as their share of the nominal capital is even less.

The general experience in developing and developed countries is that FIEs are more export-intensive and more import-intensive than domestic firms. Dunning argues that they are likely to be more trade-oriented than national companies partly because foreign production cannot take place without some trade in intermediate products, and partly because their aim may be to divert or create foreign trade (Dunning, 1993, p. 402). Looking at 'catching-up' countries, this has been confirmed by studies on Ireland (Barry and Bradley, 1997), Portugal (Corado, 1996) and Spain

Table 10.1 Exports-to-capital ratios of FIEs by manufacturing industries

ISIC Code		Czech Republic (1994)	Hungary (1996)	Slovakia (1994)	Slovenia (1996)
15	Food and beverages	**in 16**	0.92	**in 16**	1.07
16	Tobacco	1.32	1.01	1.78	*
17	Textiles	2.74	1.26	0.33	4.13
18	Wearing apparel	3.36	1.09	1.29	0.65
19	Leather	3.91	0.80	2.39	*
20	Wood	9.64	1.16	0.93	8.58
21	Paper and paper products	1.34	1.66	**in 22**	0.85
22	Publishing, printing	0.72	1.81	0.53	7.41
23	Coke and petroleum	0.00	1.00	**in 24**	*
24	Chemicals	1.26	1.07	1.24	0.86
25	Rubber and plastic	1.52	0.88	0.00	2.89
26	Other non-metallic minerals	0.89	0.89	0.54	1.20
27	Basic metals	1.50	1.13	**in 28**	5.13
28	Fabricated metals	1.47	1.25	0.73	1.43
29	Machinery n.e.c.	1.41	1.27	**in 30**	1.35
30	Office machinery	0.00	0.37	0.22	*
31	Electrical machinery	1.96	1.03	0.52	1.16
32	Radio, TV sets	2.02	1.79	2.34	13.99
33	Medical, precision, optical instruments	2.88	1.62	2.60	0.51
34	Motor vehicles, trailers	1.26	1.19	**in 35**	1.63
35	Other transport equipment	1.45	1.52	0.44	*
36	Furniture, manu-facturing n.e.c.[a]	3.02	1.57	1.07	3.42
37	Recycling	0.00	3.37	–	*
*	Industries with less than 3 FIEs	–	–	–	0.44
D	Manufacturing total	1.27	1.09	0.93	1.79

Notes: The exports-to-capital ratio is the share of FIEs in the industry's exports divided by their share in the nominal capital (in the Czech Republic equity capital) of the same industry. [a] n.e.c = not elsewhere classified.

Source: WIIW Database on FIEs; own calculations.

(Martin and Gordo, 1996). The results are the same for the CEC as well, if export intensity is defined as export sales over total sales, although data are not available for every year in every country. Manufacturing FIEs in Slovenia in 1996 exported 65 per cent of their sales, while domestic firms exported only 45 per cent. The same proportions for Hungary were 40 per cent and 22 per cent. FIEs in Slovakia in 1994 showed an export intensity of 52 per cent, as opposed to 43 per cent for domestic firms. The proportions in the Czech Republic in the same year were 41 per cent and 31 per cent respectively.

The export-intensities of FIEs and domestic firms are compared in Table 10.2 by the export intensity ratio. It can be seen that with very few exceptions, the FIEs are the more export-intensive in each industry. (The tobacco and petroleum industries stand out sharply in Hungary. This is because tobacco is almost 100 per cent in foreign hands, while the coke and petroleum branch consists of one, majority State-owned, company in which there is also a foreign stake.)

In most Hungarian sectors the export-intensity ratio is bigger than in the other countries, which apart from the strong export intensity of FIEs refers to the high foreign penetration. The ratio is especially high in the Czech Republic in the field of leather, rubber and plastic, electrical machinery, instruments and motor vehicles; in Slovenia in the printing sector; in Slovakia in the tobacco, furniture and leather branch, which means that FIEs here produce much more for exports than domestic firms.

Export activity by FIEs is rendered easier by their characteristics. First, it is easier for them to finance exports, because they have higher capital endowment than domestic firms and have better credit ratings. Second, often foreign partners also bring secured foreign markets (examples of this are given later). Highly export-intensive FIEs have helped to increase the overall export intensity of some branches to a marked extent. Good examples are the automotive or office and electrical machinery branches.

3   EFFICIENCY- AND MARKET-SEEKERS

The manufacturing branches are roughly grouped according to the distinction drawn in the introduction. One group (EO) consists of export-oriented branches, where export intensity is relatively high. This may be the target of *efficiency-seeking* investors, and includes electrical and office machinery, radio and TV sets, motor vehicles, precision instruments and furniture manufacturing. The other group (DR) consists of

Table 10.2 Export-intensity ratios of FIEs and DIEs

ISIC Code		Czech Republic (1994)	Hungary (1996)	Slovakia (1994)	Slovenia (1996)
15	Food and beverages	in 16	1.507	in 16	1.397
16	Tobacco	1.642	27.187	3.616	*
17	Textiles	1.107	2.137	1.057	1.281
18	Wearing apparel, dress	1.428	1.969	1.190	1.041
19	Leather	2.098	2.030	1.951	*
20	Wood	1.849	2.998	1.272	1.128
21	Paper and paper products	0.879	1.562	in 22	1.272
22	Publishing, printing	0.517	1.757	0.821	9.073
23	Coke and petroleum	–	58.877	in 25	*
24	Chemicals	1.477	2.250	in 25	0.976
25	Rubber and plastic	2.024	1.296	1.477	1.691
26	Other non-metallic minerals	1.158	1.457	0.701	1.345
27	Basic metals	1.405	1.931	in 28	1.329
28	Fabricated metals	0.998	2.088	0.566	1.253
29	Machinery n.e.c.	1.138	3.048	in 30	1.251
30	Office machinery	–	1.210	1.815	*
31	Electrical machinery and appliances	2.252	5.496	in 33	1.280
32	Radio, TV sets	0.640	2.793	in 33	1.286
33	Medical, precision, optical instruments	2.628	3.084	1.037	1.149
34	Motor vehicles, trailers	1.904	1.688	in 35	1.361
35	Other transport equipment	2.227	3.576	1.258	*
36	Furniture, manu-facturing n.e.c.[a]	1.827	2.840	2.360	0.960
37	Recycling	–	2.732	–	*
D	Manufacturing	1.323	1.777	1.193	1.424
*	industries with less than three FIEs	–	–	–	0.436

Notes: Export-intensity ratio: export intensity of FIEs divided by export-intensity of domestic firms. [a] n.e.c. = not elsewhere classified.

Source: WIIW Database on FIEs; own calculations.

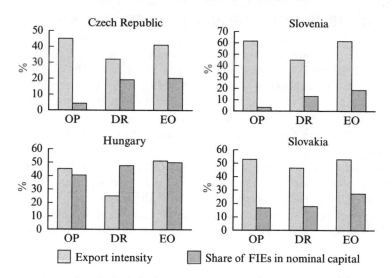

Notes: OP = outward processing industries; DR = domestic and regional market-oriented industries; EO = export-oriented industries.

Figure 10.1 Export intensity and the share of FIEs in nominal capital in manufacturing industries

branches with a characteristically medium or low export intensity, oriented towards the domestic or regional market (with exports directed to neighbouring countries). This may attract *market-seeking* investors, and includes food, beverages, tobacco, wood, paper, printing, minerals, basic and fabricated metals, and chemicals. There is also a third group (OP) covering branches that are export-oriented, but mainly and traditionally dominated by outward-processing activity. This includes textiles and clothing, and leather. (There are overlaps between the groups due to the high level of aggregation within them.)

In each country, the FIEs are present to the least extent in the OP group and to the greatest extent in the EO group, although the DR group follows closely (Figure 10.1). The special features of Hungary, with high FIE shares everywhere, are also manifested. The traditional OP branches (textile and clothing, and footwear) have not been popular with foreign investors (except in Hungary). In the EO group (for example, electrical machinery) there is also some outward-processing activity accompanied by foreign investment.

4   IMPORTS AND FOREIGN TRADE BALANCE

On the import side, surveys and case studies show that FIEs are more import-intensive than domestic firms. In several cases, FIEs play the leading role in the imports of a branch. In Hungary, the imports of FIEs increased, between 1995 and 1996, somewhat more than the average overall imports of the economy, but the increase was much less than in previous years. In 1996, the FIEs' share of total manufacturing imports was slightly higher than their share of total manufacturing exports. The FIEs accounted for over 80 per cent of the imports in tobacco, chemical, non-metallic mineral, electrical machinery and other transport equipment.

There were three branches in which less than 50 per cent of the total imports were due to FIEs: clothing, basic metals and furniture. As for the trade balance of the FIEs, this was negative in 7 of the 23 manufacturing branches: tobacco, paper, publishing, rubber, petroleum, radio and TV sets, and other transport equipment. In office machinery, where FIEs accounted for 50 per cent of the imports, there was an overall deficit, but the FIEs were in surplus. Regression figures based on an empirical survey of Hungarian manufacturers showed that majority foreign ownership does not increase the probability of greater imports. There is no significant difference in the import propensity of two firms with the same parameters, one of which is in majority foreign ownership (Kopint, 1997, p. 146).

In Slovakia's case, FIEs accounted for 44 per cent of total imports of the country and 37 per cent of total exports in 1997. The FIEs' share in imports increased by 5 per cent over 1996, but their share in exports increased by only 1 per cent. However, a significant share of the imports is taken by large firms in trade and smaller JVs that import consumer goods for the Slovak market, while the exports are supplied by manufacturers (Hosková and Vágnerová, 1998). There are no data available regarding imports of FIEs in Slovenia or the Czech Republic.

5   FIES AND THE GEOGRAPHICAL DISTRIBUTION AND PRODUCT COMPOSITION OF TRADE

The reorientation of CECs' foreign trade towards the EU, thoroughly analysed by others (Gács, 1994; Landesmann, 1994; Havlik, 1996; Brenton and Gros, 1997), took place around 1990–91. The collapse of the Comecon markets obliged firms in the CECs to seek new markets. Much of their production capacity had to be closed down or restructured. The main directions of exports became Western markets as early as 1991. Foreign investors discovered the region, so that some foreign investment was already taking place in 1990. However, major flows of FDI and the massive production by FIEs can be stated to have begun about 1991–92. So the FIEs cannot be said to have played a big part in the geographical reorientation of trade as such. They only intensified (and later modified) an already existing structure.

Turning to the present geographical distribution of trade, more than 60 per cent of the exports and imports of the four countries are with the EU. Indeed, the EU share has been increasing steadily since the major reorientation of trade, partly because of the accessions by the European Free Trade Association (EFTA) countries and partly through a real growth of trade. FIEs have contributed to the latter in two ways. On the one hand, US, Japanese and other non-EU multinational have set out to penetrate the EU market through the associated CEC countries. (The association agreements with the EU set out to establish industrial free trade, while applying rules of origin for products.) On the other hand, *efficiency-seeking* firms and multinationals from the EU found good opportunities for out-sourcing some of their activity to the four countries. Foreign investment provided new markets and contacts for privatized firms.

This is apparent in a *survey* of FIEs made in 1997 by the Czechinvest agency. More than 100 firms polled reported a steady increase in the number of their export markets. The proportion of firms exporting to five or more countries almost doubled between 1993 and 1996. A large number of FIEs were able to increase their export sales in every year. The destination pattern of the FIEs' exports was broadly similar to the pattern of origin of the FDI, the main directions being Germany, Austria and Slovakia. Apart from that, the survey confirmed that FIEs are highly export-intensive (Pomery, 1997).

FIEs also play a role in increasing trade among the four countries. Foreign investors have been able to utilize earlier contacts of the acquired domestic firms. Those aiming to conquer new markets have established a base in one of the four countries, intending to supply the whole region from there. The FIEs have contributed strongly to a revival of intra-regional trade in recent years. They are active especially in chemicals, foods and raw materials, where they treat the whole region as a domestic market (*market-seeking*).

A good example of such a regional strategy is provided by the *Unilever* group. The production capacities of Unilever (mainly in household chemicals) have been distributed around the CECs to supply the local and regional market. The group bought firms in Hungary and the Czech Republic in 1992, and also invested in Poland. Washing-up liquid production has been concentrated in Hungary, production of soaps and Pond's creams has been established in the Czech Republic, and Polish affiliates produce frozen fish fingers.[3] Ice-cream, margarine and other foodstuffs are produced simultaneously in these countries.

Our hypothesis is that FIEs have had a strong influence on the change of the *product composition* of the exports. The first 10 product groups (calculated at SITC 5-digit level, 3464 pieces of data)[4] were responsible for 25–30 per cent (less in the case of the Czech Republic – Table 10.3) of the total exports to the EU in 1997 with a considerable increase from 1993.

Table 10.3 Size and share of the first 10 SITC 5-digit product groups in the EU's imports from the four countries

| | 1993 | | 1996 | | 1997 | |
	ECU thousands	%	ECU thousands	%	ECU thousands	%
Czech Republic	769 086	16.00	1 551 639	15.97	2 170 177	18.59
Hungary	653 499	16.60	2 032 467	23.13	3 509 759	30.29
Slovakia	223 092	19.32	896 189	26.32	1 153 804	29.09
Slovenia	596 701	20.88	1 063 721	24.98	1 222 940	26.28

Source: Eurostat Comext database; own calculations.

In each country, the top product group has by far the largest share. It is interesting that in three of the four countries, the leading group is the same: motor vehicles for the transport of persons, other than public transport (SITC 78120). This accounts for 6.9 per cent of EU imports from the Czech Republic, 10.3 per cent of those from Slovakia and 12.2 per cent of those from Slovenia in 1997. In Hungary, the top product group, with 10.9 per cent, is reciprocating piston engines for cars of a cylinder capacity exceeding 1000 cc (SITC 71322). Ignition sets are in third place and motor vehicles are in fifth place, with 2.9 and 2.1 per cent respectively. Behind this obviously lie the effects of multinational affiliates in the car industry. The exports of this sector are extremely concentrated, not only on FIEs, but on a few major companies. In Hungary, more than two-thirds of the exports of road vehicles and components are made by three companies: Opel, Suzuki and Audi. In Slovenia, one single major investor, Renault is active, as is the Volkswagen affiliate Škoda in the Czech Republic. Recent statistics show that concentration has been continuing and the weight of these product groups increased further in 1997–98. So multinational producers of cars and car components have had an increasingly important role in these countries' exports in recent years.

As far as the other important product groups in the top 10 are concerned, Slovenia's includes clothing, footwear, rubber tyres and electrical machinery, and Hungary's contains telecommunications equipment, storage units for automatic data processing and electrical machinery products, as well as footwear. All these except footwear are branches where FIEs are prominent. With the Czech Republic and Slovakia, metal products such as iron and aluminium, coal, wood, clothing and footwear are found along with electrical machinery in the top 10 groups. Here the role of FIEs is important only in the last industry but not in the others.

Since the top 10 groups account for such a large and increasing share in exports at such a detailed product level, concentration can be called an important characteristic of the four countries' exports to the EU. This can be underlined by statistical calculations on concentration. Table 10.4 gives values for the Hirschman concentration coefficient,[5] which increased in all four countries between 1993 and 1997. The concentration level is the lowest in the Czech Republic, but it increased here, too.

Table 10.4 Concentration of exports (Hirschman coefficient for EU-15 imports)

	1993	1996	1997
Czech Republic	0.0757	0.0758	0.0914
Hungary	0.0777	0.1088	0.1365
Slovakia	0.0885	0.1160	0.1344
Slovenia	0.1028	0.1420	0.1412

Source: Own calculations based on SITC 5-digit nomenclature, Eurostat Comext.

As it turns out from the product structure, the increasing concentration of exports has arisen from the activity and export growth of FIEs in certain branches. Other branches have not shown such a rapid rate of increase, so that their weight in the total exports has fallen. The data show a general trend for two groups of products still important at the beginning of the 1990s to lose export shares in the period up to 1996. One group consists of textile, clothing and leather products, which are strongly associated with outward-processing and not dominated by FDI. The decrease of this group was sharpest in Hungary and Slovakia, less pronounced in the Czech Republic and Slovenia. The other group whose share tended to decrease is iron and steel and raw material products (wood, fossil fuels, cement). Meanwhile, there was a marked increase in all four countries in the electrical, office and transport machinery groups, where foreign investment had taken place.

It is worth examining how significant these changes were in the whole structure of the four countries' exports to the EU in 1993–96. The finger similarity index[6] provides one view of the structural changes (Table 10.5). The value of the index shows the extent to which the export structure in 1996 resembled that of 1993. Clearly, considerable changes have taken place over three years, as the export structures are only 60 to 70 per cent similar. The highest degree of similarity (the least change) can be seen in Slovenia and the least degree of similarity in Slovakia. In the Slovakian case, several product groups that were important in total exports in 1993 (above 1 per cent) lost share considerably by 1996. These are mainly some clothing articles, iron and steel, and cement products. Instead of these, leading positions were taken by new goods such as ignition sets, gear boxes and car components.

Table 10.5 Structural changes in exports to the EU, 1993–96

	Czech Republic	Hungary	Slovakia	Slovenia
Finger similarity index (%)	70.78	65.57	59.20	73.57

Source: Calculations based on SITC 5-digit level.

The change from traditional export products towards new products of industries dominated by FDI has been supported in Hungary by the so-called customs-free zones. Industrial customs-free zones were created under Act XXIV/1988 on foreign investment. Firms with foreign participation may establish themselves as customs-free zones under the control of the customs authorities if they export at least 80 per cent of their output outside Hungary. Within the zone, the firm is regarded as foreign for exchange-control and foreign-trade purposes; the accounts are kept in foreign currency, but the firm remains liable to Hungarian taxation, except for VAT (Antalóczy, 1998). In 1998, there were about 100 industrial customs-free zones in Hungary. Most of the companies involved were 100 per cent foreign-owned, greenfield investments acting in engineering and transport equipment producing industries. 36 per cent of Hungary's exports and 25 per cent of its imports were linked with customs-free zones, which produced a trade surplus of US\$ 1801 million which was a significant positive contribution to the country's balance of trade. The role of these zones will lessen as the general level of customs tariffs comes down and the currency regulations are liberalized. In any case they will be an important topic at Hungary's negotiations for EU entry. Even if derogation is obtained, the zones will have to transform into 'normal' companies after EU accession.

6 COMPARATIVE ADVANTAGES OF THE CECS

The changes observed in the export structures raise the question of whether the comparative advantages behind the trade of the CECs are changing as well. According to the traditional theory of comparative advantage, factor endowments induce countries to specialize their trade in goods whose production is intensive in factors they possess in abundance. In the CEC the abundant factor is a skilled, relatively cheap labour force, so that they have usually had comparative advantages in labour-intensive industries (and sometimes resource-intensive ones). So do foreign investors tend to favour these branches?

Rojec (1998) used revealed comparative advantage calculations to show that data from Slovenia do not confirm this hypothesis. Foreign investors do not seem to be seeking factor-cost advantages by entering industries where the host country has comparative advantages. They are tending to invest in relatively capital-intensive industries (paper-mills, construction materials, tobacco, electrical machinery), although the importance of labour-intensive industries (clothing, fur, wood, furniture) to the economy and trade remains high. One possible reason why Rojec's results fail to confirm the hypothesis is that foreign investors may be viewing comparative advantages differently from the calculated results. Another may be that the more capital-intensive branches chosen by foreign investors may include activities that are quite labour-intensive and require a skilled workforce (for example, assembly of car components or electrical parts). This seems to be confirmed by sectoral analysis on a more detailed level.

A study by Wolfmayer-Schnitzer (1998) classified manufactures according to factor intensity at SITC 3-digit level and defined four groups: human capital-intensive, physical capital-intensive, labour-intensive and resource-intensive industries.[7] Also distinguished within the human capital-intensive group were high-tech and medium-tech production. Within these high-tech and medium-tech groups there were more labour-intensive and more capital-intensive subgroups. The author found that the CECs' traditional field of revealed comparative advantages (RCAs) covered the resource-intensive and labour-intensive spheres. In some human capital-intensive goods disadvantages were decreasing, especially in Hungary and the Czech Republic. The last year analysed was 1994, but by the same methodology, we calculated RCA indices[8] (based on export/import ratios) for 1993, 1996 and 1997 as well, concentrating on the labour-intensive and human capital-intensive product groups in the CEC–EU trade (Table 10.6).

Table 10.6 RCAs by technology levels and factor intensities in manufacturing

	Czech Republic			Hungary		
	1993	1996	1997	1993	1996	1997
Human capital-intensive	**–0.54**	**–0.45**	**–0.32**	**–0.41**	**–0.13**	**0.06**
High-tech	–1.04	–0.83	–1.05	–0.59	–0.35	–0.18
Labour-intensive	–0.67	–0.32	–0.39	–0.07	–0.06	–1.25
Capital-intensive	–1.77	–1.76	–1.81	–1.24	–0.78	0.28
Medium-tech	–0.50	–0.46	–0.26	–0.62	–0.36	–0.16
Labour-intensive	–0.77	–0.48	–0.42	–0.47	–0.22	–0.01
Capital-intensive	–0.10	–0.43	–0.05	–0.81	–0.61	–0.50
Others	–0.26	–0.06	–0.17	0.33	0.50	0.58
Labour-intensive	**0.05**	**0.36**	**0.30**	**0.12**	**0.29**	**0.08**

	Slovak Republic			Slovenia		
	1993	1996	1997	1993	1996	1997
Human capital-intensive	**–0.83**	**–0.80**	**–0.38**	**–0.30**	**–0.25**	**–0.22**
High-tech	–1.64	–1.93	–1.68	–0.44	–0.64	–1.06
Labour-intensive	–2.23	–1.69	–1.55	0.23	–0.13	–0.46
Capital-intensive	–1.20	–2.13	–1.79	–2.46	–1.93	–2.14
Medium-tech	–0.85	–0.79	–0.31	–0.25	–0.15	–0.08
Labour-intensive	–1.26	–0.95	–0.90	0.03	0.04	–0.01
Capital-intensive	–0.30	–0.71	0.22	–0.52	–0.32	–0.14
Others	–0.15	–0.26	–0.03	–0.39	–0.50	–0.52
Labour-intensive	**–0.35**	**0.29**	**0.21**	**–0.20**	**0.22**	**0.25**

Source: Own calculations based on CEC-EU trade, SITC 5–9 groups, Eurostat Comext.

The findings in Table 10.6 reveal some interesting trends. On the one hand, the revealed comparative advantages strongly increased or were reinforced in the labour-intensive manufactured products between 1993 and 1996. The RCA index increased most in Slovakia and Slovenia and least in Hungary. From 1996 to 1997, however, a certain stagnation and a radical decrease in Hungary can be observed in the labour-intensive field. This latter decrease is caused by the fact that the import of the labour-intensive 'parts and accessories for motor vehicles' (SITC 78439) more than tripled during one year and this heavily deteriorated the foreign trade balance and the RCA value of the group.

On the other hand, there is a general improvement in the index for human capital-intensive products. The RCA index even turns into positive in Hungary for 1997, which already means a slight comparative advantage. Within the human capital-intensive group, the comparative disadvantages in high-tech products[9] decreased the most in Hungary, and remained more or less the same in the other countries. Within the high-tech subgroup, the disadvantage in general is smaller in the labour-intensive field. The only exception is Hungary, where in the capital-intensive field the RCA index turns into positive. This is caused by the automatic data processing storage units produced and exported by the IBM (4.5 per cent of total Hungarian exports in 1997).

With medium-tech products, there is a general and significant improvement in the indices. This improvement comes mainly from the capital-intensive field in three countries and from the labour-intensive field in Hungary. In Slovakia, the RCA index of the capital-intensive medium-tech product group even turns strongly into positive, which is due to the 'motor vehicles for the transport of persons' belonging to this group, which is the leading export product of the country (10.3 per cent of total exports). In Hungary, the improvement in the labour-intensive medium-tech field is caused mainly by the considerable export increase of TVs, video receivers and refrigerators. Hungary is the only country to show comparative advantages (positive RCA values) in the 'others' subgroup of the human capital-intensive group because of the fact that 'internal combustion piston engines' and 'electricity distribution equipment' belong here, these being also leading Hungarian export products.

So, it can be stated that the four countries examined have clear comparative advantages in labour-intensive goods, and rapidly decreasing comparative disadvantages in human capital-intensive goods. These disadvantages may turn into advantages in the short term (as it happened in Hungary in 1997), and this manifests the changing of the RCAs, although to different extents in each country. As we have seen, the changes are mainly caused by one or two dominant product groups produced by multinationals (principally in the automotive industry). Since the RCA index used here is calculated from the export and import ratios of products, the RCA value will rise if exports are increasing considerably faster than imports. This is just what happened in some human capital-intensive products (cars and components, electronic equipment and so on) between 1993 and 1997.

In all four countries, the production of these products is already dominated by efficiency-seeking FIEs. This shows that it was not principally the cheap labour that interested foreign investors, but the qualified labour force.[10] They invested in industries where they could utilize this endowment. Due to the activity of the FIEs, skilled labour intensity is increasingly manifest in foreign trade, so that these four countries can

serve as an example of the positive effect FDI exerts on revealed comparative advantages. Apart from that, if the background and supplier economy
are well developed and the main attractive factor becomes skilled rather
than merely cheap labour, the risk of a later FDI diversion decreases.

7   FDI AND OUTWARD-PROCESSING TRADE

Foreigners are also present in the non-skilled labour-intensive branches,
but in many cases the presence takes the form of outward-processing
co-operation rather than FDI. Outward-processing trade (OPT)[11] is
undoubtedly significant in all the countries examined. It can be seen
from Table 10.7, which shows the share of OPT in total EU imports,
that the share of outward-processing is highest in the Czech Republic
and Slovenia and that the share of OPT declined in all four countries
between 1993 and 1997.

*Table 10.7   The share of OPT in total imports by the EU and the share of
German OPT in total OPT imports, per cent*

	Czech Republic	Hungary	Slovakia	Slovenia
OPT imports/total EU imports, 1993	12.42	20.25	13.46	11.89
OPT imports/total EU imports, 1996	10.61	13.16	10.14	5.72
OPT imports/total EU imports, 1997	8.47	10.05	9.28	5.15
German OPT/total OPT imports, 1997	85.75	48.47	58.51	74.93

Source: Eurostat Comext; own calculations.

The connections between OPT and FDI are at least twofold. On the one
hand, there is a kind of substitution between these two types of co-operation
between domestic and foreign firms. OPT constitutes a form of co-operation
that avoids the risk and cost of direct investment, but may bring the same
improvements in the competitiveness of the foreign firm's products. This
classical OPT, widespread in light industry (clothing, textiles, footwear, furniture), became popular at the beginning of the 1990s in the CEC.

On the other hand, the type of OPT is often linked with FDI, mainly in
electronics and engineering. The foreign firm establishes a venture or buys

an existing company by privatization, and then essentially carries out OPT-type activity in the new affiliate. If the motivations are examined, it emerges that this type of co-operation is favoured by efficiency-seeking investors. As for the general trends, company interviews show that out-ward-processing has been increasingly connected in the 1990s to FDI in the world economy, and investors attracted mainly by low labour costs and the advantageous regulations governing OPT (Antalóczy and Sass, 1998).

The difference between the two types of OPT can be explained by the different characteristics of the products produced under them. In electronics and engineering, foreign companies are reluctant to divulge all the information and production techniques and technologies for the product. So they prefer a solution that brings the OPT-like activity 'inside' the company. Such considerations do not arise in light industry, so that the commissioning foreign firms tend not to acquire a share in the firm carrying out the outward-processing. (Where the OPT takes place as intra-firm trade, it is sometimes not registered as OPT.)

The distinction between types of OPT is important also for their different impacts on economic development. In the traditional type where OPT is not linked with FDI, the foreign company only makes use of the labour-cost differences (taking into account skills and productivity) and its extreme sensitivity to changing labour costs makes it more footloose. The room for development of the performing company and of relations between the two companies is very limited. In the second type, when OPT is linked to capital participation, there are much greater spillover effects and integration of the foreign OPT commissioning company into the domestic economy. The link with FDI and the characteristics of the product provide greater opportunities for upgrading. There is a more balanced partnership between the domestic company and other foreign affiliates or the parent, and there is a higher domestic value added.

A certain shift can be observed in the sectoral structure of registered outward-processing, away from light industry and towards engineering, as can be seen in Table 10.8. The structure is markedly different in the Czech Republic, where the clothing industry has a much smaller share, and electrical and power-generating machinery a much greater share in OPT than in the other three countries.

Besides the registered OPT, there has presumably been an increase in the 'OPT-like' activity, between a foreign parent and its local affiliate, or between affiliates mainly in electronics and engineering. According to Oláh (1998), this type of 'OPT-like' co-operation also includes some of the activity in Hungary's customs-free zones, marked by a high share of imported inputs. However, the proportion of imported inputs may fall as the contribution of local suppliers increases.

Table 10.8 *The sectoral structure of OPT (per cent of OPT imports by the EU)*

SITC Code and Industry	Czech Republic			Hungary			Slovakia			Slovenia		
	1993	1996	1997	1993	1996	1997	1993	1996	1997	1993	1996	1997
71 Power-generating machinery	4.69	4.76	2.60	1.52	1.29	2.00	0.55	0.07	0.02	0.18	0.27	0.52
72 Specialized machinery	3.04	1.95	3.51	0.48	0.64	1.06	0.75	3.71	4.83	0.60	0.85	0.62
76 Telecom. and sound recording equipment	0.82	1.93	1.51	3.00	6.31	6.76	0.74	4.56	9.03	0.09	0.00	0.01
77 Electrical machinery	13.47	16.67	22.90	10.76	11.43	13.97	2.31	4.48	6.30	2.51	1.62	0.46
78 Road vehicles	3.44	3.90	4.18	0.99	0.61	0.73	9.36	1.91	1.17	0.73	0.31	0.33
FDI-linked OPT	*25.46*	*29.21*	*34.7*	*16.75*	*20.28*	*24.52*	*13.71*	*14.73*	*21.35*	*4.11*	*3.05*	*1.94*
82 Furniture and parts	3.27	1.34	1.19	1.41	1.54	1.09	3.98	2.23	1.58	1.77	0.46	0.55
84 Clothing	37.66	33.39	27.19	59.25	57.90	54.89	70.77	70.37	65.41	83.74	84.38	83.46
85 Footwear	8.21	2.32	2.15	13.79	5.03	6.12	6.18	2.65	4.07	6.09	2.90	3.51
65 Textile yarn fabrics	4.68	9.06	7.35	3.02	6.34	4.37	1.00	2.69	2.42	0.55	1.34	0.69
Traditional type OPT	*53.82*	*46.11*	*37.88*	*77.47*	*70.81*	*66.47*	*81.93*	*77.94*	*73.48*	*92.15*	*89.08*	*88.21*

Source: Own calculations based on Eurostat Comext.

8   MAIN CONCLUSIONS

Foreign trade has an essential economic role in the four small central European countries examined in this study. In each case the dominant direction of exports and imports is the EU, into which these countries intend to integrate. By the end of the 1990s it has become obvious that firms with foreign participation play an important role in shaping the structure of foreign trade. Data show that FIEs play a bigger role in the exports of all four countries than they do in other fields (for example, capital endowment or investment). The further main conclusions to be drawn are the following.

- The two most important types of investor in the CEC are efficiency- and market-seekers. Efficiency-seekers have a high propensity to export. The small size of the countries stimulates that exports arise also from market-seeking investments to the neighbouring countries.
- A common feature that coincides with international trends is for firms with foreign participation to be more trade-intensive on average than domestic companies. Often they are found to be concentrated in more export-oriented sectors. Furthermore, some sectors have become more export- or trade-oriented as a result of the activity of FIEs.
- The activity of FIEs is apparent behind the main export product groups of the four countries. Larger greenfield investments have given a powerful impetus to exports in several branches in Hungary. FIEs are responsible for an increasing concentration of the export product structure in all four countries. Furthermore, the presence of FDI in some sectors (especially electrical machinery and cars) has caused the structure of these countries' trade with the EU to change significantly.
- The massive exports of the FIE-dominated sectors have contributed to changes in these countries' RCAs, although to differing extents. In 1997 already a comparative advantage in human capital-intensive products was revealed in the case of Hungary, and a strong decrease in disadvantages could be observed in Slovakia, Slovenia and the Czech Republic. This shows that foreign investors have been able to make use of the skilled labour pool of these countries.
- Hungary, with its high level of FDI penetration and significant greenfield investments, its FIE-dominated foreign trade and its strongly changing RCAs, presents a more positive picture than the other three countries.

- Another impact of FIEs on exports is through their outward-processing activity. In certain labour-intensive branches outward-processing dominates, seemingly as a substitute for FDI in light industry, and in connection with FDI in the engineering industry.
- Between 1993 and 1997 the export-oriented branches in which important foreign investments were made increased their production and exports rapidly. Meanwhile, several other branches stagnated or declined. This caused a concentration of the foreign trade structure. While FDI has helped CECs to integrate into the Western production systems, the concurrent product and geographical concentration of exports has made their economies more dependent and thus vulnerable.

NOTES

1. The author thanks Magdolna Sass and Miklós Szanyi for their remarks and advice.
2. The emphasis here is on two of the four types described by Dunning (1993), because the resource-seeking and strategic asset-seeking types of investment are less important to the small CECs.
3. *Business Week*, 4 May 1998 and 4 July 1994.
4. The Eurostat Comext database was used, so that exports to the EU are represented by figures for EU imports from the countries concerned.
5. The original name of the coefficient is Herfindahl–Hirschman index and the definition is the following: $H = [\sum_i s_i^2]^{1/2}$, where s_i is the share of the product group in total exports. The index varies between $1/n^{1/2}$ here (0.0169) and 1 (full concentration).
6. $F = \sum min(X_{93}, X_{96})^* 100$, where X_{93} and X_{96} are the shares of the commodity in total exports in 1993 and 1996.
7. The indicator of labour intensity was the hours worked per gross capital invested, human capital intensity is based on the share of scientists, technicians and office employees in total employment. For a product group to be assigned as intensive in some factor the indicator had to exceed the average value by 10 per cent (Wolfmayr-Schnitzer, 1998).
8. RCA = the *ln* of the relation between the export/import ratio of a specific technology class and the ratio of total exports to imports of manufactured goods. The disadvantage of this type of RCA is that it only contains the data of the exporting country and does not show its performance compared to other countries. The index can increase even if domestic demand and import decreases but export remains the same as before.
9. Certain chemicals, medicines, automatic data processing equipment, electric machinery, engines, transistors, aircraft and optical instruments belong here.
10. This statement is reinforced by the survey results described in Éltető and Sass (1998) on the motivations of foreign investors. For market-seekers, the prime motivation was to increase local market share, followed by prospects for economic development. For efficiency-seekers, the main factors were the qualified workforce and stable political situation.
11. OPT refers to the situation in which an industrial firm shifts some or all of its manufacturing (usually the labour-intensive parts that are separable from the total manufacturing process) to a foreign country. We use the definition of OPT found in customs statistics, when materials are exempt from customs tariffs if they are temporarily exported for processing. Duty need only be paid on foreign value added.

REFERENCES

Antalóczy, K. (1998), *Vámszabadterületek a világgazdaságban, az Európai Unióban és Magyarországon (Customs-free Zones in the World Economy, the European Union and Hungary)*, Budapest: Integrációs Stratégiai Munkacsoport (Strategic Task Force for European Integration).
Antalóczy, K. and M. Sass (1998), 'A bérmunka szerepe a világgazdaságban és Magyarországon' ('The role of outward processing in the world economy and in Hungary'), *Kögazdasági Szemle (Economics Review)*, August, pp. 747–70.
Barry, F. and J. Bradley (1993), 'FDI and trade: the Irish host-country experience', paper presented at the Royal Economics Society Annual Conference, University of Staffordshire, 24–6, March.
Brenton, P. and D. Gros (1997), 'Trade reorientation and recovery in transition economies', *Oxford Review of Economic Policy*, **13** (2), pp. 65–76.
Corado, Cristina, J. Rato and N. Clérigo (1996), 'FDI in Portugal', in J. Witkovska and Z. Wysokinska (eds), *Foreign Direct Investment – East and West*, Lodz: University of Lodz, pp. 24–57.
Dunning, J.H. (1993), *Multinational Enterprises and the Global Europe*, London: Addison-Wesley.
Éltető, A. (1998), 'The economic performance with firms with foreign investment in Hungary', Institute for World Economics working paper no. 94, July, p. 30.
Éltető, A. and M. Sass (1998), 'Motivations and behaviour of Hungary's foreign investors in relation to exports', *Working Paper*, no. 88, Institute for World Economics of the Hungarian Academy of Sciences, Budapest.
Gács, J. (1994), 'Hungary', in *The Economic Interpenetration between the European Union and Eastern Europe, European Economy*, **6**, 191–225.
Havlik, P. (1996), *The CEECs' Export Competitiveness in the Manufacturing Industry*, Wien: WIIW.
Hosková, A. and S. Vágnerová (1998), *Direct Foreign Investments in Slovakia with the Focus on the Banking Sphere*, Bratislava: Institute of Monetary and Financial Studies, National Bank of Slovakia.
Kopint (1997), *Konjunktúrajelentés (Business Activity Report, No. 2)*, Budapest: Kopint-Datorg.
Landesmann, M. (1994), 'Czechoslovakia', in *The Economic Interpretation between the European Union and Eastern Europe, European Economy*, **6**, 191–225.
Martin, C. and E. Gordo (1996), 'Spain in the EU: adjustments in trade and direct investment and their implications for real convergence', Working Paper, no. 127, Fundación FIES, Madrid.
Narula, R. (1996), *Multinational Investment and Economic Structure*, London and New York: Routledge.
Oláh, A. (1998), 'Van-e kapcsolat a bérmunka és a gépipar, mint húzóágazat között?' ('Is there a link between outward processing and engineering as a growth industry?'), *Ipari Szemle (Industrial Review)*, **2**, pp. 22–3.
Pomery, C. (1997), *The First Czechinvest Annual Survey on FDI in the Czech Republic*, Prague: Czechinvest.
Rojec, M. (1998), 'The impact of foreign direct investment on the efficiency and restructuring of Slovenia's manufacturing sector', paper prepared for Phare-ACE project no. P96-6183-R, mimeo.
Wolfmayr-Schnitzer, Y. (1998), 'Trade performance of CEECs according to technology classes', in *The Competitiveness of Transition Economies*, WIFO/WIIW/OECD.

11. FDI in the balance-of-payments framework

Josef Pöschl

1 INTRODUCTION

In recent years there has been a lively and controversial discussion of the causes of financial crises, first in Mexico and then in east Asia, and more recently in Russia and Brazil. Discussions also focused on measures to prevent further cases (Eichengreen *et al.* 1995; Chote, 1997; *The Economist,* 1997; Koromzay, 1997; López Gallardo, 1997a, 1997b; Milesi-Ferretti and Razin, 1997; Mundell, 1997; Obstfeld, 1995; Powell, 1997; Hahn, 1998; Tobin, 1998). Even economic miracles collapsed, and the question of how further crises could be prevented appeared to be urgent (Krugman, 1994).

Analysts identified current account deficits and the banking systems' fragility as the main financial problems underlying the recent crises. However, there are no clear indicators to warn of imminent danger, nor is there a generally accepted strategy for reducing proneness to crisis. The mere fact of a high and rising current account deficit is *not* a reliable indicator. It could either result from low and dwindling competitiveness of domestic companies or from the contrary: the country's more dynamic industries try to increase their position *vis-à-vis* foreign competitors through a massive import of advanced technology, in this way enlarging the trade deficit. A deficit may cause much more concern in the first case than in the latter.

It seems to be important how deficits in the current account are covered. This is shown in the financial account. If in a country the net inflow of FDI is the dominant factor of deficit financing, this may be a hint that the deficits are related to an upgrading of productive capacities, thus allowing for a positive assessment.

CECs generally have some trade deficits. Experts are worried because in some of the CECs also the current account deficit is high and rising. It is not just current account deficits and fragile financial systems which continue to plague CECs, but also relatively high inflation and structural

218

deficiencies. In addition, all the CECs have liberalized foreign trade almost completely and capital flows quite extensively.

Capital flows have become an important factor in CECs, both at company level and macroeconomically. In recent years, transition economies, and emerging markets in general, have found that mostly the capital account drives the current account rather than vice versa. The question of how to respond to capital inflows is controversial. Most countries have sought to resist the impact of capital inflows on the exchange rate and hence on the current account. At times, though, this has placed them in a dilemma (Koromzay, 1997).

Massive capital inflow can do even more than offset the current account deficit: it can increase currency reserves and lessen the vulnerability to currency crises. It also means availability of additional funds, better capital allocation and capital transfers. On the other hand, if the net inflow continues for a longer period, then it also tends to expand the monetary basis and may feed inflation. It may be primarily attracted by expectations of quick gains thanks to high interest rates. This can push up the exchange rate and may ultimately elevate the real exchange rate to a level causing an unsustainable deficit on the current account. As experience from the Czech Republic illustrates, high interest rates may fail to protect the economy against a currency crisis. Another example is Russia, where in summer 1998 a dramatic increase in interest rates did not prevent a currency crisis.

In developed countries, financial markets act as the brain of the economy. This means that their information role is quintessential and the question of market imperfections and limited applicability of standard welfare theorems is highly relevant (Stiglitz, 1998). Following adverse experiences in the Far East, many analysts are now questioning whether in emerging markets and transition countries the preconditions for a far-reaching liberalization of financial markets are being met.

Reversing capital liberalization now would be difficult. Governments supposedly fear this would damage the country's international reputation, so they are, together with the central banks, targeting *ex post* an improvement of the preconditions. It was not possible within just a few years to create ownership structures in the CECs enabling companies to modernize rapidly. The decisive exception was privatization relying on FDI. For this reason, the Hungarian economy now seems quite sound.

The first sections of this chapter use empirical data to discuss how vulnerable individual CECs are in terms of their balance of payments. It should become clear that although the figures are there, it is somewhat difficult to interpret them as measures of vulnerability. The circumstances in which a current account deficit emerges and the way it is financed are important.

The subsequent sections deal with the difficulties CECs face when the net inflow of FDI is not sufficient to cover the current account deficit. They may try to attract other types of capital inflow through high interest rates, arguing that this policy is instrumental in reducing their high inflation rates. However, under liberalized capital flow conditions these tactics may fail. Monetary policy keeps interest rates high, while under conditions of liberalized capital flows they should gradually approach international levels. High interest rates allow the currencies to appear stronger than the fundamentals would suggest. A case study of the Czech economy's development between 1996 and 1998 illustrates the problems that can result from such a strategy. The final section speculates how financial crises can be more effectively prevented.

2   THE NEED FOR COVERING AN IMPORT SURPLUS: A COMMON FEATURE OF ALL CECS

CECs tend to record current account deficits. Table 11.1 shows the dimension of the deficits, relating them to GDP data. In the Czech Republic, the deficit started to develop when, in 1994, the GDP began to grow, and it peaked in 1997, the year of the currency crisis. In Hungary, the deficit gradually declined in recent years from a very high level in 1994. In Poland, a methodological change produced a positive figure for 1995, but the problem reappeared in the subsequent years. Slovakia experienced a massive deterioration of the current account in 1996, a year of high GDP growth. Slovenia was the only country which never recorded a marked deficit.

The deficits in the current account followed from deficits in the trade balances. In all CECs imports usually comfortably exceeded exports. Table 11.2 shows how far export receipts were able to cover import expenditures in recent years.

Table 11.1   Current account in per cent of GDP

	1993	1994	1995	1996	1997	1998
Czech Republic	1.3	−2.0	−2.7	−7.6	−6.2	−1.9
Hungary	−9.0	−9.4	−5.6	−3.7	−2.1	−4.8
Poland	−2.7	−1.0	4.6	−1.0	−3.0	−4.4
Slovakia	−5.0	4.8	2.3	−11.2	−9.9	−10.1
Slovenia	1.5	4.2	−0.1	0.2	0.2	0.0

Source: WIIW Database.

Table 11.2 Trade balance: coverage of goods' imports through exports
(imports = 100)

	1993	1994	1995	1996	1997
Czech Republic	96.4	92.0	85.4	78.7	83.1
Hungary	71.4	67.7	84.0	84.3	91.9
Poland	85.6	95.3	92.6	75.0	70.7
Slovakia	85.4	100.9	97.4	79.4	85.7
Slovenia	97.5	95.3	89.7	90.5	91.6

Source: WIIW Database.

Imports exceeded exports in all countries apart from Slovakia in 1994. In the Czech Republic, coverage of imports by exports fell below 80 per cent in 1996, but recovered somewhat in 1997 following a currency crisis. In Hungary it reached its lowest point of 68 per cent in 1994, but the trend was reversed completely by a draconian austerity package in spring 1995. Poland seemed to have reached an alarmingly low ratio of 71 per cent in 1997 but this is partly explained by the fact that a large proportion of its exports are unregistered. The situation looks much better if this is taken into account. The country introduced 'unclassified transactions' as a special current account item in 1995. It accounted for 31 per cent of imports in the first year, but fell to 16 per cent in 1997. In Slovakia the ratio fell below 80 per cent in 1996, but improved in 1997 following a restrictive import policy. This was despite the dollar value of exports falling. Slovenia's exports have continuously covered some 90 per cent of import expenditure over the past few years.

3 INCOMPLETE COVERAGE THROUGH OTHER CURRENT ACCOUNT ITEMS

Current account items other than exports are potential sources for financing imports. These items include services (transport, travel and others), income flows and transfers. In the Czech Republic, Hungary and Slovenia, services produce a considerable surplus covering over 5 per cent of imports. On the other hand, the net result of income flows was negative in all countries in recent years except for Slovenia. This is especially true for Hungary which has to service high foreign debt. All countries had a positive balance of transfers. The extent to which the sum of exports, services, incomes, transfers and – in the case of Poland – unclassified transactions, could cover import expenditures can be seen from Table 11.3.

Table 11.3   Coverage of goods' imports through all other current account items* (imports = 100)

	1993	1994	1995	1996	1997
Czech Republic	103.1	95.5	94.6	84.4	88.4
Hungary	69.5	65.2	83.7	90.0	95.4
Poland	85.3	94.7	122.1	95.8	88.9
Slovakia	90.6	110.0	104.4	81.1	86.9
Slovenia	103.1	108.4	99.8	100.4	100.8

Note: *Exports, services, factor income, transfers and – in the case of Poland – unclassified transactions.

Source: WIIW Database.

Only in Slovenia were other current account items able to cover 100 per cent or more of imports in recent years. In 1996 and 1997, at least, all other countries showed a gap. This narrowed in the Czech Republic, Hungary and Slovakia in 1997, but widened in Poland.

4   DIFFERENT DEGREES OF DEFICIT COVERAGE THROUGH FDI

Deficits in the balance of trade and current account do not necessarily threaten stability. It would be immediately endangered if currency reserves declined considerably. Currency reserves can even expand with a current account deficit if the net inflow of capital is large enough to more than offset it. This was, for example, the case in Mexico before the 1994 crisis (López Gallardo, 1997b).

There has been much discussion about whether there is a clear indicator of the limits to a sustainable current account deficit. Some analysts say that a deficit over 4 per cent of GDP is alarming, others say 6 per cent. However, new studies indicate that there is considerable doubt whether there is such a simple answer, claiming a country's whole situation has to be taken into account. James Powell stresses that even large current account deficits should be of little concern if they reflect strong private investment (Powell, 1997). Equity financing, and FDI in particular, is securer than debt financing. This means that one important aspect is how the current account deficit is financed. Balance-of-payments statistics differentiate between three main groups of capital flows: FDI, portfolio investment and 'other investment'.

The groups differ in many respects. If a country experiences an external shock, for example, it makes a difference how the current account deficit was financed in the past. If it relied mainly on borrowing, then the country itself must bear most of the burden from the shock. With equity financing (especially FDI), asset prices can adjust, so that foreign investors share part of the negative impact. This is the case because different types of capital flow exhibit different degrees of volatility: very high in the case of short-term debt and portfolio investment, but much lower in the case of FDI.[1] FDI expresses an investor's long-term engagement in a country. In the CECs, FDI flows are mainly one-way, into the countries. They may be massive one year, but modest in another. However, a massive reversal of such flows is hardly feasible, therefore a country's stability is not immediately threatened by a high current account deficit if there is sufficient FDI to finance the deficit.

Tables 11.4 and 11.5 shows (i) to what extent FDI financed import expenditure in recent years, and (ii) to what extent total current account items plus FDI financed imports. The maximum figure for financing

Table 11.4 Coverage of goods' imports through net inflow of FDI (imports = 100)

	1993	1994	1995	1996	1997
Czech Republic	3.8	4.3	10.0	5.0	4.7
Hungary	20.5	9.8	28.9	11.8	7.7
Poland	3.7	3.0	4.6	8.4	7.9
Slovakia	2.1	2.6	1.5	1.2	0.7
Slovenia	1.8	1.8	1.8	1.9	3.2

Table 11.5 Coverage of goods' imports through net inflow of exports, services, income and transfer, FDI* (imports = 100)

	1993	1994	1995	1996	1997
Czech Republic	106.9	99.8	104.6	89.5	93.1
Hungary	90.1	75.0	112.7	101.8	103.1
Poland	89.0	97.7	126.7	104.3	96.8
Slovakia	92.7	112.6	106.0	82.3	87.6
Slovenia	104.9	110.2	101.6	102.3	104.0

Note: *Plus unclassified transactions in the case of Poland.

Source: WIIW Database.

imports through FDI was achieved by Hungary in 1995 with 29 per cent. FDIs contribution to covering import expenditure in 1997 was rather significant in Poland and Hungary, less impressive in the Czech Republic and negligible in Slovakia.

From a balance-of-payments point of view, no threat to stability seems to exist in Hungary and Slovenia. Poland's situation also looks quite healthy, though the trend is negative. The 1997 figures for the Czech Republic and Slovakia indicate a stability problem, though this was less acute than in 1996.

One interesting argument was raised by John A. Tatom, who maintains that a current account deficit is less alarming if a country is growing rapidly (Tatom, 1997). In his opinion, faster-growing economies are likely to have higher rates of return on capital and, therefore, attract a capital inflow that has its counterpart in a current account deficit. The higher the growth, the larger the sustainable current account deficit. Tatom uses a simple criterion of whether the deficit (in per cent of GDP) exceeds the growth rate by two percentage points or more. Table 11.6 applies this criterion to CECs.

Table 11.6 Gap between current account deficit in per cent of GDP and GDP growth rate, (percentage points)

	1993	1994	1995	1996	1997	1998
Czech Republic	−1.9	−1.2	−3.7	3.7	5.2	4.6
Hungary	9.6	6.5	4.0	2.4	−2.3	−0.4
Poland	−1.1	−4.2	−11.6	−5.1	−3.8	−0.5
Slovakia	8.9	−9.8	−9.6	4.6	3.4	6.4
Slovenia	−4.4	−9.5	−4.0	−3.3	−4.4	−4.4

Source: WIIW Database.

In Table 11.6, a negative number contains a positive message. It means that the current account deficit is lower than the GDP growth rate. In Poland, for example, the current account deficit in 1997 was 3.0 per cent of GDP, and thus 3.8 percentage points lower than the growth rate (6.8 per cent). According to Tatom's rule of thumb, a positive figure higher than two indicates an unhealthy situation. This was the case for Hungary until 1996, and in the Czech Republic and Slovakia from 1996 onwards. This indicator is no substitute for others, covering instead an additional facet.

Tatom stresses that the relationship between current account deficit and competitiveness is not simple (Tatom, 1997). Some analysts interpret a deficit as an indicator of domestic companies' low competitiveness. This can but need not be the case. It is possible for both trade and current account deficits to worsen, while acceleration in economic growth largely concentrates on export- and import-competing sectors and is led by them. Companies may be in urgent need of rapidly expanding their productive equipment, possibly covering this in part by importing investment goods, resulting in above average capacity and output growth in these sectors. Tatom's examples include the US electrical equipment, non-electrical machinery and transport equipment industries in the early 1980s. Trade and current account deficits ballooned in these industries even more than in the economy as a whole; at the same time, production and productivity growth were higher than the manufacturing sector average.

5 FEEDBACK EFFECTS: FDI MAY BOTH COVER AND AMPLIFY CURRENT ACCOUNT DEFICITS

FDI tends to stimulate imports. It frequently finances new projects, or expands and modernizes existing production facilities and is in these cases inevitably associated with substantial imports of new and advanced machinery and intermediate goods. Such kinds of import contribute to diversifying, deepening, or upgrading the industrial base and thus accelerate structural change (United Nations, 1997, pp. 85–94).

The first phase of FDI generally brings about an increase in imports. At a later stage of such a project, after the targeted company has been modernized, exports may also increase. The net effect on the balance of trade depends on the project's purpose and the nature of activity (United Nations, 1997, pp. 85–94):

- With foreign affiliates seeking to establish themselves in a market, imports will exceed exports, especially in the project's initial phase when imports also include equipment.
- Foreign affiliates based on resource or efficiency-seeking are more likely to export more than they import.
- Finally, in the case of strategic asset-seeking investments, consequences for foreign trade largely depend on the type of activity. In Asia, for example, exports were low in the chemical industry, but high in electrical machinery.

In a second phase local sourcing usually increases because transnational corporations are eager to fully integrate host countries' suppliers into their group network (Naujoks and Schmidt, 1995).

A considerable proportion of FDI concentrates on service sectors and trade and has in this way an impact on the volume of visible and invisible imports and exports. In a more indirect way, the category of 'other services' is also heavily influenced by capital flows, especially FDI in the current period and earlier, irrespective of which industry it was directed at.[2] Foreign investment companies often make use of services from abroad (consulting, auditing and so on), and other services are likely to increase in importance within the balance of payments in the future.

Capital inflows also influence income flows registered on the current account.[3] Their impact tends to increase over time. The reasons for this are twofold: such payments rise in line with the accumulated stock of inward FDI, and FDI projects only become profitable after some time. All kinds of capital inflow have important effects on the current account, not just directly but also indirectly through their impact on GDP and exchange rates.

6   MACROECONOMIC ENVIRONMENT: FACTORS (NOT) IMPEDING FDI

A glance at different exchange rate policies gives the impression that stability considerations did not impact FDI to any larger degree. This seems to be true with regard to the stability of both the price level and the exchange rate. Hungary and Poland recorded relatively high rates of inflation, but attracted at the same time more FDI than the Czech Republic, Slovakia and Slovenia, countries with relatively low inflation. In the same way, there is no evidence that devaluation deterred foreigners from investing in CECs. Hungary attracted most FDI into the region in the first half of the 1990s, with Poland being equally successful in more recent years. The Czech Republic and Slovakia attracted much less FDI despite maintaining constant exchange rates. Slovenia's case also shows that the opposite is not necessarily true: depreciation is not automatically linked with high FDI inflow. The exchange rate environment does not seem to exert a major influence on FDI. Also, CECs with lower budget deficits were not those that were more successful in attracting FDI.

In recent years, both the Czech Republic and Hungary had to face a severe economic crisis. In 1997, the Czech currency crisis initiated an overall economic crisis resulting in a GDP stagnation (in 1997) and even decline (in 1998). The standard interpretation is that the crisis uncovered significant structural shortcomings of the Czech economy and FDI declined dramatically. This was not the case in Hungary, when in 1995 an austerity package depressed GDP growth in a similar way, but less (down to +1.5 per cent in 1995 and +1.3 per cent in 1996). This quasi-stagnation did not curb FDI inflow at all. Quite the contrary, it reached its highest ever level in 1995 (US$ 4.4 billion).

7 COVERING TRADE DEFICITS THROUGH CAPITAL INFLOWS OTHER THAN FDI

At least, superficially, massive inflow of portfolio and other investment has clear positive aspects.[4] Additional funds become available and better capital allocation and more technology transfer are possible. It has a positive impact on currency reserves thus lessening vulnerability to currency crises. On the other hand, if it continues over a longer period of time, it tends to increase the monetary basis, frequently seen as causing an overheating of the economy (Chote, 1997) and, in this way, an upward pressure on inflation. It may, therefore, threaten the competitiveness of domestic producers of tradable goods in the national and international markets. Potential future problems in debt servicing are an additional threat. Under exchange rate flexibility, inflationary pressure may be at least partially offset by the resulting currency appreciation. Relative to non-tradable goods, prices of imported goods will decrease so that the share of non-tradables in total consumption is likely to decline.

Under a regime of fixed exchange rates, a massive inflow of capital could stimulate monetary authorities to reduce the assumed inflationary impact through sterilization activities (Ul Haque *et al.*, 1997). Other interventions could entail more restrictive fiscal policies or currency appreciation. Each of the three instruments (sterilization, fiscal austerity and appreciation) can be inappropriate in a specific situation. Sterilization is not possible if the central bank does not have the right instruments and if financial markets are not developed sufficiently. Fiscal policy measures are slow. Fiscal austerity does not necessarily improve the current account. There is ample evidence that the 'twin deficits' hypothesis is generally wrong. Current account deficits are not always caused by actions that raise fiscal deficits. Indeed, evidence suggests that this is hardly ever the case (Tatom, 1997). Finally, appreciation may have an undesired effect on the competitiveness of domestic firms. Controlling capital flows may be useful for a limited period of time (Ul Haque *et al.*, 1997). It can be used to restrict foreign currency holdings, thus limiting the domestic financial institutions' mediation of foreign capital inflow and reducing the proportion of short-term capital.

A report to Commonwealth finance ministers recommends several steps to be taken before a country liberalizes its capital account (Chote, 1997):[5]

- cutting government borrowing, inflation and current account deficits;
- strengthening domestic financial markets;
- tackling other structural economic distortions.

CECs have liberalized their capital markets despite the fact that they continue to be plagued by relatively high inflation, current account deficits, weak financial systems and structural deficits. Reversing capital liberalization now, however, would be difficult. Instead, CECs should try to reach the required standards as soon as possible. The banking sector's inefficiency also has an adverse impact at the micro-level. In an investment survey conducted in the Czech Republic, managers of FIEs earmarked inadequate quality of banking services as a major barrier to investing and modernizing (Mertlík, 1997). Their domestic counterparts were much less inclined to do so.

8   PROBLEMS IN DEFENDING THE EXCHANGE RATE PEG IN A SITUATION WHERE FDI DOES NOT COVER THE CURRENT ACCOUNT DEFICIT

The question of whether emerging market countries should peg their exchange rates remains. Even IMF executive directors have become much less enthusiastic about fixed exchange rate regimes (Chote, 1997). Two aspects are important here: exchange rate pegs can be the quickest and most effective way of breaking self-fulfiling expectations of high inflation, but at the same time they can be dangerous in emerging markets where investors prefer the security of short-term debt and borrowing in a foreign currency.

Doubts about interest rates' suitability for defending currencies are also growing. A sharp rise in interest rates has a major effect on demand when short-term borrowing prevails. This means weak banking systems are placed under more pressure, not least because a marked increase in interest rates lowers the overall level of economic activity. Bank closures are quite likely to reduce credit availability, destroy informational capital, increase uncertainty and decrease the net worth of banks. Later, if the exchange rate peg is broken, devaluation raises the cost of servicing foreign debt, thus depressing the economy still further. Robert Chote suggests a country should have an exit strategy to escape its peg (Chote,

1997). Julio Gallardo stresses the importance of securing high capital utilization as a precondition for growth resumption, rather than emphasizing high rates of investment and savings as a precondition for crisis management (López Gallardo, 1997a).

Joseph Stiglitz points out that some countries confronted with an exchange rate crisis see themselves as facing a trade-off between adverse effects of exchange rate depreciation and interest rate increases (Stiglitz, 1998). This, however, has no empirical justification, as tests have found, if anything, a positive interest rate differential is associated with an appreciating currency, but this result only concerns normal times. If periods of crisis are also included then the results are mixed, with negative correlation between interest rates and exchange rates in some cases, and positive in others. Stiglitz argues that an increase in the interest rate may discourage capital inflows if potential investors regard it as an emergency measure by the central bank to defend a given exchange rate peg. In such a case there is no trade-off and the higher interest rates weaken the economy directly, actually exacerbating the exchange rate's fall. Jeffrey Sachs is also sceptical about defending an exchange rate through high interest rates, as he made clear in a recent interview: 'Because such defences don't work, they lead to a lot of damage' (Sachs, 1998).

9   THE CECS' POLICY RESPONSE TO BALANCE-OF-PAYMENTS PROBLEMS

In recent years, Slovenia targeted a balanced current account, demonstrating in the process that it is indeed possible to keep it balanced. The main instrument was exchange rate policy, based on managed floatation of the Slovenian currency. From a balance-of-payments point of view, there was no need for FDI. In fact, capital flows were kept low so that their impact on the exchange rate was rather limited. Furthermore, real GDP growth was modest, so limiting import growth.

The other countries in the region emphasized fighting inflation rather than balancing the current account. The Czech Republic, and in a more pragmatic manner Slovakia, too, attempted to keep the nominal exchange rate constant, thus allowing no opportunity for depreciation related price boosts for imported goods. This policy failed in the Czech Republic in 1997, and in October 1998 it was abandoned by Slovakia. Hungary and Poland, starting from high initial inflation, have decided to follow a policy of pre-announced permanent devaluation (crawling peg).

It may well be that policy makers in countries with high inflation and liberalized capital markets are in a trap. If they use high interest rates as the traditional instrument for fighting inflation then they may face difficulties. It is intended to restrict the monetary base, but may actually attract massive capital inflow if foreign investors expect higher gains in that country than in others. For those who contract deals in terms of CEEC currencies, the nominal rate of interest and the expected rate of depreciation are significant. The gap between the discount rate and depreciation rate between 1993 and 1997 may serve as a rough indicator for some types of portfolio investments lower profitability limits (Table 11.7).

Table 11.7 Discount rate minus depreciation rate

	1993	1994	1995	1996	1997
Czech Republic	10.6	7.9	5.1	13.0	11.8
Hungary	12.3	12.1	−7.6	6.3	13.3
Poland	3.7	−0.1	4.5	16.1	18.9
Slovakia	9.3	5.8	4.7	10.6	13.6
Slovenia	−13.3	0.0	5.9	1.2	7.6

Source: WIIW Database.

In 1997, the discount rate was over 10 percentage points higher than the rate of depreciation in all countries except Slovenia. For those foreign portfolio investors who think that this proportion will not narrow very much, these countries must be interesting. For international lenders of money, confidence in being repaid is also decisive (Stiglitz, 1998). For both reasons short-term capital may be prevailing.

A massive inflow of capital may cause upward pressure on the exchange rate even if the current account exhibits a considerable deficit. In this way it can lead to a further widening of the current account deficit. Indeed, strong real currency appreciation may ultimately threaten the competitiveness of enterprises. There is a strong tendency towards real appreciation in CECs (Table 11.8), but above a certain degree it can overtax the competitive position of enterprises.

The policy of high interest rates appears to be problematic under the circumstances of full capital account mobility. It would be interesting to ask what the more viable alternatives are. This is difficult to answer, but there is some evidence that inflation declined in those CECs where growth rates were significantly positive, and increased where economic development came to a standstill or turned negative.

Table 11.8 *Real depreciation (+): depreciation rate adjusted by producer*
price index (PPI)

	1993	1994	1995	1996	1997
Czech Republic	−10.8	−4.5	−3.0	−6.9	−3.5
Hungary	−0.8	5.1	4.8	−5.2	−11.8
Poland	−5.1	2.2	−3.9	−5.8	−5.9
Slovakia	−12.4	−3.5	−3.6	−5.7	−8.9
Slovenia	8.0	−1.5	−7.7	1.9	−3.5

Source: WIIW Database.

10 CASE STUDY: HUNGARY'S FDI AND FDI-RELATED BALANCE-OF-PAYMENTS FLOWS

To be able to service high foreign debt, Hungary had to secure massive compensating capital inflows. Starting from the early 1990s, the country was very successful in attracting direct foreign investment and gained a leading position among CECs in this respect. In the earlier years, a high proportion of FDI inflows targeted the manufacturing sector, for example, 56 per cent in 1991. Later, the proportion gradually decreased to less than 40 per cent in 1996[6] whereas the shares of services and public utilities increased.

In Hungary's manufacturing the share of FIEs already amounted to 55 per cent of output in 1994; 66 per cent of exports and 79 per cent of investment. On the other hand, their share in the manufacturing's total employment was only 37 per cent, a fact that indicates that they achieved much higher labour productivity than the rest of the sector.

Figure 11.1 shows how FDI and selected FDI-related balance-of-payments flows developed from 1994 to 1998.[7] It also gives the impression that a high inflow of FDI in 1995[8] was followed by a jump in total exports and technology imports (SITC 7) two years later. However, such a reasoning would be over simplistic. In Spring 1995, a crisis led the government and national bank to introduce tough austerity measures. As can be seen from the figure, this resulted in a stagnation of total exports as well as SITC 6 and SITC 7 imports, but did not stop the FDI inflow. GDP growth only recovered in 1997. It is obvious from this figure that in 1997 the Hungarian economy was able to respond in a very pronounced way to widening export opportunities. At the same time, only a modest increase in the import of intermediate goods (SITC 6) contrasted with a

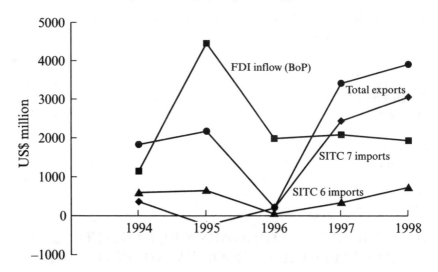

*Figure 11.1 Changes in Hungary's FDI inflows and in FDI-related trade
flows, 1994–98*

very strong increase in the import of machinery (SITC 7, which includes
transport equipment), pointing to a massive rise in investment.[9]

With the increasing stock of FDI implying an enlarging participation
of FIEs, within the current account both the net inflow of 'other services
excluding government services'[10] and the net inflow of income from
direct investment became markedly negative. This is shown in Figure 11.2
and reflects exactly what one would expect from a massive inflow of FDI
in the longer run. The deficits in these two balance-of-payments positions
are still relatively low and can be expected to amount in 1998 to some
4 per cent of imports each.

In countries that have accumulated high FDI inflows, after some years the
outflow of profits can be expected to increase, and the import of business-
related services is likely to rise. One of the influences impacting these flows is
the fact that transnational enterprises search for a cost- and tax-saving allocation of revenues. Thus, in the longer run, the positive balance-of-payments
effect of a continuing net inflow of FDI will be paralleled by increasing negative effects on the balance of income and services. This fact does not reduce
the positive long-run impact of FDI in other fields such as the business
sector's integration into international networks and the import of advanced
technology. As Figure 11.3 shows, in Hungary's balance of payments the
negative impact of accumulated former FDI is in its dimension approaching
the positive effect of new FDI.

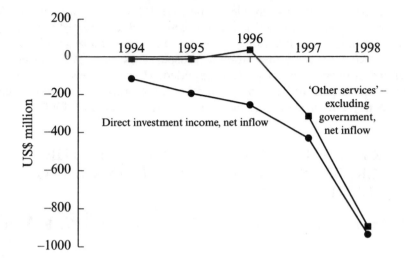

Figure 11.2 Hungary's FDI-related service and income flows, net, US$ million

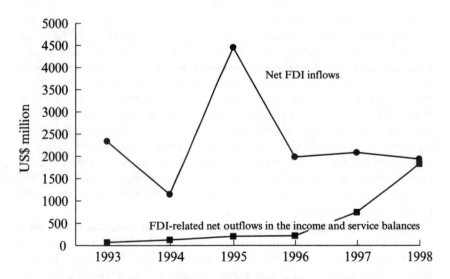

Figure 11.3 Hungary's net FDI inflows and FDI-related net outflows in the income and service balances

The overall pattern seems clear. The FDI inflow into Hungary is likely to have boosted imports of investment goods and contributed to a strong upsurge in exports, including a rise in the share of more sophisticated goods. After the economy started to prosper, imports of business-related services and transfers of profits expanded. However, these balance-of-payments items do not only increase in connection with cyclical prosperity, but also as a long-term result of accumulated FDI inflow.

11   CASE STUDY: THE CZECH WAY INTO THE CRISIS – STIMULATING DEBT FINANCING RATHER THAN FDI

The starting conditions for the transformation of the Czech and the Hungarian economies were different in many aspects, one of them being a high foreign indebtedness of Hungary and a low one in (former) Czechoslovakia. As a consequence, to be able to service its debt, Hungary had to attract the inflow of foreign capital – primarily FDI. Meanwhile, it seems that this necessity may have been good luck for the Hungarian economy. The Czech government under the leadership of Václav Klaus thought that domestic forces would be able to do most of the restructuring job. The Czech privatization campaign was hindering rather than favouring a massive inflow of FDI. As the Czech Republic has always been the most developed of those countries, a lot of companies were attractive for foreign investors, and supposedly they often found more indirect ways when direct access was closed. Nevertheless, large parts of the Czech business sector proved not to be able to restructure sufficiently and suffered from low or unfavourable access to international markets and networks. Under these circumstances, when the economy started to become more dynamic, exports were not able to keep up with imports, and the balance-of-payments problem escalated rapidly, as becomes obvious from Tables 11.1 to 11.4. Unfortunately, the policy response to the problem was inappropriate.

Statistical evidence (Table 11.9) may lead to the conclusion that after 1995 two forces simultaneously strangulated Czech GDP growth: the real interest rate's rise to a level between 9 per cent and 10 per cent, and the koruna's permanent real appreciation. We use an industry-oriented concept of real interest rate, defining it as a gap (in percentage points) between nominal interest rate and industrial producer price inflation. In a similar way, real appreciation measures the increase in Czech industrial producer prices relative to German producer price inflation, taking into account shifts in the nominal exchange rate.

Table 11.9 Real interest rate, real depreciation and growth in the Czech Republic, 1995–97; nominal interest rate, nominal depreciation, Czech and German producer price inflation

	Mar. 1995	June 1995	Sept. 1995	Dec. 1995	Mar. 1996	June 1996	Sept. 1996	Dec. 1996	Mar. 1997	June. 1997	Sept. 1997	Dec. 1997
Nominal interest rate [a]	13.5	13.1	13.3	13.1	12.8	13.4	14.0	13.6	13.6	20.4	15.8	15.8
Depreciation rate *vis-à-vis* DM (year on year)	7.0	4.3	3.1	3.2	-1.7	-3.2	-4.9	-5.4	-5.8	2.6	5.4	9.9
Czech producer price inflation (year on year)	7.3	7.6	7.8	7.6	5.7	5.0	4.2	4.2	4.3	4.3	5.3	5.6
German producer price inflation[b]	1.7	2.2	2.2	1.4	-0.1	-0.6	-0.7	-0.3	0.5	1.4	1.4	1.1

Notes:
[a] on new credits.
[b] year on year approximate figures for 1997.

Real interest rate, real depreciation and GDP growth

	Mar. 1995	June 1995	Sept. 1995	Dec. 1995	Mar. 1996	June 1996	Sept. 1996	Dec. 1996	Mar. 1997	June. 1997	Sept. 1997	Dec. 1997
Real interest rate [a]	6.2	5.5	5.5	5.5	7.1	8.4	9.8	9.4	9.3	16.1	10.5	10.2
Real depreciation [b]	1.4	-0.9	-2.3	-2.7	-7.1	-8.4	-9.3	-9.5	-9.2	-0.2	1.5	5.3
GDP growth, year on year	6.6	6.8	6.7	5.4	4.6	4.7	3.4	3.2	1.2	0.5	-0.1	2.2

Notes:
[a] Nominal interest rate on new credits minus change in industrial producer prices (year on year).
[b] *Vis-à-vis* the DM, calculated with Czech and German producer price changes.

Sources: Czech Statistical Office; German Statistical Office.

As Table 11.9 shows, annual GDP growth was close to 7 per cent in the second quarter of 1995, when the real interest rate was 5.5 per cent and real appreciation insignificant. Then the real interest rate climbed to almost 10 per cent in 1996, and annual real appreciation was close to 10 per cent from the second quarter of 1996 through to the first quarter of 1997. The GDP growth rate gradually declined correspondingly, falling to 0.5 per cent in the second quarter of 1997, the period of the currency crisis. In the third quarter, GDP even fell slightly (by 0.1 per cent) because of the damage caused by flooding in Moravia and due to an extremely high real interest rate. In the last quarter of 1997, the interest rate was back to a little over 10 per cent, and real depreciation *vis-à-vis* Germany amounted to over 5 per cent. Not surprisingly, GDP grew by 2.2 per cent in that quarter.

Growth resumed in the last quarter of 1997 indicating that Czech enterprises were quick to respond to the fact that a lower exchange rate improved their competitiveness both at home and abroad. In this way, the currency crisis in May 1997 changed the overall trend in foreign trade development via the resulting depreciation. As Table 11.10 illustrates, export revenues covered less than 80 per cent of import expenditures in the first quarter of 1997, but 93 per cent one year later.

Table 11.10 Foreign trade developments from 1993 to 1998

Annually	1993	1994	1995	1996	1997
Exports in % of imports	98.9	93.0	85.7	79.0	83.8

Quarterly	Q1 97	Q2 97	Q3 97	Q4 97	Q1 98	Q2 98	July–Aug. 98
Exports in % of imports	79.6	84.2	86.6	84.2	92.9	92.4	91.3

Source: WIIW Database.

This reversal in the trend resulted from the fact that real export growth surpassed that of imports from the second quarter of 1997 onwards (Table 11.11).

Despite the high growth of exports, the GDP declined in the first quarter and even more in the second quarter of 1998 (by 0.9 per cent and

Table 11.11 Real changes in exports and imports in per cent

	Q1 1996	Q2 1996	Q3 1996	Q4 1996	Q1 1997	Q2 1997	Q3 1997	Q4 1997	Q1 1998	Q2 1998
Exports	6.8	4.1	5.5	5.5	1.3	11.7	11.3	15.5	27.4	12.3
Imports	12.4	9.2	20.0	10.5	7.5	9.4	2.4	7.7	17.3	7.9

Source: Czech Statistical Office.

2.4 per cent, respectively). The reason for that was a shrinking domestic demand – private consumption by 4.5 per cent in the first half of 1998, public consumption by 1.5 per cent and gross investment by 6.3 per cent. While industrial production showed a considerable rise (6.7 per cent) in the first six months of 1998, construction output (–4 per cent) and retail trade revenues (at constant prices –6.7 per cent) fell. Fiscal and monetary austerity, introduced in the context of the currency crisis in May 1997, showed its full impact in 1998. The export growth proved to be remarkably robust, even when in spring 1998 the exchange rate returned to levels as high as those observed in 1995 and 1996 (Table 11.12). Export performance may have ameliorated because of the more positive business climate in the EU and also due to structural improvement in part of the export sector. Internationally, the confidence in the stability of the koruna strengthened so that the high interest rates attracted foreign capital again. Data for August 1998 record a stagnation of imports (in Czech koruna, Kč, year on year) and, probably under the impact of a strong koruna (Table 11.12), a much lower increase in exports than observed in the first half of the year. Year on year, in August the increase in industrial output was not more than 1.1 per cent. Over the previous month, producer prices sank in August and stagnated in September. Consumer prices followed roughly the same pattern.

Between March and June 1998, the koruna fluctuated at levels around 18.6 per DM. A further strengthening of the koruna was most probably impeded by signals of a Russian currency crisis in May, and uncertainties connected with the Czech parliamentary elections in

Table 11.12 Average exchange rate (midpoint)

	Jan. 1995	Jan. 1996	Jan. 1997	Jan. 1998	Feb. 1998	Mar. 1998	Apr. 1998	May 1998	June 1998	July 1998	Aug. 1998
Kč/DM	18.2	18.4	16.9	19.5	19.0	18.6	18.6	18.3	18.6	17.8	18.0

Source: Czech National Bank.

June. In July and August the tendency towards further nominal appreciation, originating in net capital inflow, became clearly visible. At the end of September, there was no visible impact of the recent Russian crisis – the exchange rate was very close to the August average. The Czech National Bank tried to weaken the koruna a little several times in the second half of July, but without much success. This is hardly surprising in view of the large gap between Czech and international interest rates and with investors not expecting a significant devaluation over the next few months. To the decline in the consumer as well as the producer price index, the Czech National Bank responded with some small cuts in interest rates.

The Czech National Bank regards its influence on interest rates as the appropriate instrument to fight inflation. In 1998 consumer price inflation will be back above 10 per cent after years of single digit rates (since 1995). The jump in the consumer price index is the outcome of an increase in the upper limits of regulated prices. Market-determined prices do not move much any more – inflationary pressure in the Czech Republic has become rather low.

There is a certain danger that monetary policy is too restrictive, keeping interest rates at an unnecessarily high level. If we look for potential future difficulties, there is a possibility that capital inflow could push the koruna up to a point which would once again produce an unsustainable current account deficit, possibly provoking a sudden reversal of capital flows. However, a potential future economic crisis will not necessarily start from balance-of-payments problems or sudden capital market developments. It may emerge from difficulties within the business sector which could infect commercial banks.

In the prevailing depressed climate, the volume of classified loans increased in the first half of 1998 by 7.2 per cent and their share in the overall volume of loans reached 28.9 per cent. Some of the big companies are heavily indebted loss-makers. In the next few years, the government will not have much opportunity left for managing their survival, in one way or the other. These companies will also have less support from commercial banks than in the past since the latter will have to observe the rules of prudent banking more carefully, even if there is some delay with the privatization of the big banks. In the worst case it could lead to a severe crisis since the banks themselves would suffer negative feedback through a mass collapse of their clients. In the given situation it may not be easy to find foreign investors who might take over or become strategic investors in major financial and non-financial companies, but it is nevertheless important for the future development and integration into the EU.

12   POLICY RECOMMENDATIONS FOR CECS

International capital flows have undoubtedly become an important factor, not only in the macroeconomic framework but also at firm level. They are potentially very fruitful, but can also cause major disturbances. We still have no clear indicators which would warn us that a country is in acute danger, nor a widely accepted strategy for reducing proneness to crisis. What we have gained, however, is better knowledge about the potential damage which could follow from a policy which tries to finance a dramatically widening current account deficit by attracting massive short-term capital inflow rather than FDI.

The majority of tradable goods CECs produce are perceived internationally as low-quality products. Their prices have adjusted to international markets, and now we can observe an ongoing inflationary process which can be expected to slowly establish the 'right' ratio between domestic prices of tradable and non tradable goods. Not surprisingly, CECs have so far failed in their attempts to extinguish inflation quickly through strict control of the money supply. There were two main reasons for this. First, money supply tended to grow more than targeted. Second, the real GDP growth rate has also been affected by such a policy – to assume it would only affect prices would be too simple. It could cause real GDP to fall, for example, in which case even zero growth of money supply could easily be connected with inflation. There is a high probability that a very restrictive monetary policy will not reach its money supply target and the real effects possibly outpace the anti-inflationary impact.

Policy makers may believe they face a trade-off between targeting a low deficit on the current account through repeated currency devaluation, and a strict fight against inflation by keeping the interest rate high and thus above international levels. However, if in the latter case the interest rate differential attracts so much capital inflow that the resulting real appreciation starts worsening the current account, a sudden crisis might follow. The currency could come under pressure, and a devaluation could again feed inflation. A monetary policy which avoids triggering a large current account deficit will probably enjoy a lower likelihood of currency crisis.

It was wrong to assume that it would be sufficient to implement a Western-style monetary system in the CECs and control monetary supply in the traditional way. The commercial banks were not comparable to long-established Western banks. The overall situation was very exceptional compared to the usual environment in which Western banks act. Their activities differed from usual Western banking business. By Western standards, their lending activity was completely irregular. The business carrying least risk for these commercial banks was to lend to big, formerly State-owned companies, irrespective of how unsuccessful they were. Banks hardly investigated their clients' viability, relying more on collateral. If borrowing is very expensive, non-viable firms mainly apply for loans, knowing that they will most probably never repay them. Western institutions and methods were simply copied when the monetary system was transformed. This made money scarce but did not prevent its wrong allocation. Commercial banks in CECs could have done with, and still need, much better guidelines for their lending business. This would be helpful in controlling the supply and use of money, together with involving strategic partners from the West.

There is empirical evidence for CECs that economic growth is the best background for gradually reducing inflation. When a country fell back into stagnation in recent years it always meant an inflationary push. Firms have a better chance of approaching Western standards during a period of economic growth. Labour productivity is more likely to rise, capacity utilization improves, companies increase their profits and can use them to modernize their equipment. Tough anti-inflationary policy has a negative effect on enterprises. It increases their difficulties in servicing their loan obligations and these are huge anyway in some transition countries. It limits their room for manoeuvre in financing new investment projects, and since such a policy also implies a relatively strong currency, it has a curbing impact on exports and stimulates imports. It also attracts loans from abroad. There is a certain risk that the exchange rate gets stuck at a level not commensurate with the economy's fundamentals.

Exchange rate policy is closely connected with interest rate policy. As such it should try and avoid a situation where potentially volatile capital inflow finances an increasing gap in the current account. It should instead focus on keeping the current account deficit under control by achieving a deficit coverage mainly through FDI and simultaneously avoid attracting massive inflow of short-term capital.

CECs are likely to face balance-of-payments troubles as long as free mobility of capital is paralleled by high rates of inflation. The individual countries will gradually lose their inflation with the formation of a country-specific, internationally competitive industrial nucleus. It will be characterized by high labour productivity and a stronger position on international markets. The structural weakness of CEEC economies is only partly inherited from their communist past. It is also a consequence of the fact that it was not possible within just a few years to develop ownership structures which would have enabled companies to be modernized quickly. The decisive exception was privatization relying on FDI. For this reason, the Hungarian economy now seems quite sound. By following this example, the CECs could improve their competitiveness and integration into international networks.

NOTES

1. FDI influences the current account via exports and imports, dividends and distributed profits, interest on intra-company loans, licence fees and loyalties, and it influences the capital account in the form of equity capital, changes in inter-company claims and liabilities, and borrowing from offshore capital markets.
2. Other services include a broad variety of transactions between residents and non-residents: communication, construction, insurance services, computer and information services, royalties and licence fees, intermediary and auxiliary financial services, trading and trade-related services, miscellaneous business, professional and technical services (various forms of consulting, auditing and so on), personal, cultural and recreational services, and government services such as embassies and consulates. Some of these service transactions will be of growing importance in the future.
3. Income transactions between residents and non-residents include employee compensation and investment income, that is, receipts and payment on external financial assets and liabilities – mainly income on equity (dividends) and on debt (interest). Investment income results from direct, portfolio or other investment as registered in the financial accounts of previous periods. Investment income is closely linked with flows within financial accounts and with the international investment situation.

    The scheme subdivides income flows originating from FDI into income on equity and income on debt. The latter is identical with interest payment, while income on equity consists of (1) dividends and distributed branch profits, and (2) reinvested earnings and undistributed branch profits. Income flows originating from portfolio investment are also composed of income on equity, meaning dividends here, and income on debt, namely interest payments connected with (1) bonds and notes, or (2) money market instruments and financial derivatives (IMF *Balance of Payments Manual*, Washington, 1993).
4. A massively increased inflow of capital may follow from internal pull factors such as an autonomous increase in domestic demand for money and increases in domestic capital productivity. Alternatively, it may stem from external push factors such as an international reduction in interest rates.
5. In investigating the Mexican crisis in 1994, Julio Gallardo maintains that capital controls or a two-tier currency market would be necessary (López Gallardo, 1997a). The latter would restrict sharp fluctuations to capital transactions and leave the fundamentals untouched.
6. These FDI data are based on the enterprises' tax declarations and differ considerably from data in the balance-of-payments statistics.
7. The problem with Hungarian foreign trade statistics is that from 1996 onwards a new methodology was applied, with the effect that statistics offer parallel figures for 1996 – one calculated in the old methodology, the other in the new one. In Figure 11.1 the 1997 figures are related to the new methodology figures for 1996. For estimating the full year 1998 figures, the half year data 1998 were multiplied by two.
8. The high FDI figure for 1995 originates from foreign investment in industries supplying electricity, gas and water.
9. SITC 6 and SITC 7, as well as total exports, are in Figure 11.1 labelled as 'FDI-related trade flows'. Of course, FDI is only one of the factors determining the magnitude of these flows.
10. A high proportion of these services can be assumed to be FDI-related.

REFERENCES

Chote, R. (1997), 'World economy: Thai crisis highlights lessons of Mexico', *Financial Times*, 19 September.

The Economist (1997), 'Something horrible out there – will eastern Europe be the next region to suffer exchange-rate turmoil?', 18 October, pp. 91 ff.

Eichengreen, B., Andrew K. Rose and C. WypIosz (1995), 'Exchange market mayhem: the antecedents and aftermath of speculative attacks', *Economic Policy*, **21**, October, pp. 251–312.

Hahn, F.R. (1998), 'Währungskrisen – Herausforderung für Theorie und Politik', Austrian Institute of Economic Research, *Monatsberichte*, **9**, pp. 583–90.

IMF (1993), *IMF Balance of Payments Manual*, Washington, DC: IMF.

Koromzay, V. (1997), 'Some observations on current accounts and international adjustment', paper presented at the conference on Current Account Imbalances in East and West: Do they Matter?, Vienna, 16–18 November.

Krugman, P. (1994), 'The myth of Asia's miracle', *Foreign Affairs*, November/December, **73** (6), pp. 62–78.

López Gallardo, J. (1997a), 'Growth resumption and long-run growth in Lantinamerican Economies – a modest proposal', *Cuadernos de trabajo* 38, Maestría en Ciencias Economicas, UNAM, Mexico.

López Gallardo, J. (1997b), 'Mexico's financial modernisation and financial fragility', *BNL Quarterly Review*, **201**, June.

Mertlik, P. (1997), 'Investment survey: the Czech Republic', manuscript in the framework of Phare-ACE Project P95-2226-R, Prague, August.

Milesi-Ferretti, G.M. and A. Razin (1997), 'Reversals in current account deficits and currency crises', paper presented at the Conference on Current Account Imbalances in East and West: Do they Matter?, Vienna, 16–18 November.

Mundell, R.A. (1997), 'The international adjustment mechanism of the balance of payments', *Zagreb Journal of Economics*, **1**, pp. 3–57.

Naujoks, P. and K.-D. Schmidt (1995), 'Foreign direct investment and trade in transition countries: tracing links', paper prepared for the Conference on Corporate Adjustment, Market Failures and Industrial Policies in the Transition, Prague, 4–6 May.

Obstfeld, M. (1995), 'Models of currency crises with self-fulfiling features', *Working Paper* no. 5285, National Bureau of Economic Research, Cambridge MA, October.

Pohl, G., G.T. Jedrzejczak and R.E. Anderson (1995), *Creating Capital Markets in Central and Eastern Europe*, The World Bank, April.

Powell, J. (1997), 'Current accounts: imbalances and monetary policy in Canada', paper presented at the Conference on Current Account Imbalances in East and West: Do they Matter?, Vienna, 16–18 November.

Sachs, J. (1998), interviewed in the *Prague Business Journal*, 13–19 July, p. 15.

Stiglitz, J.E. (1998), 'Knowledge for development – economic science, economic policy, and economic advice', paper prepared for the Annual World Bank Conference on Development Economics, Washington DC, 20–21 April.

Tatom, J.A. (1997), 'Do current account imbalances matter?', paper presented at the conference on Current Account Imbalances in East and West: Do they Matter?, Vienna, 16–18 November.

Tobin, J. (1998), 'Financial globalization: can national currencies survive?', paper prepared for the Annual World Bank Conference on Development Economics, Washington DC, 20–21 April

Ul Haque, N., D. Mathieson and S. Sharma (1997), 'Die Ursachen von Kapitalzuflüssen und politische Reaktionen', *Finanzierung und Entwicklung*, **34** (1), March, pp. 3–6.

United Nations (1997), *World Investment Report 1997 – Transnational Corporations, Market Structure and Competition Policy*, New York and Geneva.

Index